걸프 사태

유엔안전보장이사회 동향 2

걸프 사태

유엔안전보장이사회 동향 2

한국학술정보

| 머리말

걸프 전쟁은 미국의 주도하에 34개국 연합군 병력이 수행한 전쟁으로, 1990년 8월 이라크의 쿠웨이트 침공 및 합병에 반대하며 발발했다. 미국은 초기부터 파병 외교에 나섰고, 1990년 9월 서울 등에 고위 관리를 파견하며 한국의 동참을 요청했다. 88올림픽 이후 동구권 국교 수립과 유엔 가입 추진 등 적극적인 외교 활동을 펼치는 당시 한국에 있어 이는 미국과 국제 사회의 지지를 얻기 위해서라도 피할 수 없는 일이었다. 결국 정부는 91년 1월부터 약 3개월에 걸쳐 국군의료지원단과 공군수송단을 사우디아라비아 및 아랍 에미리트 연합 등에 파병하였고, 군 · 민간 의료 활동, 병력 수송 임무를 수행했다. 동시에 당시 걸프 지역 8개국에 살던 5천여 명의 교민에게 방독면 등 물자를 제공하고, 특별기 파견 등으로 비상시 대피할 수 있도록 지원했다. 비록 전쟁 부담금과 유가 상승 등 어려움도 있었지만, 걸프전 파병과 군사 외교를 통해 한국은 유엔 가입에 박차를 가할 수 있었고 미국 등 선진 우방국, 아랍권 국가 등과 밀접한 외교 관계를 유지하며 여러 국익을 창출할 수 있었다.

본 총서는 외교부에서 작성하여 30여 년간 유지한 걸프 사태 관련 자료를 담고 있다. 미국을 비롯한 여러 국가와의 군사 외교 과정, 일일 보고 자료와 기타 정부의 대응 및 조치, 재외동포 철수와 보호, 의료지원단과 수송단 파견 및 지원 과정, 유엔을 포함해 세계 각국에서 수집한 관련 동향 자료, 주변국 지원과 전후복구사업 참여 등 총 48권으로 구성되었다. 전체 분량은 약 2만 4천여 쪽에 이른다.

2024년 3월

한국학술정보(주)

| 일러두기

· 본 총서에 실린 자료는 2022년 4월과 2023년 4월에 각각 공개한 외교문서 4,827권, 76만 여 쪽 가운데 일부를 발췌한 것이다.

· 각 권의 제목과 순서는 공개된 원본을 최대한 반영하였으나, 주제에 따라 일부는 적절히 변경하였다.

· 원본 자료는 A4 판형에 맞게 축소하거나 원본 비율을 유지한 채 A4 페이지 안에 삽입하였다. 또한 현재 시점에선 공개되지 않아 '공란'이란 표기만 있는 페이지 역시 그대로 실었다.

· 외교부가 공개한 문서 각 권의 첫 페이지에는 '정리 보존 문서 목록'이란 이름으로 기록물 종류, 일자, 명칭, 간단한 내용 등의 정보가 수록되어 있으며, 이를 기준으로 0001번부터 번호가 매겨져 있다. 이는 삭제하지 않고 총서에 그대로 수록하였다.

· 보고서 내용에 관한 더 자세한 정보가 필요하다면, 외교부가 온라인상에 제공하는 『대한민국 외교사료요약집』 1991년과 1992년 자료를 참조할 수 있다.

| 차례

정 리 보 존 문 서 목 록

기록물종류	일반공문서철	등록번호	2017060005	등록일자	2017-06-05
분류번호	731.33	국가코드	XF	보존기간	30년
명 칭	걸프사태 관련 유엔안전보장이사회 동향, 1990-91. 전5권				
생 산 과	국제연합과/중동1과	생산년도	1990~1991	담당그룹	
권 차 명	V.3 1991.1-2월				
내용목차	* 1991.1.14 유엔 사무총장, 이라크 방문 결과 보고(안보리) 1.17 미국, 대이라크 선제 공격 - 비공식 비공개 안보리 회의 개최 1.22 주유엔 대사, 한국의 다국적군(의료진) 파견 결정 통보(유엔사무총장 앞 서한) 1.31 주유엔 대사, 한국의 다국적군 추가 지원 내역 통보 (유엔사무총장 앞 서한) 1.31 UNIIMOG 임기 1개월 연장(1991.1.31 임기 만료) 결의안 (안보리 결의 685호) 채택 2.27 주유엔 이라크대사, 휴전 관련 제의 (안보리 의장에게 전달) 안보리 결의안 수락 통보 2.27 Bush 미국 대통령, 다국적군 공격작전 중지 조치 발표				

0001

원 본

외 무 부

종 별 :

번 호 : UNW-0011 일 시 : 91 0104 1800

수 신 : 장 관(국연,중근동,기정)

발 신 : 주 유엔 대사

제 목 : 안보리(대이락 제재위)

안보리결의 661 호에 따라 안보리내에 설치된 대이락 제재위는 금 1.4.오후 1991년 중동 제재위 의장국으로 오스트리아를 선출하였음.(1990년의장국은 핀랜드)끝

(대사 현홍주-국장)

국기국 1차보 중아국 정문국 안기부

PAGE 1 91.01.05 09:25 WG

외신 1과 통제관

0002

원

주 국 련 대 표 부

주국련 203132- 003

수신 장 관

참조 국제기구조약국장

제목 안보리 대이락 제재위 보고서

90.12.20자 및 90.12.21자의 안보리 대이락 제재위 보고서를 별첨 송부합니다.

첨 부 : 상기 제재위 보고서 각 1부. 끝.

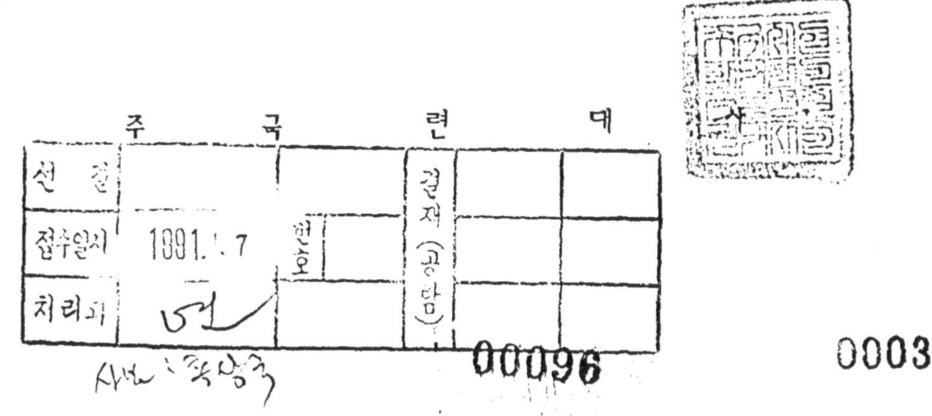

주 국 련 대

선 결			결재(공람)		
접수일시	1991. 1. 7	번호			
처리과					

00096

0003

UNITED
NATIONS

S

Security Council

Distr.
GENERAL

S/22021/Add.1
21 December 1990

ORIGINAL: ENGLISH

LETTER DATED 19 DECEMBER 1990 FROM THE CHAIRMAN OF THE SECURITY COUNCIL COMMITTEE ESTABLISHED BY RESOLUTION 661 (1990) CONCERNING THE SITUATION BETWEEN IRAQ AND KUWAIT ADDRESSED TO THE PRESIDENT OF THE SECURITY COUNCIL

Addendum

Letter dated 21 December 1990 from the Chairman of the Security Council Committee established by resolution 661 (1990) concerning the situation between Iraq and Kuwait addressed to the President of the Security Council

I have the honour to refer to my letter dated 19 December 1990 by which I submitted the first set of recommendations to the Security Council adopted by the Security Council Committee established by Security Council resolution 661 (1990) in response to requests for assistance under the provisions of Article 50 of the Charter of the United Nations.

At its 22nd meeting, on 20 December 1990, the Committee adopted without objection as further recommendations to be made to the President of the Security Council the draft decisions submitted by the Working Group with regard to Sri Lanka, Yemen, Czechoslovakia, Poland, Mauritania, Pakistan, the Sudan, Uruguay, Viet Nam, Bangladesh and the Seychelles. The recommendations are set out hereunder. In accordance with the decision taken at the Committee's 21st meeting and at the request of applicant States, the Committee is transmitting with the relevant recommendation any additional explanatory material provided by those States.

(Signed) Marjatta RASI
Chairman
Security Council Committee established by resolution 661 (1990) concerning the situation between Iraq and Kuwait

90-37111 2205b (E) /...

0004

Annex I

Recommendation by the Security Council Committee established by resolution 661 (1990) concerning the situation between Iraq and Kuwait with regard to Sri Lanka

The Security Council Committee established by resolution 661 (1990) concerning the situation between Iraq and Kuwait,

Having dealt with the communications received from Sri Lanka under Article 50 of the Charter of the United Nations,

Recalling Security Council resolution 661 (1990) of 6 August 1990 in which the Council decided to impose sanctions in accordance with Chapter VII of the Charter of the United Nations, as well as Security Council resolutions 660 (1990) of 2 August 1990, 662 (1990) of 9 August 1990, 664 (1990) of 18 August 1990, 665 (1990) of 25 August 1990, 666 (1990) of 13 September 1990, 667 (1990) of 16 September 1990, 669 (1990) of 24 September 1990, 670 (1990) of 25 September 1990 and 674 (1990) of 29 October 1990,

Recalling also the provisions of Articles 25, 49 and 50 of the Charter of the United Nations,

Noting the information given by Sri Lanka a/ regarding the measures taken to give full effect to the sanctions as laid down in resolution 661 (1990) and concerning the special economic problems it has been confronted with as a result of the implementation of those measures,

Having heard the representative of Sri Lanka,

Expressing concern at the special economic problems confronting Sri Lanka as a result of the severance of its economic relations with Iraq and occupied Kuwait as required by Security Council resolution 661 (1990), which are particularly difficult in terms of its commercial and financial losses, as well as costs associated with the repatriation and rehabilitation of Sri Lankan workers returning from Kuwait and Iraq,

Recognizing that the continued full implementation of Security Council resolution 661 (1990) by Sri Lanka, as well as other States, will support measures to ensure compliance with paragraph 2 of that resolution and to restore the authority of the legitimate Government of Kuwait,

1. Commends the Government of Sri Lanka for the measures it has taken to comply with resolution 661 (1990);

---

a/ S/21627, S/21710 and S/21984.

0005

/...

2. Recognizes the urgent need to assist Sri Lanka in coping with its special economic problems resulting from the severance of its economic relations with Iraq and occupied Kuwait as required by Security Council resolution 661 (1990), especially those losses resulting from undelivered Sri Lankan products to Iraq and Kuwait, as well as costs associated with the repatriation and rehabilitation of Sri Lankan workers returning from Kuwait and Iraq;

3. Appeals to all States on an urgent basis to provide immediate technical, financial and material assistance to Sri Lanka to mitigate the adverse impact on its economy of the application by Sri Lanka of sanctions against Iraq pursuant to Security Council resolution 661 (1990);

4. Invites the competent organs and specialized agencies of the United Nations system, including the international financial institutions and the regional development banks, to review their programmes of assistance to Sri Lanka with a view to alleviating its special economic problems arising from the application of sanctions against Iraq pursuant to Security Council resolution 661 (1990);

5. Requests the Secretary-General, on a regular basis, to seek information from States and the concerned organs and agencies of the United Nations system on action taken to alleviate the special economic problems of Sri Lanka and to report thereon to the Security Council.

0006 /...

Enclosure

Revised memorandum, dated 30 November 1990, on the adverse economic and other consequences resulting from the imposition of sanctions under Security Council resolution 661 (1990) a/

[Original: English]

On 5 September 1990, Sri Lanka submitted to the Security Council a memorandum covering the period ending 31 December 1990 setting out the adverse repercussions following the imposition of sanctions under Security Council resolution 661 (1990) (see S/21710, annex). However, as the problem seems unresolved and is likely to remain so for an indeterminate period, it has become necessary to revise the original memorandum. A revision was also necessitated by the fact that increases in the price of oil have exceeded original forecasts. This revised memorandum addresses both of those factors.

Sri Lanka has an open economy, which to a great extent depends on the performance of imports and exports, both of which are presently under severe stress owing to internal as well as external factors. The imposition of sanctions under Security Council resolution 661 (1990) has further aggravated this situation. This development will in turn lead to severe economic hardships as well as political and social instability.

Sri Lanka is currently engaged in combating terrorism and a substantial amount of its resources is being diverted for this purpose. Terrorism in Sri Lanka, which has threatened the well-entrenched democratic way of life and governance and the territorial integrity of the country, has retarded economic growth. The decline in resources for economic growth will in turn further weaken Sri Lanka's ability to counter this. Further, other priority sectors, which are equally important in providing the basic needs of the people, will be deprived of much-needed resources. A consequence of this would be continued political and social instability.

The adverse effects consequent on the observance of the sanctions are particularly felt in the following areas.

A. Export of tea

Tea is the second largest source of foreign exchange earnings and accounted for 15 per cent of total current account receipts in 1989. The Middle East absorbs approximately 55 per cent of tea exports. Iraq and Kuwait together accounted for around 12.15 per cent of the total exports and Iraq has been the second largest buyer of Sri Lankan tea. Consequent on the loss of the market in these two countries, Sri Lanka experienced a fall in tea prices owing to a lack of demand from a major buyer.

---

a/ S/21984, annex I.

0007

/...

In the second half of 1989, the value of tea exported to Iraq and Kuwait was $US 25.6 million and $5.7 million, respectively. The general oversupply of tea on the world market will drastically reduce Sri Lanka's earnings from tea owing to a decline in prices. In 1991, the decline in the tea export price from $2 to $1.20 per kilogram would imply a drop in earnings of $37 million. In 1992 and 1993, prices are projected to remain 13 per cent below the originally expected price - about $60 million less in total earnings than projected earlier. The indirect effects of a fall in prices would amount to another $15 million per year.

B. Other exports and imports

The total value of other exports to Iraq and Kuwait in 1989 was around $1 million. This market is completely closed to Sri Lankan exports since the eruption of the Gulf crisis. The loss of export markets can in no way be compensated for by a redirection of exports because of limited market accessibility and the prohibitive cost of breaking into new markets in an environment of protection.

C. Remittances by Sri Lankan expatriates in the Middle East

It is estimated that over 100,000 Sri Lankans were employed in Kuwait and a sizeable number in Iraq. While worker remittances from abroad are the third largest foreign exchange earner and were estimated at $360 million for 1991, remittances from Kuwait and Iraq constituted a fair share of the total, estimated at about $90 million annually.

The steady flow of remittances from these expatriates cushioned the adverse impact of the increase in oil prices.

This cushion no longer exists.

The loss of income-generating capacity from worker remittances cannot be limited to the dollar value of its loss. The sustenance of dependants, increases in national savings, enhanced investment activities and the growth of entrepreneurship at the small-scale enterprise level have now been greatly reduced. The impact can be seen in the decline in the activities of financial institutions as a result of the decline in savings and a reduction of their capacity to recover loans that have been financed on the understanding that there will be a steady flow of foreign remittances.

Based on the above assumption, the impact of the loss of remittances, excluding indirect repercussions, is expected to be $53 million in 1990. The overall impact in 1991, 1992 and 1993 is expected to be $207 million, $193 million and $125 million, respectively.

D. Price of crude oil

The anticipated increase in the cost of crude oil imports over the estimate made prior to the Gulf crisis, despite a 9 per cent reduction in volume, is $58.4 million for 1990. The average price of Sri Lanka's crude oil imports for the balance of the year is estimated at $32 per barrel, which is more than 50 per cent higher than the prices prevailing during the first half of the year. This increase is mainly a result of a shortfall created by the removal of Iraqi and Kuwaiti oil from the market. The average for 1991 is assumed to be $29 per barrel. In 1991, the impact will be felt fully and the bill for crude oil imports is expected to go up from $246 million to $377 million. The impact of this increase in 1991 is expected to be $131 million. The oil price shock has several indirect effects on other prices. Apart from an increase in import prices, there will be a general rise in local costs. Transportation costs have already risen. Marginal enterprises are likely to go out of business and industrial production will slacken.

E. Inflation and economic growth

Sri Lanka is already experiencing inflation, an average annual rate of 18.7 per cent. The impact of the escalation of the price of oil on Sri Lanka's import prices will add further pressure on inflation and raise the cost of industrial production. In the context of continuing inflationary pressure, the monetary policies will no doubt remain tight but this will lead to slower economic growth.

F. Socio-economic conditions

With the large-scale return to Sri Lanka of displaced workers from the Middle East, the high unemployment rate in the country, estimated at around 18 per cent, will be further aggravated. This could result in a reduction in the quality of life of lower-income groups of the population owing to the considerable reduction in remittances received from family members employed overseas. There could also be an adverse social impact on account of readjustment problems faced by the workers returning from the Middle East who have become accustomed to a different lifestyle based on high-income levels enjoyed overseas. The cost of rehabilitating the returning migrant workers is still to be fully determined. The cost of the repatriation of Sri Lankan workers from the Gulf financed by external assistance has not yet been fully determined, but is estimated to be $25 million. In addition to this, Sri Lanka has up to now incurred expenditure amounting to $5 million.

G. Overall economic situation

Sri Lanka is currently in the process of implementing an economic restructuring programme in collaboration with the International Monetary Fund (IMF), the World Bank and other multilateral donor agencies. The recent escalation of terrorist activities is already adding pressure on the operation of the restructuring programme. Compliance with resolution 661 (1990) will take these programmes further off course. The restructuring programme was based on the optimistic estimates of the earnings from tea exports and expatriate worker remittances, as well as the continuation of normal trends in respect of fuel prices, etc. The unexpected fall in foreign exchange earnings combined with the increase in the price of imports will have severe adverse implications on the balance of payments and economic stability of Sri Lanka and thereby impose severe constraints on the working of the programme.

* * *

The cumulative effect of compliance with the Security Council resolution is not easily quantifiable. The invisible and indirect consequences and the time-span are equally important in gauging the overall effect of the sanctions on society as a whole.

Further, the impact of sanctions on an economy such as that of Sri Lanka, which is experiencing severe constraints, will be far more damaging than on a strong or larger economy capable of absorbing losses arising out of compliance with the sanctions.

Sri Lanka has been severely affected by the Gulf crisis because of several factors. Apart from the loss of a growing and lucrative tea market and the loss of remittances from migrant workers, the savings and investment capabilities of Sri Lankans have been reduced owing to reduced income generation. Additionally, the negative multiplier effects of the loss of income have an adverse impact on small-scale enterprises, finance companies and wholesale and retail businesses. Further, the returnees from Kuwait and Iraq will add to the unemployment problem, with adverse social consequences. Above all, the upsurge in oil prices puts tremendous pressure on the balance of payments, which is already under severe strain. The oil price increase alone is expected to increase Sri Lanka's external payments by as much as 20 per cent of export earnings. In addition, the increased air fares, together with higher insurance costs, will reduce tourist income while increased freight charges will raise prices of imports to Sri Lanka.

On the above basis, the impact of the Gulf crisis during the period from August 1990 to the end of 1993 is expected to be well beyond $1 billion. With all the ongoing readjustment efforts, the economy is not in a position to absorb a loss of revenue of this magnitude and to continue with its economic programmes, even at minimum levels, unless substantial economic assistance is made available to cushion these losses. If this assistance is not forthcoming Sri Lanka will suffer irreparable political, economic and social consequences.

Hence, the Security Council is requested to take immediate action to facilitate the mobilization of resources from bilateral, multilateral and other sources.

Annex II

Recommendation by the Security Council Committee established by resolution 661 (1990) concerning the situation between Iraq and Kuwait with regard to Yemen

The Security Council Committee established by resolution 661 (1990) concerning the situation between Iraq and Kuwait,

Having dealt with the communications received from Yemen under Article 50 of the Charter of the United Nations,

Recalling Security Council resolution 661 (1990) of 6 August 1990 in which the Council decided to impose sanctions in accordance with Chapter VII of the Charter of the United Nations, as well as Security Council resolutions 660 (1990) of 2 August 1990, 662 (1990) of 9 August 1990, 664 (1990) of 18 August 1990, 665 (1990) of 25 August 1990, 666 (1990) of 13 September 1990, 667 (1990) of 16 September 1990, 669 (1990) of 24 September 1990, 670 (1990) of 25 September 1990 and 674 (1990) of 29 October 1990,

Recalling also the provisions of Articles 25, 49 and 50 of the Charter of the United Nations,

Noting the information given by Yemen a/ regarding the measures taken to give full effect to the sanctions as laid down in resolution 661 (1990) and concerning the special economic problems it has been confronted with as a result of the implementation of those measures,

Having heard the representative of Yemen,

Expressing concern at the special economic problems confronting Yemen, a least developed country, as a result of the severance of its economic relations with Iraq and occupied Kuwait as required by Security Council resolution 661 (1990), which are particularly difficult in terms of its commercial and financial losses, as well as costs associated with the repatriation and rehabilitation of Yemeni expatriates,

Recognizing that the continued full implementation of Security Council resolution 661 (1990) by Yemen, as well as other States, will support measures to ensure compliance with paragraph 2 of that resolution and to restore the authority of the legitimate Government of Kuwait,

1. Commends the Government of Yemen for the measures it has taken to comply with resolution 661 (1990);

---

a/ S/21615 and S/21748.

0011 /...

2. Recognizes the urgent need to assist Yemen in coping with its special economic problems resulting from the severance of its economic relations with Iraq and occupied Kuwait as required by Security Council resolution 661 (1990), especially those losses resulting from undelivered Yemeni products to Iraq and Kuwait and undelivered oil shipments from Iraq and Kuwait, as well as costs associated with the repatriation and rehabilitation of Yemeni expatriates;

3. Appeals to all States on an urgent basis to provide immediate technical, financial and material assistance to Yemen to mitigate the adverse impact on its economy of the application by Yemen of sanctions against Iraq pursuant to Security Council resolution 661 (1990);

4. Invites the competent organs and specialized agencies of the United Nations system, including the international financial institutions and the regional development banks, to review their programmes of assistance to Yemen with a view to alleviating its special economic problems arising from the application of sanctions against Iraq pursuant to Security Council resolution 661 (1990);

5. Requests the Secretary-General, on a regular basis, to seek information from States and the concerned organs and agencies of the United Nations system on action taken to alleviate the special economic problems of Yemen and to report thereon to the Security Council.

Enclosure I

Letter dated 9 September 1990 from the Minister for Foreign Affairs of Yemen addressed to the Secretary-General a/

[Original: Arabic]

1. I have the honour to inform you that, as a member of the international community, the Republic of Yemen is aware that the resolutions of the Security Council are of a binding character. Our representative to the Security Council has already expressed commitment to Council resolution 661 (1990), and we should here like to affirm that the Republic of Yemen has adopted appropriate measures to comply with its provisions.

2. After careful study of the present and future impact of compliance with the resolution, the competent authorities have determined that there have been harmful consequences for the national economy and grave economic difficulties for Yemen and its population which will be aggravated as a direct result of such compliance. This situation constitutes one involving "special economic problems" under the terms of Article 50 of the Charter of the United Nations. In this connection, permit me to call your attention to the far-reaching relations that have linked our country with both Iraq and Kuwait and to the degree of Yemeni economic dependence on the refining of Iraqi and Kuwaiti petroleum, on expatriate remittances and on the assistance, grants and loans accorded to it by those two countries. The extent of that dependence can be gauged from the attached memorandum.

While my Government is most desirous of meeting its obligations under the Charter in good faith, at the same time it realizes the enormity of the burdens imposed on Yemen by compliance with resolution 661 (1990). By virtue of the present letter it officially requests that the Security Council enter into consultations, on an urgent basis, with a view to finding a solution to the problems that will arise out of the implementation of measures under Chapter VII of the Charter.

---

a/ S/21748, annex I.

Enclosure II

Memorandum on the economic and financial impact on the Republic of Yemen as a result of the imposition of restrictions on economic relations with Iraq and Kuwait a/

[Original: Arabic]

This memorandum explains the economic losses that Yemen has already suffered and will continue to suffer as a result of the imposition of restrictions on trade and on transactions in the services and financial sectors with Iraq and Kuwait.

These losses can be classified under the following headings:

Refining of Iraqi and Kuwaiti petroleum at the Aden refinery, and easements accorded by Iraq and Kuwait to Yemen with respect to petroleum for domestic consumption.

Annual grants provided by Iraq and Kuwait in support of the budget.

Assistance and donations for the funding of projects.

Exports to Iraq and Kuwait.

Concessional loans from the Arab Fund for Economic and Social Development (AFESD) and the Kuwait Fund for Arab Economic Development (KFAED).

Remittances from Yemenis working in Kuwait and Iraq.

Compulsory repatriation of Yemeni expatriates in Kuwait.

1. Refining of Iraqi and Kuwaiti petroleum at the Aden refinery, and easements accorded by Iraq and Kuwait to Yemen with respect to petroleum for domestic consumption

Yemen has contractual ties with both Iraq and Kuwait for the refining of petroleum at the Aden refinery. Any commitment not to refine Iraqi and Kuwaiti petroleum, as required by the contracts in effect, would cause large-scale losses, exemplified by the loss of refining fees and port fees, the costs of the unemployment arising out of the suspension of these contracts and the cost of the interest payments that we should have to assume as a result of the failure to utilize Iraqi and Kuwaiti easements relating to petroleum for domestic consumption. This represents a loss in the order of $39,994,675 for the remainder of 1990. Under the contracts in force, the loss would rise to some $219,663,000 in 1991.

---

a/ S/21748, annex II.

0014

/...

We should further like to indicate here that the quantity of petroleum for the refinement of which contracts have been concluded with Iraq and Kuwait for 1990 is as follows:

Iraq: 2.5 million tons.

Kuwait: 1 million tons.

For both Iraq and Kuwait, this quantity would increase in 1991 to 6 million tons, since contracts have already been concluded with Iraq on refining 5 million tons in 1991, including 2.5 million tons in accordance with the agreement with the Iraqi party allocating this quantity for the domestic consumption of petroleum products, on the understanding that the cost of the shipments purchased would be paid one year after the date of delivery.

2. Annual grants provided by Iraq and Kuwait in support of the budget

Yemen receives regular annual financial support for certain items in its budget from both Iraq and Kuwait, in the following manner:

Iraq

$50 million a year. The remaining allocation of such support for 1990 is $25 million. The loss for 1990 will therefore be $25 million and, in 1991, the loss will increase to $50 million.

Kuwait

$18,336,203 a year, principally in support of university-level and general education services and health care. These amounts have been subject to an annual increase in accordance with the increasing costs of the services that they fund.

3. Assistance and donations for the funding of projects

Both Iraq and Kuwait implement various projects on a regular annual basis, and current financial obligations for projects under implementation are as follows:

Iraq

$70 million for the implementation of a project for a conference centre, a five-star hotel, large meeting halls and their ancillary services.

Kuwait

$8,643,555 for the construction, repair and development of hospitals.

0015 /...

4. Exports

Yemen's non-petroleum commodity exports for 1990 are estimated at $201 million. Most of these exports are products of the agriculture and fisheries sector, and it had been anticipated that exports to Iraq and Kuwait would reach more than $100 million. With a halt to exports to Kuwait and Iraq, the anticipated losses for the last five months of 1990 are estimated at $42 million. It had been anticipated that, in 1991, such exports would increase at a rate of between 15 and 20 per cent. The sharp drop in the exportation of goods will have an impact on the balance of trade and on economic activity, and unemployment in Yemen, which is already very high, will increase with the influx of expatriates returning from Kuwait.

5. Concessional loans from AFESD and KFAED

Total unutilized loans for projects under implementation or definitively agreed upon are in the order of $US 396,450,000, broken down as follows:

1. KFAED	$108 000 000
2. AFESD (based in Kuwait)	$288 450 000
Total	$396 450 000

Reference should here also be made to the fact that the actual losses may exceed the amounts mentioned above since most of the loans in question represent a share in the funding of projects in which other sources of funding also participate so that, with the loss of financing from the two Funds, other sources of funding are also likely to be lost. The above figure also does not include other project funding arrangements with the two Funds on which agreement had been reached but with respect to which the constitutional procedures for ratification had not been completed, some of which had been in the final stages of consideration.

6. Remittances from expatriates

The national economy will be affected by greater disequilibrium in the balance of payments because of the suspension of remittances from Yemeni expatriates working in Kuwait, which amount to some $250 million. The authorities concerned also estimate that further reductions in remittances from expatriates in other areas of the Gulf because of recent developments in the region will lead to the loss of at least another $150 million.

0016 /...

7. Compulsory repatriation of expatriates from Kuwait

The number of Yemeni expatriates in Kuwait was about 35,000, most of whom have now returned. This is causing an increasingly severe unemployment problem and imposes on the State additional costs and problems in their absorption and in providing them with assistance as a result of the loss of their incomes. In another respect, the influx of returnees continues to involve an enormous financial outlay on transport, since the State has assumed the costs of their homeward travel. It is clear from the foregoing that the direct consequences of the country's compliance with the implementation of resolution 661 (1990) will cost it not less than $1.384 billion.

All of the losses set forth above will also give rise to other, indirect losses in terms of the performance of the national economy as a whole and the enormous difficulties that the Yemeni balance of payments will face at a delicate stage of our history in which we are encountering great economic difficulties and assuming great burdens. Such losses will be exemplified in increasing unemployment, the failure to implement projects and their increased cost, increasing burdens on the general State budget and a fall in the level of interaction with the economies of neighbouring countries. Losses arising out of such indirect effects are estimated at $300 million.

Accordingly, the imposition of the embargo will place burdens on the Yemeni economy that it will be unable to sustain. The Republic of Yemen therefore calls for the provision of the following:

1. The crude oil necessary to ensure the functioning of the Aden refinery at its planned level of operation and on the same terms as previously.

2. Petroleum for domestic consumption on preferential terms.

3. Grants to compensate for those previously provided by Iraq and Kuwait whether in support of the budget or in order to finance projects and ensure their implementation.

4. Long-term concessional loans in order to ensure the implementation of those projects that were being financed by KFAED and AFESD.

5. Concessional loans and other sources of support in order to overcome the anticipated sharp fall-off in the external sector as a result of reduced remittances from expatriates and the drop in exports and with a view to curtailing the negative impact of this situation on the level of performance of the national economy.

Annex III

Recommendation by the Security Council Committee established by resolution 661 (1990) concerning the situation between Iraq and Kuwait with regard to Czechoslovakia

The Security Council Committee established by resolution 661 (1990) concerning the situation between Iraq and Kuwait,

Having dealt with the communications received from Czechoslovakia under Article 50 of the Charter of the United Nations,

Recalling Security Council resolution 661 (1990) of 6 August 1990 in which the Council decided to impose sanctions in accordance with Chapter VII of the Charter of the United Nations, as well as Security Council resolutions 660 (1990) of 2 August 1990, 662 (1990) of 9 August 1990, 664 (1990) of 18 August 1990, 665 (1990) of 25 August 1990, 666 (1990) of 13 September 1990, 667 (1990) of 16 September 1990, 669 (1990) of 24 September 1990, 670 (1990) of 25 September 1990 and 674 (1990) of 29 October 1990,

Recalling also the provisions of Articles 25, 49 and 50 of the Charter of the United Nations,

Noting the information given by Czechoslovakia a/ regarding the measures taken to give full effect to the sanctions as laid down in resolution 661 (1990) and concerning the special economic problems it has been confronted with as a result of the implementation of those measures,

Having heard the representative of Czechoslovakia,

Expressing concern at the special economic problems confronting Czechoslovakia as a result of the severance of its economic relations with Iraq and occupied Kuwait as required by Security Council resolution 661 (1990), which are particularly difficult in terms of commercial and financial losses incurred by Czechoslovakia,

Recognizing that the continued full implementation of Security Council resolution 661 (1990) by Czechoslovakia, as well as other States, will support measures to ensure compliance with paragraph 2 of that resolution and to restore the authority of the legitimate Government of Kuwait,

1. Commends the Government of Czechoslovakia for the measures it has taken to comply with resolution 661 (1990);

---

a/ S/21750, S/21837 and S/AC.25/1990/9.

0018

/...

2. Recognizes the urgent need to assist Czechoslovakia in coping with its special economic problems resulting from the severance of its economic relations with Iraq and occupied Kuwait as required by Security Council resolution 661 (1990), especially those losses resulting from undelivered Iraqi oil shipments to Czechoslovakia in payment for outstanding debts incurred by Iraq towards Czechoslovakia and other financial and commercial losses;

3. Appeals to all States on an urgent basis to provide immediate technical, financial and material assistance to Czechoslovakia to mitigate the adverse impact on its economy of the application by Czechoslovakia of sanctions against Iraq pursuant to Security Council resolution 661 (1990);

4. Invites the competent organs and specialized agencies of the United Nations system, as well as the international financial institutions and the regional development banks, to provide assistance to Czechoslovakia with a view to alleviating its special economic problems arising from the application of sanctions against Iraq pursuant to Security Council resolution 661 (1990);

5. Requests the Secretary-General, on a regular basis, to seek information from States and the concerned organs and agencies of the United Nations system on action taken to alleviate the special economic problems of Czechoslovakia and to report thereon to the Security Council.

0019

/...

Enclosure I

Letter dated 2 October 1990 from the Permanent Representative of Czechoslovakia to the United Nations addressed to the President of the Security Council a/

[Original: English]

I have the honour to reiterate again that the Czech and Slovak Federal Republic fully supports and strictly complies with all the Security Council resolutions concerning the situation between Iraq and Kuwait. The Government, as stated before, has undertaken the corresponding steps and measures aimed at ensuring that all Czech and Slovak institutions and organizations fully adhere to the provisions of those resolutions.

However, this position in support of the international solidarity against the flagrant violation of the Charter of the United Nations and of other international legal norms by Iraq entails a considerable economic impact on the Czechoslovak economy. At a time when my country is following the path of democratic social transformation and fundamental economic reforms, the increasing losses incurred in the wake of the implementation of Security Council resolution 661 (1990) constitute a threat to the successful transition to the principles of a market economy.

As stated in the letter of the Minister for Foreign Affairs, Mr. Jiří Dienstbier (see S/21750), the overall losses are estimated at about $US 2 billion.

1. Direct economic loss

A. The freezing of outstanding claims against Iraq as of 31 December 1990 in the total amount of $US 400 million.

A contract has already been concluded with Iraq for oil deliveries in 1990 as a compensation for outstanding claims in the amount of $US 44 million. Besides, the Iraqi side was willing to compensate the remaining outstanding claims by gradual oil deliveries (in 1990 in the amount of an additional $US 100 million).

B. Other claims, which will become payable in subsequent years, in the amount of $US 150 million.

C. Suspension of the contracts already in effect, as follows:

- Engineering plant in Daura, in the amount of $US 82 million,

- Isomerization plant in Baiji, in the amount of $US 18 million,

---

a/ S/21837, annex.

0020

/...

- Ceramics plant in Ramadi, in the amount of $US 42 million,

- Oil refinery in Stred, in the amount of $US 185 million,

- Tractor parts manufacturing plant, in the amount of $US 45 million,

- Other contracts in the amount of $US 20 million.

The above combined loss incurred by Czechoslovakia amounts to $US 392 million (note: most equipment for the aforementioned ventures has already been produced).

D. Other unspecified direct loss as a result of open contracts being at an advanced stage of preparation, in the approximate amount of $US 300 million.

The total direct loss for the Czechoslovak economy amounts to more than $US 1.1 billion.

2. Indirect economic loss

A. An increase of oil prices by $US 1 per barrel represents a loss of $US 100 million per year. Thus, the estimated minimum loss would be between $US 400 million and $US 600 million per year for the Czech and Slovak Federal Republic.

B. The estimated internal impact (including possible close-outs of production enterprises) on the Czechoslovak economy amounts approximately to $US 400 million per year.

Thus the total indirect loss incurred by the Czechoslovak economy amounts approximately to $US 1 billion.

Czechoslovakia expects that the Security Council Committee established by resolution 661 (1990) will work out and submit to the Security Council in a very short time recommendations that will help partially to eliminate in a concrete manner the losses of the most affected countries.

I should be grateful if the text of this letter could be circulated as a document of the Security Council.

0021

/...

Enclosure II

Letter dated 19 November 1990 from the Permanent Representative of Czechoslovakia to the United Nations addressed to the President of the Security Council a/

[Original: English]

I have the honour to reaffirm that the Czech and Slovak Federal Republic has adopted concrete measures aimed at strict implementation of Security Council resolution 661 (1990), which are contained, *inter alia*, in Security Council document S/AC.25/1990/9. However, this position entails considerable negative consequences for the Czechoslovak economy exactly at the time of a resolved transition to the principles of market economy. Therefore, the Czech and Slovak Federal Republic has exercised its right and consulted, in accordance with Article 50 of the Charter, on the possibilities of alleviating its economic losses.

Following up to my letter of 2 October 1990 (S/21837), I wish to present some additional information in this regard:

	(In United States dollars)
Loss incurred in 1990	
Frozen assets of Czechoslovak foreign trade corporations in Iraq and Kuwait	586 million
Failed contracts due to the embargo	403 million
Effects of oil price increases on Czechoslovak balance of payments in feeely convertible currencies	592 million
Total	1 581 billion

The overall value of contracts under preparation with Iraq and Kuwait is estimated to be 2 billion Czechoslovak koruny (about $US 120 million).

Loss in 1991

The minimum estimated loss for 1991 caused by increased oil prices is $US 1 billion.

I should be grateful if the text of this letter could be circulated as a document of the Security Council.

---

a/ S/22019.

0022 /...

Annex IV

Recommendation by the Security Council Committee established by resolution 661 (1990) concerning the situation between Iraq and Kuwait with regard to Poland

The Security Council Committee established by resolution 661 (1990) concerning the situation between Iraq and Kuwait,

Having dealt with the communications received from Poland under Article 50 of the Charter of the United Nations,

Recalling Security Council resolution 661 (1990) of 6 August 1990 in which the Council decided to impose sanctions in accordance with Chapter VII of the Charter of the United Nations, as well as Security Council resolutions 660 (1990) of 2 August 1990, 662 (1990) of 9 August 1990, 664 (1990) of 18 August 1990, 665 (1990) of 25 August 1990, 666 (1990) of 13 September 1990, 667 (1990) of 16 September 1990, 669 (1990) of 24 September 1990, 670 (1990) of 25 September 1990 and 674 (1990) of 29 October 1990,

Recalling also the provisions of Articles 25, 49 and 50 of the Charter of the United Nations,

Noting the information given by Poland a/ regarding the measures taken to give full effect to the sanctions as laid down in resolution 661 (1990) and concerning the special economic problems it has been confronted with as a result of the implementation of those measures,

Having heard the representative of Poland,

Expressing concern at the special economic problems confronting Poland as a result of the severance of its economic relations with Iraq and occupied Kuwait as required by Security Council resolution 661 (1990), which are particularly difficult in terms of commercial and financial losses incurred by Poland,

Recognizing that the continued full implementation of Security Council resolution 661 (1990) by Poland, as well as other States, will support measures to ensure compliance with paragraph 2 of that resolution and to restore the authority of the legitimate Government of Kuwait,

1. Commends the Government of Poland for the measures it has taken to comply with resolution 661 (1990);

---

a/ S/21808, S/21918 and S/AC.25/1990/41.

2. Recognizes the urgent need to assist Poland in coping with its special economic problems resulting from the severance of its economic relations with Iraq and occupied Kuwait as required by Security Council resolution 661 (1990), especially those losses resulting from undelivered Iraqi oil shipments to Poland in payment for outstanding debts incurred by Iraq towards Poland and other financial and commercial losses;

3. Appeals to all States on an urgent basis to provide immediate technical, financial and material assistance to Poland to mitigate the adverse impact on its economy of the application by Poland of sanctions against Iraq pursuant to Security Council resolution 661 (1990);

4. Invites the competent organs and specialized agencies of the United Nations system, as well as the international financial institutions and the regional development banks, to provide assistance to Poland with a view to alleviating its special economic problems arising from the application of sanctions against Iraq pursuant to Security Council resolution 661 (1990);

5. Requests the Secretary-General, on a regular basis, to seek information from States and the concerned organs and agencies of the United Nations system on action taken to alleviate the special economic problems of Poland and to report thereon to the Security Council.

/...

0024

Enclosure I

Memorandum dated 20 September 1990 by the Government of the Republic of Poland for the Security Council Committee established by resolution 661 (1990) concerning the situation between Iraq and Kuwait on losses sustained by Poland resulting from the application of economic sanctions on Iraq a/

[Original: English]

The Council of Ministers of the Republic of Poland, in full support of Security Council resolution No. 661 of 6 August 1990, and overwhelmed by the resolve to implement its provisions, adopted a decree suspending all trade turnover and financial flow with Iraq as of 13 August 1990. In fact, the trade turnover suspension had been introduced earlier, almost immediately following the adoption of the said resolution. Also, sea and air transport communications were suspended thereafter.

The implementation of the above resolution has serious social and economic implications for Poland, as Iraq had for many years been Poland's major trading partner among Near and Middle Eastern countries. Since Poland belongs to heavily indebted countries, these implications are even more painful.

The Government of the Republic of Poland presents below the estimated direct and indirect losses resulting from Poland's participation in international sanctions against Iraq. Their full and long-term estimate is still being completed and will be presented separately at a later date.

Losses incurred by Poland, in the opinion of the Government, should be considered in the context of the country's dramatic economic and social situation, and in view of the extensive programme of radical reforms, under way for almost a year. The reforms are being carried out with the assistance of the international community, world financial institutions (IMF, WB) as well as a number of States (the Group of 24) who have addressed direct assistance to Poland. The introduction by the Government of restrictive monetary and financial policy, following the advice by United Nations specialized agencies has already contributed to bringing down the rate of inflation. The property and structural changes which have been initiated and which require great financial outlays, are expected to contribute to increasing economic efficiency. However, the Polish nation has been paying a very high price for those implemented changes. The 30 per cent drop in production and a similar drop in the already low living standards, and almost a million unemployed undermine further success of the reforms. Their realization - in the opinion of the Government of Poland - depends, to a considerable extent, on external factors, including stable co-operation and economic exchanges with abroad.

---

a/ S/21808, annex.

Meanwhile, changes in the conditions of trade with the Soviet Union, including limitations in the supply of crude oil and the shift to convertible currency accounts have aggravated the country's balance of payments. In this situation Iraq was expected to be an increasingly important oil supply source for Poland (circa 1.3 million tonnes by the end of this year in repayment for the debts owed by Iraq to Poland).

Last year, turnover with Iraq reached 367 million USD. Nevertheless, the network of economic ties with the country, developed over a period of many years, was based not only on the commodity trade exchange but also on important investment contacts entered upon by Polish companies individually, or as subcontractors, with large-scale financial and material inputs, the loss of which is particularly severe.

At the beginning of the conflict, 3,700 Polish nationals were employed on Iraq and Kuwaiti territory, of whom 1,700 had returned home on an emergency as by 14 September.

General losses are estimated at ca 2.4 billion USD.

In the short run, most perceptible is the suspension of payment of Iraqi debts to Poland, amounting to over 500 million USD. This means also the suspended delivery of 750,000 tonnes of crude oil which was to be supplied by the end of this year, and apparently no further deliveries in the years to come. Considering sharply increased oil prices, it means that Poland will have to spend an additional 170 million USD before the end of this year. Further costs of the trade embargo on Iraq and occupied Kuwait total:

- immediately perceptible by companies lost export values - 219 million USD
- financial loss in bank accounts, advance payments, guarantees for arrears, others - 183 million USD
- rolling contracts at signature stage, for the carrying out of which contractors had assembled equipment and ordered supplies - 1 515 million USD

The above list does not include the values of machinery, equipment, means of transport as well as other properties and possessions left by Polish enterprises in Kuwait, as well as their decapitalization, the degree of which will depend on the duration of the conflict. Also, the possessions left by Polish nationals in Iraq and Kuwait have not been taken into account, nor potential transfers of their savings and of bank deposits, due to the emergency departure for the home country, nor evacuation costs. It was also not possible to present from the quantitative angle the negative implications of severed economic links on the companies which were largely dependent on exports to the Iraqi market.

0026

/...

Considering the above, the Government of the Republic of Poland has repeatedly expressed its concern about the negative, multi-faceted and long-term consequences of the crisis in the Persian Gulf which would constitute a serious threat to the economic development of the country. Favourable changes in the Polish economy as well as the process of reforms might be slowed down. Liquid fuel prices increase threatens a revival of inflation, halted with such difficulty and at such high social cost. Envisaged implications for the Polish balance of payments in a situation where indebtedness will reach 43 billion USD by the end of 1990, the bankruptcies of enterprises (including those involved in investments in Iraq and Kuwait) as well as a sharp rise in the price of fuels may have grave consequences both in the economic and political sphere.

Their impact on the unprecedented peaceful process of democratic reforms and market transition in Poland taking into account their importance for all the countries of Central and Eastern Europe, might influence negatively the security and stability of the entire subregion. While the economic consequences of the crisis are relatively easy to estimate, the political and the social ones are difficult to access and - according to the records of the session of the Council of Ministers held on 13 August - Government is following them with utmost concern.

The Government of the Republic of Poland expresses its hope that the international community will show understanding for the particularly unfavourable situation in which Poland has found herself for the reasons beyond her control as a result of the conflict, and that it will contribute - by decisions of the Security Council and other competent international bodies - to alleviate the wide-scale consequences of our country's participation in the sanctions imposed by the United Nations Security Council, taking relevant immediate and long-term measures, including writing off a part of the Polish debt.

Poland counts therefore on international solidarity to offset the losses sustained by the States which are paying a high social and economic price at home for implementing the decisions of the Security Council. The Government of the Republic of Poland strongly supports the decisions of the Council charging its Special Committee with the task of investigating the losses sustained by Member States of the Organization as well as recommending measures to alleviate their losses. We expect that an international mechanism will soon be elaborated and agreed upon to ease the lot of most severely affected countries thus to demonstrate - in making - international solidarity to all the victims of the conflict.

0027

/...

Enclosure II

Reply of the Polish Government to the questionnaire on the national measures relating to the implementation of Security Council resolution 661 (1990) a/

[Original: English]

1. Legislative framework

(a) (i) The Polish Customs Law of 28 December 1989 (*Journal of Laws* No. 75, item 445 of 1989);

(ii) The Polish Law on Foreign Exchange Regulations and the Penal-Fiscal Act of 26 October 1971;

(b) No new legislation has been enacted;

(c) (i) The Council of Ministers Regulation of 13 August 1990 concerning the temporary ban on trade with Iraq and Kuwait;

(ii) The resolution of the Council of Ministers of the Republic of Poland dated 13 August 1990 on the implementation by the organs of State administration of Security Council resolution 661 (1990) of 6 August 1990 concerning the armed conflict between Iraq and Kuwait.

2. Control of imports or activities that would promote or are calculated to promote imports or trans-shipments of goods from Iraq and Kuwait

(a) Ministers, organs of State administration (heads of central organs of State administration) and governors of the provinces (*voivodes*) are under the obligation to undertake, within the scope of their competence, all necessary action aimed at ensuring the implementation of Security Council resolution 661 (1990). Supervision of the implementation of the resolution is vested with the Minister of Foreign Economic Relations in consultation with the Minister for Foreign Affairs;

(b) A ban was instituted on:

(i) The introduction into Poland of any commodities or products originating in, or coming from, Iraq or Kuwait;

(ii) The export from Poland to the said countries of any commodities or products originating in, or coming from, Poland.

---

a/ S/AC.25/1990/41.

0028

/...

Excluded from the application of the above measures are:

(i) Commodities and products intended strictly for medical purposes as well as foodstuffs supplied out of humanitarian considerations;

(ii) Commodities or products that originate in, or come from, Iraq or Kuwait and were exported before 7 August 1990.

Positions 30 and 44 were deleted from annex 5 of the Council of Ministers Regulation of 30 December 1989 regarding customs duties on commodities imported from abroad (Journal of Laws No. 75, item 448).

3. Control of exports or activities that would promote or are calculated to promote sales or supply of products and commodities to Iraq and Kuwait

(a) The same authorities as those named in paragraph 2 (a) above are responsible for implementing the control of such exports or activities as required by Security Council resolution 661 (1990);

(b) The same measures as those specified in paragraph 2 (b) above apply.

4. Control of financial or economic resources

(a) There is an effective system of control to prevent transfers of financial or economic resources covered by Security Council resolution 661 (1990) under the relevant provisions of the Polish Law on Foreign Exchange Regulations and the Penal-Fiscal Act of 26 October 1971;

(b) No specific legislative measures were necessary as the Minister for Finance is under the obligation to undertake all necessary action aimed at ensuring the implementation of Security Council resolution 661 (1990).

5. Enforcement

In the case of breaches of Security Council resolution 661 (1990) by individuals and companies, enforcement provided by the appropriate regulations of Polish Law will be applied.

In the specific case of unauthorized import or export of goods, the enforcement foreseen in the Polish Customs Law will be applied. As regards unauthorized movement of funds, penalties will be administered in accordance with the relevant provisions of the Polish Law on Foreign Exchange Regulations and the Penal-Fiscal Act of 26 October 1971.

6. Other

(a) In a memorandum dated 20 September 1990 the Government of Poland informed the Security Council Committee that the implementation of resolution 661 (1990) had serious social and economic implications for Poland, as Iraq had for many years been Poland's major trading partner among the Near and Middle Eastern countries.

0029 /...

These implications are particularly painful since Poland belongs to the heavily indebted countries. The losses incurred by Poland have a highly negative impact on the process of fundamental economic change that is currently taking place in this country. According to latest calculations, Poland estimates its losses at approximately $US 2.9 billion;

The Government of Poland is confident that the Security Council will make the necessary recommendations enabling Poland to overcome these difficulties;

(b) See items 1, 2 and 3;

(c) No specific measures to protect the assets of the legitimate Government of Kuwait were necessary owing to the absence of any such assets in Poland.

Annex V

Recommendation by the Security Council Committee established by resolution 661 (1990) concerning the situation between Iraq and Kuwait with regard to Mauritania

The Security Council Committee established by resolution 661 (1990) concerning the situation between Iraq and Kuwait,

Having dealt with the communications received from Mauritania under Article 50 of the Charter of the United Nations,

Recalling Security Council resolution 661 (1990) of 6 August 1990 in which the Council decided to impose sanctions in accordance with Chapter VII of the Charter of the United Nations, as well as Security Council resolutions 660 (1990) of 2 August 1990, 662 (1990) of 9 August 1990, 664 (1990) of 18 August 1990, 665 (1990) of 25 August 1990, 666 (1990) of 13 September 1990, 667 (1990) of 16 September 1990, 669 (1990) of 24 September 1990, 670 (1990) of 25 September 1990 and 674 (1990) of 29 October 1990,

Recalling also the provisions of Articles 25, 49 and 50 of the Charter of the United Nations,

Noting the information given by Mauritania a/ regarding the measures taken to give full effect to the sanctions as laid down in resolution 661 (1990) and concerning the special economic problems it has been confronted with as a result of the implementation of those measures,

Having heard the representative of Mauritania,

Expressing concern at the special economic problems confronting Mauritania, a least developed country, as a result of the severance of its economic relations with Iraq and occupied Kuwait as required by Security Council resolution 661 (1990), which are particularly difficult in terms of commercial and financial losses incurred by Mauritania,

Recognizing that the continued full implementation of Security Council resolution 661 (1990) by Mauritania, as well as other States, will support measures to ensure compliance with paragraph 2 of that resolution and to restore the authority of the legitimate Government of Kuwait,

1. Commends the Government of Mauritania for the measures it has taken to comply with resolution 661 (1990);

---

a/ S/21789, S/21818, S/AC.25/1990/20 and S/AC.25/1990/39.

/...

0031

2. Recognizes the urgent need to assist Mauritania in coping with its special economic problems resulting from the severance of its economic relations with Iraq and occupied Kuwait as required by Security Council resolution 661 (1990), especially those losses resulting from suspended capital flows from Kuwait and other commercial and financial losses;

3. Appeals to all States on an urgent basis to provide immediate technical, financial and material assistance to Mauritania to mitigate the adverse impact on its economy of the application by Mauritania of sanctions against Iraq pursuant to Security Council resolution 661 (1990);

4. Invites the competent organs and specialized agencies of the United Nations system, including the international financial institutions and the regional development banks, to review their programmes of assistance with Mauritania with a view to alleviating its special economic problems arising from the application of sanctions against Iraq pursuant to Security Council resolution 661 (1990);

5. Requests the Secretary-General, on a regular basis, to seek information from States and the concerned organs and agencies of the United Nations system on action taken to alleviate the special economic problems of Mauritania and to report thereon to the Security Council.

/...

Enclosure

Letter dated 24 September 1990 from the Minister for Foreign Affairs and Co-operation of Mauritania addressed to the Secretary-General a/

[Original: French]

Pursuant to my letter No. 1077 of 18 September 1990, by which I assured you of the determination of the Islamic Republic of Mauritania to comply with the provisions of Security Council resolution 661 (1990), I have the honour to set out below the problems which the Islamic Republic of Mauritania faces as a result of the implementation of that embargo, taking into account Mauritania's economic and financial relations with Iraq and Kuwait.

I. RELATIONS WITH IRAQ

1. While trade relations with Iraq were relatively insignificant, a $5 million contract was to have been carried out for the delivery of fish, exports of which would have amounted to $10 million.

2. In addition, Mauritania and Iraq were involved in joint ventures in the fishing industry (capital of $20 million) and the mining industry (capital of $70 million); the investment and export programmes for these ventures will be deferred, resulting in a loss of jobs and major funding.

3. Iraq was providing Mauritania with a subsidy and various forms of assistance equivalent to $100 million (training, technical assistance, medicines, agricultural equipment, school supplies, etc.).

4. Transfers from Mauritanian workers in Iraq amounted to $3 million.

The embargo against Iraq will thus cause Mauritania to suffer a loss the direct effects of which will cost $63 million, a figure that could reach $100 million if other effects on the economy are taken into account.

II. RELATIONS WITH KUWAIT

1. Traditionally, Kuwait has been one of the most important donors to Mauritania: current projects being financed by the Kuwaiti Fund for Arab Economic Development and projects for which Fund resources have been committed total $37.85 million and $49.1 million respectively. If the effect of the embargo on the Arab Fund for Economic and Social Development (AFESD), with headquarters in Kuwait, is also taken into consideration, these figures reach $125.7 million and

---

a/ S/21818, annex.

0033

/...

$132.9 million respectively, or a total of $258.6 million, which accounts for 40 per cent of the country's total investment programme. Moreover, the Inter-Arab Investment Guarantee Corporation was to have underwritten a major programme for the renovation of Mauritania's fishing fleet costing nearly $50 million.

The drying up of this financial flow as a result of the embargo has an impact that goes far beyond mere numbers, since, in the final analysis, it is the development of Mauritania's very economy that is being sold short, particularly when one considers that such financing is often combined with financing from other sources. The halting of flows from Kuwait casts doubts on the availability of a significant portion of flows from other sources.

2. Kuwait also invested in Mauritania through joint ventures in real estate, the mining industry and processing industries; cutting off the influx of capital to joint ventures will stop their development programmes, eliminating even more jobs. Total unpaid capital stands at $16 million.

Moreover, the effect of the embargo on the increase in crude oil prices has already caused Mauritania's oil bill to rise by $15 million, and this will no doubt be followed by a rise in domestic prices and the price of imported goods.

3. Trade with Kuwait is relatively limited and involves primarily silver, gold and gems. Kuwaiti charity organizations provided assistance through official and unofficial channels totalling $5 million.

Losses sustained in 1990 as a result of the embargo against Kuwait will total $127 million as a result of direct effects and $329 million when other effects on the economy are taken into account.

- In conclusion, the consequences of implementing the embargo will be serious for a country as poor as Mauritania, which must also face the problem of desertification.

- Mauritania's development programme will be interrupted and all the adjustments the country has undertaken for nearly six years will be called into question.

- There will be a significant rise in unemployment as enterprises are closed and/or dozens of projects are halted.

- The disequilibrium in the balance of payments will grow more pronounced: net flows from Iraq and Kuwait were largely positive.

There is thus reason to fear that the programme to rehabilitate the Mauritanian economy cannot be carried out according to schedule unless special assistance to offset lost aid can be secured. It is for this reason that, in accordance with Article 50 of Chapter VII of the Charter of the United Nations, which stipulates that, "if preventive or enforcement measures against any state are taken by the Security Council, any other state, whether a Member of the United Nations or not, which finds itself confronted with special economic problems

/...

0034

arising from the carrying out of those measures shall have the right to consult the Security Council with regard to a solution of those problems", the Government of the Islamic Republic of Mauritania deems it necessary to request the Security Council to help it find solutions that will safeguard the economic and social interests of Mauritania.

0035 /...

Annex VI

Recommendation by the Security Council Committee established by resolution 661 (1990) concerning the situation between Iraq and Kuwait with regard to Pakistan

The Security Council Committee established by resolution 661 (1990) concerning the situation between Iraq and Kuwait,

Having dealt with the communications received from Pakistan under Article 50 of the Charter of the United Nations,

Recalling Security Council resolution 661 (1990) of 6 August 1990 in which the Council decided to impose sanctions in accordance with Chapter VII of the Charter of the United Nations, as well as Security Council resolutions 660 (1990) of 2 August 1990, 662 (1990) of 9 August 1990, 664 (1990) of 18 August 1990, 665 (1990) of 25 August 1990, 666 (1990) of 13 September 1990, 667 (1990) of 16 September 1990, 669 (1990) of 24 September 1990, 670 (1990) of 25 September 1990 and 674 (1990) of 29 October 1990,

Recalling also the provisions of Articles 25, 49 and 50 of the Charter of the United Nations,

Noting the information given by Pakistan a/ regarding the measures taken to give full effect to the sanctions as laid down in resolution 661 (1990) and concerning the special economic problems it has been confronted with as a result of the implementation of those measures,

Having heard the representative of Pakistan,

Expressing concern at the special economic problems confronting Pakistan as a result of the severance of its economic relations with Iraq and occupied Kuwait as required by Security Council resolution 661 (1990), which are particularly difficult in terms of its commercial and financial losses, as well as costs associated with the repatriation and rehabilitation of Pakistani workers returning from Iraq and Kuwait,

Recognizing that the continued full implementation of Security Council resolution 661 (1990) by Pakistan, as well as other States, will support measures to ensure compliance with paragraph 2 of that resolution and to restore the authority of the legitimate Government of Kuwait,

1. Commends the Government of Pakistan for the measures it has taken to comply with resolution 661 (1990);

---

a/ S/21734, S/21776, S/21832, S/21875 and S/AC.25/1990/65.

/...

0036

2. Recognizes the urgent need to assist Pakistan in coping with its special economic problems resulting from the severance of its economic relations with Iraq and occupied Kuwait as required by Security Council resolution 661 (1990), especially those losses resulting from undelivered oil shipments from Iraq and Kuwait and other commercial and financial losses, as well as costs associated with the repatriation and rehabilitation of Pakistani workers returning from Iraq and Kuwait;

3. Appeals to all States on an urgent basis to provide immediate technical, financial and material assistance to Pakistan to mitigate the adverse impact on its economy of the application by Pakistan of sanctions against Iraq pursuant to Security Council resolution 661 (1990);

4. Invites the competent organs and specialized agencies of the United Nations system, including the international financial institutions and the regional development banks, to review their programmes of assistance to Pakistan with a view to alleviating its special economic problems arising from the application of sanctions against Iraq pursuant to Security Council resolution 661 (1990);

5. Requests the Secretary-General, on a regular basis, to seek information from States and the concerned organs and agencies of the United Nations system on action taken to alleviate the special economic problems of Pakistan and to report thereon to the Security Council.

Enclosure I

Memorandum on economic and financial impact on Pakistan, resulting from restrictions on economic relations with Iraq and Kuwait a/

[Original: English]

The implementation of United Nations Security Council resolution 661 (1990) has had an immediate and adverse impact on Pakistan's economy. The following are the direct consequences for Pakistan's economy:

(1)	Evacuation and rehabilitation of Pakistanis	$ 70 million
(2)	Loss of home remittances	$300 million
(3)	Loss of export receipts	$100 million
(4)	Increase in the price of oil	$600 million

1. Evacuation and rehabilitation of Pakistanis

Official assessment indicates that 100,000 Pakistanis in Kuwait and Iraq have to be evacuated. About 10,000 Pakistanis are expected to travel back to Pakistan by their own vehicles or through other means of road transportation. The remaining 90,000 will travel by air or sea. The passage by a Pakistan International Airlines flight from Amman to Karachi costs 7,500 Pakistan rupees, and from Riyadh to Karachi PRs 6,000 while the approximate cost by sea journey also comes to PRs 7,000 per person. The average transportation cost for bringing back a Pakistani from various stations in the Middle East to Karachi is estimated roughly at PRs 7,000. The expenditure thus expected to be incurred on travel by air and sea would therefore be PRs 630 million.

Those returning by their own vehicles or other means of road transportation will need to be provided PRs 10,000 per head to meet the cost of gasoline, hire charges for buses, temporary shelter and food charges in Turkey, the Islamic Republic of Iran and the Syrian Arab Republic. About PRs 100 million will be incurred on 10,000 persons travelling by road.

To facilitate internal movement within Pakistan and to meet other expenses for reaching the final destination, the Government has decided to pay PRs 6,000 to each person at the time of entry into Pakistan. The total burden of the cash grant would amount to PRs 600 million.

---

a/ S/21776, annex.

0038

The evacuees reaching Riyadh and Amman were transported from the borders, lodged in camps and provided food, blankets and medical aid before their embarkation on planes and ships. While all the evacuees in Riyadh have been cleared, there is a continuous flow to Amman. The cost of running camps at these places is estimated at $3.5 million, i.e., about PRs 70 million. Similarly, reception camps have been established at Taftan for overland evacuees and at Karachi for those returning by sea or air. The cost per head presently is estimated at PRs 1,000, with a total cost of PRs 100 million. Thus, camps and associated relief inputs will cost about PRs 170 million.

The summary of expenditure on the facilities noted above is given below.

		Millions of Pakistan rupees
a.	Travel expenditure at PRs 7,000 per head for 90,000 persons by air/sea	630
b.	Travel expenditure of 10,000 evacuees moving by land route at PRs 1,000 per head	100
c.	Expenditure on camps in Amman and Riyadh	70
d.	Payment at entry point for 100,000 evacuees at PRs 6,000 per head	600
e.	Reception camps at Karachi, Taftan: transportation and food	100
	Grand total	1 500
		(Approximately $70 million)

The majority of expatriate Pakistanis have both the skill and enterprise for gainful absorption into the economy. To facilitate the process, schemes for their rehabilitation are under preparation. The cost to the federal budget will be known when returns and estimates are firmed up.

2. Loss of home remittances

Pakistan was receiving home remittances of about $170 million annually from Kuwait. As a result of the crisis, Pakistanis in Kuwait and Iraq are returning home. Due to disturbed conditions in the Gulf area, home remittances from other Gulf countries are also expected to decline. The total loss in home remittances is presently estimated at $300 million.

0039 /...

3. Loss of export receipts

The embargo on trade with occupied Kuwait and Iraq will cause a loss of $100 million in the form of export receipts.

4. Increase in the price of oil

The Gulf crisis will have a serious impact on the already tenuous balance-of-payments position of Pakistan since most of the refined petroleum products were being imported from Kuwait. Import payments are estimated to go up very significantly due to the increase in oil prices. The budget for 1990/91 projects a crude oil price at $17 per barrel, fuel oil at $85 per ton and other petroleum products at $160 per ton. As a result, POL (petroleum, oil and lubricants) import payments for the year 1990/91 are expected to add a burden of $600 million to the projection of $1,304 million incorporated in the budget as shown in the following table:

POL imports

	Budget	Projections (Revised)
Crude oil		
Value (millions of dollars)	470.0	664.0
Volume (millions of barrels)	27.7	27.7
Price (dollars per barrel)	17.0	24.0
Fuel oil		
Value (millions of dollars)	161.0	227.0
Volume (millions of tons)	1.9	1.9
Price (dollars per ton)	85.0	119.0
Others		
Value (millions of dollars)	673.0	950.0
Volume (millions of tons)	4.2	4.2
Price (dollars per ton)	160.0	226.0

/...

0040

Thus, loss of exports, a surge in oil prices and a drop in home remittances will increase Pakistan's current account deficit by about $1 billion in 1990/91. With foreign exchange liquid reserves of $500 million, sufficient to cover only a two weeks' import bill, it will not be possible for Pakistan to absorb the loss. In addition, an outlay of $70 million (PRs 1,500 million) which includes some foreign exchange expenditure on travel, camps and other operations, is required for Pakistanis returning from Kuwait and Iraq.

To overcome these unforeseen problems, Pakistan would need additional assistance of about $1,100 million by way of quick disbursing aid to support the deteriorating balance-of-payments position and also for the evacuation of Pakistanis from Kuwait and Iraq.

It is hoped that donor countries, the United Nations and international agencies would extend all possible assistance so that Pakistan can overcome these problems.

0041 /...

Enclosure II

Letter dated 12 October 1990 from the Permanent Representative of Pakistan to the United Nations addressed to the President of the Security Council a/

[Original: English]

In a letter dated 14 September (S/21776), I had conveyed to the President of the Security Council a memorandum on economic and financial impact on Pakistan resulting from the restrictions on economic relations with Iraq and Kuwait, pursuant to Security Council resolution 661 (1990). In that memorandum it was estimated that as a result of these restrictions, Pakistan's current-account deficit would increase by about $1 billion in 1990/91.

Since then, the price of oil and related products has increased considerably. It is estimated that as a result of these increases, Pakistan would now have to pay an extra $1,596 million during the current financial year for oil imports alone, as shown in the following table:

Petroleum, oil and lubricants (POL) imports

	Budget	Projections
Crude oil		
Value (millions of dollars)	470.0	915.0
Volume (millions of barrels)	27.7	27.7
Price (dollars per barrel)	17.0	36.0
Fuel oil		
Value (millions of dollars)	161.0	317.0
Volume (millions of tons)	1.9	1.9
Price (dollars per ton)	85.0	173.0

---

a/ S/21875.

/...

0042

	Budget	Projections
Others		
Value (millions of dollars)	673.0	1 668.0
Volume (millions of tons)	4.2	4.2
Price (dollars per ton)	160.0	397.0
Freight (millions of dollars)	10.0	10.0
(millions of dollars)	1 314.0	2 910.0

Thus, as a result of loss of exports to Iraq and Kuwait ($100 million), a drop in home remittances ($300 million), expenditure on repatriation of Pakistanis from Kuwait and Iraq ($70 million), and oil price increases ($1,596 million), Pakistan's current-account deficit will increase by approximately $2 billion in 1990/91. Consequently, Pakistan would need additional assistance of over $2,100 million by way of quick disbursing aid to support the deteriorating balance-of-payments position and for the evacuation of Pakistanis from Kuwait and Iraq.

0043

/...

Annex VII

Recommendation by the Security Council Committee established by resolution 661 (1990) concerning the situation between Iraq and Kuwait with regard to the Sudan

The Security Council Committee established by resolution 661 (1990) concerning the situation between Iraq and Kuwait,

Having dealt with the communications received from the Sudan under Article 50 of the Charter of the United Nations,

Recalling Security Council resolution 661 (1990) of 6 August 1990 in which the Council decided to impose sanctions in accordance with Chapter VII of the Charter of the United Nations, as well as Security Council resolutions 660 (1990) of 2 August 1990, 662 (1990) of 9 August 1990, 664 (1990) of 18 August 1990, 665 (1990) of 25 August 1990, 666 (1990) of 13 September 1990, 667 (1990) of 16 September 1990, 669 (1990) of 24 September 1990, 670 (1990) of 25 September 1990 and 674 (1990) of 29 October 1990,

Recalling also the provisions of Articles 25, 49 and 50 of the Charter of the United Nations,

Noting the information given by the Sudan a/ regarding the measures taken to give full effect to the sanctions as laid down in resolution 661 (1990) and concerning the special economic problems it has been confronted with as a result of the implementation of those measures,

Having considered the information given by the Sudan,

Expressing concern at the special economic problems confronting the Sudan, a least developed country, as a result of the severance of its economic relations with Iraq and occupied Kuwait as required by Security Council resolution 661 (1990), which are particularly difficult in terms of commercial and financial losses incurred by the Sudan, as well as costs associated with the repatriation and rehabilitation of Sudanese workers returning from Iraq and Kuwait,

Recognizing that the continued full implementation of Security Council resolution 661 (1990) by the Sudan, as well as other States, will support measures to ensure compliance with paragraph 2 of that resolution and to restore the authority of the legitimate Government of Kuwait,

1. Commends the Government of the Sudan for the measures it has taken to comply with resolution 661 (1990);

---

a/ S/21675 and S/21930.

0044 /...

2. Recognizes the urgent need to assist the Sudan in coping with its special economic problems resulting from the severance of its economic relations with Iraq and occupied Kuwait as required by Security Council resolution 661 (1990), especially those losses resulting from undelivered Iraqi products to the Sudan and suspended capital flows from Kuwait, in addition to other commercial and financial losses, as well as costs associated with the repatriation and rehabilitation of Sudanese workers returning from Iraq and Kuwait;

3. Appeals to all States on an urgent basis to provide immediate technical, financial and material assistance to the Sudan to mitigate the adverse impact on its economy of the application by the Sudan of sanctions against Iraq pursuant to Security Council resolution 661 (1990);

4. Invites the competent organs and specialized agencies of the United Nations system, including the international financial institutions and the regional development banks, to review their programme of assistance to the Sudan with a view to alleviating its special economic problems arising from the application of sanctions against Iraq pursuant to Security Council resolution 661 (1990);

5. Requests the Secretary-General, on a regular basis, to seek information from States and the concerned organs and agencies of the United Nations system on action taken to alleviate the special economic problems of the Sudan and to report thereon to the Security Council.

0045

/...

Enclosure

Memorandum on the adverse economic and financial impact on the Sudan resulting from the Gulf crisis a/

[Original: English]

Sudan has faced a deteriorating economic situation during the last few years resulting from recurrent drought and rainfall shortages, influx of refugees and displaced people, as well as the armed conflict in the southern part of the country.

Despite all efforts exerted by the Government to mitigate the situation by adopting stringent economic reforms, the economic situation was lately aggravated by the Gulf crisis that laid adverse, direct and indirect economic and financial impact on the Sudanese economy.

Following is a brief outline of the direct and indirect impact:

	United States dollars (Millions)
A. Direct impact:	
1. The Gulf crisis is creating severe problems to the Sudanese economy. The most immediate of these problems have already been felt in the sharp increase in oil prices. At the current price of $40 per barrel, the country will have to pay an additional $200(M)	200
2. As for wheat which could have been bought at a highly favourable price ($130/ton) from Saudi Arabia, the country will lose $60 million, i.e., 9 months' supply of 450 tons	60
3. Another direct consequence of the crisis is the freezing of the trade protocol with Iraq and the expected delay in the implementation of the trade protocol with Jordan; the size of the two protocols is $100(M)	100
4. Export earnings are also expected to shrink considerably since the Gulf States have recently become an important market for some of our traditional export commodities. The drop in the expected revenue from these exports is now anticipated as follows:	360

---

a/ S/21930, annex.

0046 /...

		United States dollars (Millions)
	(Brought forward)	360
(a) Livestock	70	
(b) Vegetables and fruit	20	
(c) Sesame	15	
(d) Sorghum	70	175
5. The second area where the economy is expected to suffer is the remittances from the Sudanese working in the Gulf and who used to be a major source of import financing. Revenue from this source is anticipated to drop by about 30 per cent as a result of the atmosphere of uncertainty created by the crisis. Moreover, those who returned home have lost their jobs, properties and probably their savings; and have already started to exert an additional pressure on our meagre resources and services. Loss in remittances plus expenses on those who returned to reach $300(M)		300
6. Project aid from the Kuwaiti Fund and the Arab Fund has, for practical reasons, come to a halt. Drawings from these two institutions are estimated at $200(M) during fiscal year 1990/91. These were allocated to finance most urgently needed and vital projects whose main objectives are to boost production of essential commodities and eliminate serious infrastructural bottle-necks		200
7. General increase in freight and insurance is estimated at $20(M)		20
8. Expected increases in exports of industrial countries due to higher oil prices are estimated at $130(M)		130
Total direct adverse financial impact of the Gulf crisis on the Sudan's external account is estimated at		1 185

0047

/...

B. Indirect impact:

The Gulf crisis has also an indirect impact on the country's general budget and the performance of its economy at large. Subsidies on petrol, wheat and medicine are expected to reach L.S. 4 billion (about $1 billion). This will incur more borrowing from the banking system and hence cause an increase in the supply of money. Such measures will lead to higher rate of inflation, with all its adverse consequences on incentives to producers and the performance of the economy on the macro level.

Annex VIII

Recommendation by the Security Council Committee established by resolution 661 (1990) concerning the situation between Iraq and Kuwait with regard to Uruguay

The Security Council Committee established by resolution 661 (1990) concerning the situation between Iraq and Kuwait,

Having dealt with the communications received from Uruguay under Article 50 of the Charter of the United Nations,

Recalling Security Council resolution 661 (1990) of 6 August 1990 in which the Council decided to impose sanctions in accordance with Chapter VII of the Charter of the United Nations, as well as Security Council resolutions 660 (1990) of 2 August 1990, 662 (1990) of 9 August 1990, 664 (1990) of 18 August 1990, 665 (1990) of 25 August 1990, 666 (1990) of 13 September 1990, 667 (1990) of 16 September 1990, 669 (1990) of 24 September 1990, 670 (1990) of 25 September 1990 and 674 (1990) of 29 October 1990,

Recalling also the provisions of Articles 25, 49 and 50 of the Charter of the United Nations,

Noting the information given by Uruguay a/ regarding the measures taken to give full effect to the sanctions as laid down in resolution 661 (1990) and concerning the special economic problems it has been confronted with as a result of the implementation of those measures,

Having heard the representative of Uruguay,

Expressing concern at the special economic problems confronting Uruguay as a result of the severance of its economic relations with Iraq and occupied Kuwait as required by Security Council resolution 661 (1990), which are particularly difficult in terms of its commercial and economic losses,

Recognizing that the continued full implementation of Security Council resolution 661 (1990) by Uruguay, as well as other States, will support measures to ensure compliance with paragraph 2 of that resolution and to restore the authority of the legitimate Government of Kuwait,

1. Commends the Government of Uruguay for the measures it has taken to comply with resolution 661 (1990);

---

a/ S/21775 and S/AC.25/1990/34.

0049

/...

2. Recognizes the urgent need to assist Uruguay in coping with its special economic problems resulting from the severance of its economic relations with Iraq and occupied Kuwait as required by Security Council resolution 661 (1990), especially those losses resulting from undelivered Uruguayan products to Iraq and Kuwait;

3. Appeals to all States on an urgent basis to provide appropriate assistance to Uruguay to mitigate the adverse impact on its economy of the application by Uruguay of sanctions against Iraq pursuant to Security Council resolution 661 (1990);

4. Invites the competent organs and specialized agencies of the United Nations system, including the international financial institutions and the regional development banks, to review their programmes of assistance to Uruguay with a view to alleviating its special economic problems arising from the application of sanctions against Iraq pursuant to Security Council resolution 661 (1990);

5. Requests the Secretary-General, on a regular basis, to seek information from States and the concerned organs and agencies of the United Nations system on action taken to alleviate the special economic problems of Uruguay and to report thereon to the Security Council.

Enclosure I

Letter dated 13 September 1990 from the Permanent Representative of Uruguay to the United Nations addresssed to the President of the Security Council a/

[Original: Spanish]

Upon instructions from my Government, I have the honour to refer to the application to Uruguay of the provisions of Article 50 of the Charter of the United Nations, in the light of the economic difficulties which my country is facing as a result of the application against Iraq of the measures provided for by the Security Council in its resolution 661 (1990).

The Government of Uruguay, a country which has a deep-rooted law-abiding tradition and respects the decisions of United Nations bodies, has taken the necessary steps to ensure that its authorities and citizens comply with the embargo imposed against Iraq under the provisions of the above-mentioned resolution.

The implementation of this embargo has serious adverse consequences for our national interests by aggravating the progressive economic deterioration which has been affecting our country for several years.

Indeed, the flow of trade between Uruguay and Iraq had recently provided sizable benefits to our economy, owing to a succession of trade balances favourable to Uruguay. The volume of trade may not seem significant in absolute terms, but in the context of our national economy it represents significant amounts, particularly if it is borne in mind that the economy is greatly dependent on exports and has been facing a grave economic crisis for a number of years.

The suspension of this trade seriously affects our interests, since we have had to cancel export orders already placed as well as ongoing negotiations.

The interruption of lamb exports is having particularly grave repercussions on the Uruguayan economy, since this product, in the light of the present state of Uruguay's production and export sectors, is vital to the economy of the country.

It is for these reasons that I am turning to the Security Council, on behalf of my Government and in exercise of the right granted by Article 50 of the Charter of the United Nations, in order to initiate consultations with the Council with a view to solving these problems faced by Uruguay as a result of the implementation of resolution 661 (1990).

---

a/ S/21775.

Enclosure II

Aide-mémoire on Uruguay's presentation to the Working Group of the Committee established by Security Council resolution 661 (1990) a/

[Original: English]

Uruguay is a small country with a long and well-established tradition of honouring its international obligations as part of its commitment to strengthening international law. It therefore immediately abided by the sanctions imposed by resolution 661 (1990) and others and enacted the necessary domestic legislation to enforce the embargo against Iraq. This action was taken without hesitation, in spite of the serious, immediate and direct effects it would have upon the country's economy.

These effects are particularly negative given the present situation and prospects of the Uruguay economy.

Economic situation of Uruguay

The economy of my country is and always has been heavily dependent on external factors. This is mainly due to the limitations of our doemstic market plus our need to import two mainstays for our economic development: capital goods and oil. Thus, in order to finance our development we have to expand our exports.

Uruguay is essentially an agricultural and agro-industrial country. We rely heavily on the export of agricultural commodities. Under normal free market conditions our natural and human resources would allow us to harbour good expectations. However, discriminatory practices in the international markets and the emergence of extraordinary circumstances beyond our control can jeopardize our best efforts and highlight Uruguay's vulnerability to external factors.

To guard against these risks it was necessary to diversify and to find new markets. One of the results of this drive was that the countries of the Middle East and of the Persian Gulf, particularly Iraq became important trade partners.

The ever-present need to increase our exports became even more imperative on account of our foreign debt and our determination not to default on its payments.

Note should be taken that all these challenges have to be met within the context of difficult economic and social problems.

Having opted for an economic model based on an open economy, Uruguay has engaged in a policy that entails very important structural adjustments such as reducing state intervention and expenditure and the adoption of measures directed at curtailing inflation, all of which have a high social and political cost.

---

a/ S/22026, annex.

In view of this situation, it is not difficult to understand the disastrous effects of the Gulf crisis on Uruguay's economy. Nor is it surprising that the main international organizations dealing with world and regional economic and financial problems - such as the World Bank and the "Latin American Economic System" organization - have singled Uruguay out as one of the countries most affected by the current oil crisis.

Uruguay imports 100 per cent of its fuel requirements and uses it mainly for the transportation of goods and the generation of electricity. Therefore, the first impact of the crisis came as a sudden sharp rise in the price of its imports. The cost of Uruguay's oil imports for 1990 rose by almost $42 million, or the equivalent of 3 per cent of all estimated imports for 1990. The estimates for 1991 are no better but depend mostly on future developments of the crisis. In any case, additional expenditures for next year would equal 1 per cent of the gross national product.

This disastrous situation will serve as a framework to understand the very negative impact of the applications of the sanctions imposed on Iraq by the Security Council and duly observed by Uruguay.

Effects of the Security Council imposed embargo

For several years, the private sector in Uruguay, with official support, had tried to penetrate Middle East markets, particularly Iraq, and had begun to be increasingly successful as far as volume, prices and payment conditions were concerned.

Over the last few years Iraq became a very important buyer of beef, mutton and rice. As far as mutton is concerned, Iraq became the primary importer from Uruguay, rising from 2,000 tons to more than 15,000 tons in 1989. This represents 29 per cent of total mutton exports. The value of immediate losses as a result of the conflict is estimated at $22 million. However, since the market as a whole can be presumed to be lost because of this situation, at least in the foreseeable future, the actual figure would be closer to $34 million for 1990-1991. This is equal to 1 per cent of total exports for 1990 or 2 per cent of total exports estimated for 1991.

Efforts at replacing this market have so far proved very difficult, despite intense bilateral efforts, owing to well known obstacles in the international market. Given the disappointing result of the General Agreement on Tariffs and Trade's Uruguay Round, particularly regarding agricultural products, the prospects are not encouraging.

The effect on the country's economy, however, is belied by these apparently minor figures. First, such large purchases are very important inputs to the stock management equation. Secondly, the mutton industry was highly dependent on these exports and as a direct result of no longer being able to sell to Iraq, private companies have been left on the verge of bankruptcy and have been forced to lay off up to 50 per cent of the work force. Since this industry is the economic backbone

0053 /...

of certain areas of the country, the ensuing social and related economic effects are potentially devastating to these areas owing to their multiplying effect and therefore to the economy as a whole.

In summary, the simple and very probable continuation of this situation will mean that Uruguay will lose $53.8 million from its trade balance in 1990 and $112 million in 1991. This latter figure is equal to 1.3 per cent of the gross national product or 5 per cent of estimated exports for this year.

This loss of income has obvious negative effects on Uruguay's capacity to save, invest and import, and on a wider sense on its economic growth, its unemployment rate and price levels.

In conclusion, the resulting damage to the Uruguayan economy is qualitatively and in terms of its own proportions very serious.

In our opinion, this whole situation is clearly covered by the provisions of Article 50 of the Charter of the United Nations, that is to say that there exists a special economic problem arising from the carrying out of the sanctions imposed by the Security Council.

Annex IX

Recommendation by the Security Council Committee established by resolution 661 (1990) concerning the situation between Iraq and Kuwait with regard to Viet Nam

The Security Council Committee established by resolution 661 (1990) concerning the situation between Iraq and Kuwait,

Having dealt with the communications received from Viet Nam under Article 50 of the Charter of the United Nations,

Recalling Security Council resolution 661 (1990) of 6 August 1990 in which the Council decided to impose sanctions in accordance with Chapter VII of the Charter of the United Nations, as well as Security Council resolutions 660 (1990) of 2 August 1990, 662 (1990) of 9 August 1990, 664 (1990) of 18 August 1990, 665 (1990) of 25 August 1990, 666 (1990) of 13 September 1990, 667 (1990) of 16 September 1990, 669 (1990) of 24 September 1990, 670 (1990) of 25 September 1990 and 674 (1990) of 29 October 1990,

Recalling also the provisions of Articles 25, 49 and 50 of the Charter of the United Nations,

Noting the information given by Viet Nam a/ regarding the measures taken to give full effect to the sanctions as laid down in resolution 661 (1990) and concerning the special economic problems it has been confronted with as a result of the implementation of those measures,

Having heard the representative of Viet Nam,

Expressing concern at the special economic problems confronting Viet Nam as a result of the severance of its economic relations with Iraq and occupied Kuwait as required by Security Council resolution 661 (1990), which are particularly difficult in terms of its commercial and financial losses,

Recognizing that the continued full implementation of Security Council resolution 661 (1990) by Viet Nam, as well as other States, will support measures to ensure compliance with paragraph 2 of that resolution and to restore the authority of the legitimate Government of Kuwait,

1. Commends the Government of Viet Nam for the measures it has taken to comply with resolution 661 (1990);

2. Recognizes the urgent need to assist Viet Nam in coping with its special economic problems resulting from the severance of its economic relations with Iraq

---

a/ S/21696, S/21810, S/21821, S/AC.25/1990/16 and S/22004.

0055

/...

and occupied Kuwait as required by Security Council resolution 661 (1990), especially those losses resulting from undelivered Vietnamese products to Iraq and other commercial and financial losses;

3. Appeals to all States on an urgent basis to provide immediate technical, financial and material assistance to Viet Nam to mitigate the adverse impact on its economy of the application by Viet Nam of sanctions against Iraq pursuant to Security Council resolution 661 (1990);

4. Invites the competent organs and specialized agencies of the United Nations system, including the international financial institutions and the regional development banks, to review their programmes of assistance with Viet Nam with a view to providing assistance to Viet Nam so as to alleviate its special economic problems arising from the application of sanctions against Iraq pursuant to Security Council resolution 661 (1990);

5. Requests the Secretary-General, on a regular basis, to seek information from States and the concerned organs and agencies of the United Nations system on action taken to alleviate the special economic problems of Viet Nam and to report thereon to the Security Council.

0056

/...

Enclosure

Memorandum on the economic, commercial and financial impact on Viet Nam resulting from restrictions on economic relations with Iraq and Kuwait a/

[Original: English]

As an underdeveloped country whose economy was devastated during many years of war, Viet Nam's strict implementation of Security Council resolution 661 (1990) has had an immediate and serious impact on Viet Nam's fragile economy, especially at a time when Viet Nam has begun a renewal process with a view to transforming its economy from a system of bureaucratic and centralized management based on State subsidies into an economy of commodity production and at a time when Viet Nam has begun implementing the plan for the voluntary repatriation of Vietnamese refugees.

The following are some of the losses inflicted on Viet Nam's economy as a result of Viet Nam's strict implementation of Security Council resolution 661 (1990):

	(United States dollars)
A. Direct impact	
1. Losses in exports to Iraq	
(a) Goods already shipped but that could not reach Iraq	500 000
(b) Goods to be delivered as per contracts already signed but that now must be cancelled	6 500 000
(c) Value of contracts ready for signing with Iraq but that now will have to be dropped	3 500 000
2. Total loss for the Government of Viet Nam due to abrupt termination of contracts of 16,305 Vietnamese workers working in Iraq	112 602 290
3. Value of contracts already signed with Iraq for a further 10,000 Vietnamese workers to work in Iraq that are now suspended	53 080 000

a/ S/22004, annex.

0057

/...

	(United States dollars)
4. Total value of loans and credits which Kuwait provided Viet Nam for the construction of an irrigation project and some other projects in the central highland areas of Viet Nam. All this has now been suspended	30 000 000
B. Indirect impact	
1. Total local costs in Viet Nam incurred due to the return of 16,305 workers (costs in terms of settlement allowances, employment arrangements, job retraining, etc.)	8 528 600
2. Additional costs for oil imports until the end of 1990 owing to the increase in oil price	100 000 000
3. Additional costs incurred for imports of chemical fertilizers	12 500 000
4. Additional costs incurred for imports of various chemicals, plastics and iron, etc. (approximate)	50 000 000
Total	377 210 890

5. Other impact on the country's economy that cannot be estimated yet:

(a) Transportation costs increased by:

(i) 70 per cent for road transport;

(ii) 13 per cent for rail transport;

(iii) 30 per cent for maritime transport;

(b) Additional production cost for coal mining (estimated increase from 80,000 Vietnamese dongs to 120,000 dongs per ton);

(c) Additional production cost for power generation (increased from 167 dongs/KW to 213 dongs).

The overall impact of the Gulf crisis on such an economy in transition as that of Viet Nam is extremely damaging. This is in terms not only of adverse effects on the country's socio-economic development efforts and plans, but also of direct effects on the current living conditions of the people.

It is in this context that Viet Nam seeks assistance from the United Nations and international agencies to overcome those difficulties.

0058 /...

Annex X

Recommendation by the Security Council Committee established by resolution 661 (1990) concerning the situation between Iraq and Kuwait with regard to Bangladesh

The Security Council Committee established by resolution 661 (1990) concerning the situation between Iraq and Kuwait,

Having dealt with the communication received from Bangladesh under Article 50 of the Charter of the United Nations,

Recalling Security Council resolution 661 (1990) of 6 August 1990 in which the Council decided to impose sanctions in accordance with Chapter VII of the Charter of the United Nations, as well as Security Council resolutions 660 (1990) of 2 August 1990, 662 (1990) of 9 August 1990, 664 (1990) of 18 August 1990, 665 (1990) of 25 August 1990, 666 (1990) of 13 September 1990, 667 (1990) of 16 September 1990, 669 (1990) of 24 September 1990, 670 (1990) of 25 September 1990 and 674 (1990) of 29 October 1990,

Recalling further the provisions of Articles 25, 49 and 50 of the Charter of the United Nations,

Noting the information given by Bangladesh a/ regarding the measures taken to give full effect to the sanctions as laid down in resolution 661 (1990) and concerning the special economic problems it has been confronted with as a result of the implementation of those measures,

Having heard the representative of Bangladesh,

Expressing concern at the special economic problems confronting Bangladesh, a least developed country, as a result of the severance of its economic relations with Iraq and occupied Kuwait as required by Security Council resolution 661 (1990), which are particularly difficult in terms of its commercial and financial losses, as well as costs associated with the repatriation and rehabilitation of Bangladeshi workers returning from Kuwait and Iraq,

Recognizing that the continued full implementation of Security Council resolution 661 (1990) by Bangladesh, as well as other States, will support measures to ensure compliance with paragraph 2 of that resolution and to restore the authority of the legitimate Government of Kuwait,

1. Commends the Government of Bangladesh for the measures it has taken to comply with resolution 661 (1990);

---

a/ S/21856.

0059

/...

2. Recognizes the urgent need to assist Bangladesh in coping with its special economic problems resulting from the severance of its economic relations with Iraq and occupied Kuwait as required by Security Council resolution 661 (1990), especially those losses resulting from undelivered Bangladeshi products to Iraq and Kuwait as well as costs associated with the repatriation and rehabilitation of Bangladeshi workers returning from Kuwait and Iraq;

3. Appeals to all States on an urgent basis to provide immediate technical, financial and material assistance to Bangladesh to mitigate the adverse impact on its economy of the application by Bangladesh of sanctions against Iraq pursuant to Security Council resolution 661 (1990);

4. Invites the competent organs and specialized agencies of the United Nations system, including the international financial institutions and the regional development banks, to review their programmes of assistance with Bangladesh with a view to alleviating its special economic poblems arising from the application of sanctions against Iraq pursuant to Security Council resolution 661 (1990);

5. Requests the Secretary-General, on a regular basis, to seek information from States and the concerned organs and agencies of the United Nations system on action taken to alleviate the special economic problems of Bangladesh and to report thereon to the Security Council.

0060 /...

Enclosure

Memorandum on the economic and financial impact on Bangladesh resulting from restrictions on economic relations with Iraq and Kuwait a/

[Original: English]

Bangladesh has been abiding by Security Council resolution 661 (1990). The implementation of the resolution has had immediate and adverse repercussions on the economy of Bangladesh. The memorandum explains the economic losses that Bangladesh would face as a result of the imposition of sanctions against Iraq and Kuwait. The impact of sanctions has caused serious damage to the economy and development efforts of Bangladesh. The adverse consequences are felt most acutely in the following areas:

(a) Cost of repatriation and rehabilitation of Bangladeshis displaced from Iraq and Kuwait;

(b) Loss of remittances;

(c) Increase in the price of oil;

(d) Loss of exports;

(e) Loss of aid.

1. Repatriation and rehabilitation of Bangladeshis

According to estimates, 100,000 Bangladeshis were employed in Kuwait and Iraq. Bangladesh is obliged to bear the burden of their repatriation. The cost of such repatriation is tentatively estimated at about $US 36 million. Stranded Bangladeshis are being airlifted from Jordan, Turkey and Saudi Arabia. In addition to these costs, and loss of remittances, the Government will have to spend an enormous amount to rehabilitate the returnee Bangladeshis. With Bangladesh's fragile economy, it will be an extremely difficult task to absorb them into the economy. It will aggravate the already high unemployment situation in the country and put an unbearable social burden on the country.

2. Loss of remittances

The Gulf crisis has stopped annual remittances of $US 160 million from Bangladeshis employed in Kuwait and Iraq. The situation has caused a large exodus of Bangladeshis from the area.

---

a/ S/21856, annex.

3. Increase in the price of oil

Bangladesh has been most seriously affected by the rise in the price of oil as most of its requirements are met from imports from the Middle East. The additional cost of petroleum, oil and lubricants to the economy at the current price would be very high. Computation of the exact amount is rendered difficult owing to the continual rise in oil prices.

4. Loss of exports

Kuwait and Iraq have been important trading partners of Bangladesh. The embargo will result in an annual loss of exports to these countries in the amount of $US 120 million.

5. Loss of aid

The crisis has resulted in the loss of $US 56 million from Kuwait lined up for various projects in Bangladesh.

Besides these, the crisis and its prolongation will mean for Bangladesh an estimated revenue loss of about taka 10 billion or $US 278 million in 1990-1991.

Conclusion

External shocks emanating from the Gulf crisis will have debilitating effects on the long-term growth prospects, balance of payments, employment and price levels of Bangladesh. Unless such losses, which may amount to $1.5 billion, are compensated for, Bangladesh will be forced to curtail imports drastically. It will affect the Government's ability to continue with the implementation of the structural adjustment import liberalization programme as well as the development programme.

It is in this context that Bangladesh hopes that donor countries, the United Nations and multilateral agencies will consider rendering all possible assistance to Bangladesh to overcome these problems.

/...

Annex XI

Recommendation by the Security Council Committee established by resolution 661 (1990) concerning the situation between Iraq and Kuwait with regard to Seychelles

The Security Council Committee established by resolution 661 (1990) concerning the situation between Iraq and Kuwait,

Having dealt with the communication received from Seychelles under Article 50 of the Charter of the United Nations,

Recalling Security Council resolution 661 (1990) of 6 August 1990 in which the Council decided to impose sanctions in accordance with Chapter VII of the Charter of the United Nations, as well as Security Council resolutions 660 (1990) of 2 August 1990, 662 (1990) of 9 August 1990, 664 (1990) of 18 August 1990, 665 (1990) of 25 August 1990, 666 (1990) of 13 September 1990, 667 (1990) of 16 September 1990, 669 (1990) of 24 September 1990, 670 (1990) of 25 September 1990 and 674 (1990) of 29 October 1990,

Recalling further the provisions of Articles 25, 49 and 50 of the Charter of the United Nations,

Noting the information given by Seychelles a/ regarding the measures taken to give full effect to the sanctions as laid down in resolution 661 (1990) and concerning the special economic problems it has been confronted with as a result of the implementation of those measures,

Having heard the representative of Seychelles,

Expressing concern at the special economic problems confronting Seychelles as a result of the severance of its economic relations with Iraq and occupied Kuwait as required by Security Council resolution 661 (1990), which are particularly difficult in terms of commercial and financial losses incurred by Seychelles,

Recognizing that the continued full implementation of Security Council resolution 661 (1990) by Seychelles, as well as other States, will support measures to ensure compliance with paragraph 2 of that resolution and to restore the authority of the legitimate Government of Kuwait,

1. Commends the Government of Seychelles for the measures it has taken to comply with resolution 661 (1990);

2. Recognizes the urgent need to assist Seychelles in coping with its special economic problems resulting from the severance of its economic relations

---

a/ S/21891.

0063

/...

with Iraq and occupied Kuwait as required by Security Council resolution 661 (1990), especially those losses resulting from undelivered Kuwaiti oil shipments to Seychelles and other commercial and financial losses incurred by Seychelles;

3. *Appeals* to all States on an urgent basis to provide immediate technical, financial and material assistance to Seychelles to mitigate the adverse impact on its economy of the application by Seychelles of sanctions against Iraq pursuant to Security Council resolution 661 (1990);

4. *Invites* the competent organs and specialized agencies of the United Nations system, including the international financial institutions and the regional development banks, to review their programmes of assistance to Seychelles with a view to alleviating its special economic problems arising from the application of sanctions against Iraq pursuant to Security Council resolution 661 (1990);

5. *Requests* the Secretary-General, on a regular basis, to seek information from States and the concerned organs and agencies of the United Nations system on action taken to alleviate the special economic problems of Seychelles and to report thereon to the Security Council.

Enclosure

Presentation made on 17 December 1990 by the Chargé d'affaires a.i. of Seychelles to the Working Group of the Security Council Committee established by resolution 661 (1990) concerning the situation between Iraq and Kuwait

[Original: English]

The Seychelles is a geographically remote, sea-locked multi-island developing country with limited resources relying for its economic prosperity on the performance of its principal tourism and fisheries sectors. The economy is, as a result, highly vulnerable to exogenously determined forces.

As a consequence of Seychelles' location, economic structure and concomitant import dependence, it has been placed in an extremely difficult economic position because of the Iraq annexation of Kuwait and the implementation of Security Council resolution 661 (1990).

The Government of Seychelles has fully complied with the provisions of Security Council resolution 661 (1990) adopted on 6 August 1990, to impose economic sanctions on Iraq.

The observance by Seychelles of the United Nations sanctions régime against Iraq has had significant adverse consequences for the Seychelles economy. Some of those effects have been experienced immediately while other detrimental impacts will be manifested in the coming period owing to the time lags.

This brief, preliminary assessment seeks to show that the Seychelles' situation warrants financial assistance from the international community for as long as Security Council resolution 661 (1990) remains in force.

The immediate impact of the political crisis in the Gulf sharply raised aircraft fuel and insurance premiums, engendering in turn a hike in the cost structure of the tourism industry, the mainstay of the economy. The re-export of oil, mostly as bunker sales to the locally based tuna fishing fleet and to a lesser extent to transiting aircraft, was sharply disrupted. The lucrative oil re-export business, and with it, the foreign exchange margin, which had by and large financed the domestic consumption of petroleum products in recent years, went into a downturn.

Although it may be argued to the contrary that there is an unexpected benefit concerning the re-export of oil, this would be erroneous.

Because of the crisis any increase in bunkering costs has been off-set by maintaining very low licensing fees for foreign purse seiners, e.g., the recent agreement between the Seychelles Fishing Authority and Nippon Maru, where the licence fee was held at the same level as at 1986 prices.

The energy requirements of Seychelles are met through imports of petroleum, which is one of the major commodities significantly affecting the balance of

0065 /...

payments. The cost of petroleum imports accounts for more than 25 per cent of the country's import bill or 169 million Seychelles rupees, a/ or $US 30 million (1989).

Therefore the whole economy depends on getting the cheapest possible petroleum at favourable terms of credit and from the closest distance.

Prior to the political crisis in the Gulf region, Seychelles was entirely dependent on Kuwait for oil supplies. Those supplies were transacted under preferential terms and conditions. Kuwaiti oil was purchased on 45 days' credit which permitted Seychelles 15 days extra grace to pay refining costs, instead of the normal 30 days.

The price was based on a five-day arithmetic mean of oil spot prices in the Arab free-on-board (FOB) market for all products, with the exception of motor gasoline.

Also, because the supply was assured in addition to the extra 15 days' credit, it was necessary for Seychelles to maintain only minimum stocks of all fuel types. Those stocks could be replenished easily because of Kuwait's proximity to Seychelles, being only 10 days sailing time away. As a consequence of the aforesaid, the country did not experience a bunching of payments or a liquidity problem.

The political crisis in the Gulf and Seychelles' adherence to United Nations sanctions against Iraq effectively severed the country's regular supply of oil and simultaneously resulted in the loss of the Kuwaiti oil-financing facility.

Seychelles has been especially affected by the steep rise in the price of oil since it has no alternative sources of energy or oil refineries of its own. In this regard, it will be recalled that the price of refined oil has increased to an even greater extent than that of crude oil.

On 31 July 1990, the country's stock was at the minimum requirement level. Also, two cargo loads of oil were on order from Kuwait in August, amounting to 12,000 tons at pre-crisis prices. As a result of the political situation in the Gulf, that arrangement could not be finalized.

Seychelles was compelled to purchase, in August, on the open Bahrain spot market with only 30 days' credit, instead of 45 days. To meet the situation, the Seychelles Petroleum began stockpiling at high cost from August 1990 onwards. This means that, in the last quarter of 1990, Seychelles has spent an extra $2 million.

In addition, the need to make bulk purchases of petroleum products on the spot market gave rise to a liquidity problem and this will be reflected in the balance of payments in 1991.

---

a/ SR 5.50 = $US 1.00.

0066

/...

Given the current situation, provisional estimates for 1991 indicate that the purchase of petroleum imports would result in an additional cost of $12.5 million, giving rise to a loss of $4.1 million.

The quantification on the balance of payments given below is based on actual performance up to July 1990, and assumes that payments for imports and oil imports will rise by 15 per cent.

The following forecast can be made: based on actual performance up to July 1990, and assuming a 15 per cent rise in the price of imports, the overall balance of payments is expected to post a deficit of SR 36 million ($6.5 million), giving rise to a cumulative deficit of SR 72 million ($13 million) for 1990 and 1991.

Seychelles is almost wholly dependent on tourism earnings. 1988 earnings from tourism were SR 515 million. The gross domestic product (GDP) as current market prices in 1988 was SR 1,523.9 million. Thus, tourist income alone as a percentage of GDP was around 33 per cent at current market prices in 1988. The gross national product (GNP) was SR 1,430.3 million in 1988, indicating tourist earnings as 36 per cent of GNP.

However, the value added to GDP from the tourist sector in the form of transport, hotel services, etc., has not been included in these percentages.

There are other relevant aspects to the tourist industry which must be mentioned here. These aspects are: (a) tourist bookings for 1990 do not give a picture of the impact of the crisis on Seychelles because over 75 per cent of tourist arrivals were pre-booked and planned long before; (b) a large percentage of the remaining 25 per cent is low-budget tourists who spend very little foreign exchange in the country; and (c) around 80 per cent of tourist income is spent on imports, of which imports for the tourist trade stand at a very high percentage. Most of the big hotels have raised their rates by from 3 to 8 per cent and the small hotels by 7 per cent.

The impact of the crisis on domestic prices and trade tax as at 5 September 1990 has been estimated as follows:

(a) The price of gasoline is up from SR 5.21 ($0.9) per litre to SR 6.51 ($1.18) per litre;

(b) AV gas is up from SR 5.87 ($1.06) per litre to SR 7.00 ($1.3) per litre;

(c) Jet A-I is up from SR 2.98 ($0.54) per litre to SR 3.77 ($0.68) per litre;

(d) Spirit-type jet fuel is up from SR 5.87 ($1.06) per litre to SR 7.00 ($1.27) per litre.

As at 5 September 1990, trade tax losses, which by the nature of the tax mechanism are exactly equal to the additional foreign exchange cost of domestic fuel consumption, are expected to be SR 11.5 million ($2.0 million) from August to December 1990.

0067 /...

The fiscal effects of trade tax losses and other spill-over effects are expected to add to the total budgetary cost to the Government in the region of SR 8 to SR 50 million ($2 million-$9 million) in 1990.

The need to pay spot cash for oil as and when necessary is creating and will fuel a liquidity problem which cannot be quantified at this time.

In conclusion, time-lagged detrimental impacts in the future would be exacerbated by possible economic fluctuations in the world economy, such as a recession accompanied with inflation. Thus, the impact on the economy particularly the balance of payments and budget via tourism earnings cannot be fully quantified at this moment in time.

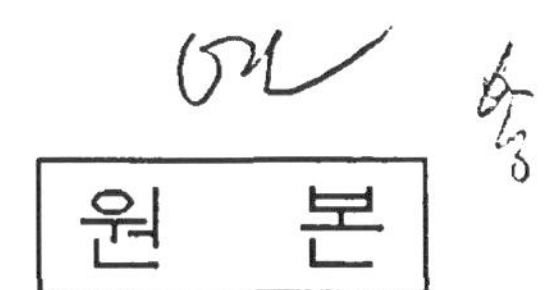

원 본

외 무 부

종 별 :

번 호 : UNW-0044 일 시 : 91 0110 0700

수 신 : 장관 (국연)

발 신 : 주유엔대사

제 목 : 유엔사무총장 이락 방문

데 꾸에야르 유엔사무총장은 이락-쿠웨이트 사태중재를 위해 1.10.중 뉴욕을 출발, 금주내에 사담후세인 이락 대통령을 만날 계획이라고 1.9. 저녁공식 발표함. 끝

(대사 현홍주-국장)

국기국 정문국 1차보 미주국 중아국 안기부

PAGE 1

91.01.11 01:21 CG
외신 1과 통제관

0069

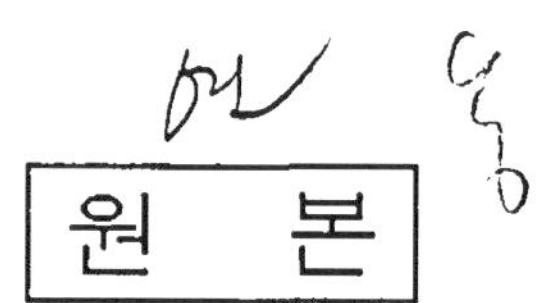

원 본

외 무 부

종 별 :

번 호 : UNW-0048 일 시 : 91 0110 1800

수 신 : 장 관 (국연,중근동)

발 신 : 주 유엔 대사

제 목 : 유엔사무총장 이락방문

연: UNW-0044

1. 유엔사무총장은 금 1.10. 20:00 경 특별기편으로 당지 출발, 제네바에 도착하여 EC 12개국 외무장관과의 회담, 비동맹 의장국인 유고 외무장관과의 회담을 가진후 토요일 바그다드 도착예정임.

2. 금일 오전 사무총장은 일본 가이후 총리, 고르바쵸프 소 대통령의 이락사태 중재 성공을 기원하는 메세지를 당지 주재 대사들을 통해 전달받았으며 부쉬 대통령도전화통화로 사무총장의 성공을 기원하였음.

3. 사무총장은 후세인 대통령과의 회담시 이락군대에 대신하여 유엔평화 유지군을 쿠웨이트에 배치하는 제안을 포함하여 사태해결을 위한 모든 가능한 방법을 협의할것으로 알려짐.

4. 동 총장은 내주 월요일 당지에 귀임하여 안보리에 회담결과를 보고예정임.끝

(대사 현홍주-국장)

국기국 1차보 중아국 정문국 안기부 그차보 미주국 대외국

PAGE 1

91.01.11 08:17 FC

외신 1과 통제관

0070

F 청부문

United Nations

Press Release

Department of Public Information • News Coverage Service • New York

SG/T/1638
11 January 1991

SECRETARY-GENERAL, ON WAY TO BAGHDAD, HOLDS TALKS WITH PRESIDENT MITTERRAND IN PARIS; EEC AND SWISS FOREIGN MINISTERS, NON-ALIGNED CHAIRMAN IN GENEVA

(Received from a spokesman accompanying the Secretary-General.)

GENEVA, 11 January -- Secretary-General Javier Perez de Cuellar arrived in Geneva Friday on his way to Baghdad following a short stopover in Paris during which he met for half an hour with President François Mitterrand of France.

During the meeting, which took place at the Elysee Palace, President Mitterrand pledged the full support of France for the mission of the Secretary-General. The Secretary-General said he "enormously appreciated this support". They also discussed the situation in the Persian Gulf following the failure of the Geneva talks last Wednesday. French Foreign Minister Roland Dumas accompanied the Secretary-General to the meeting and further discussions were held between them on the same topics.

The Secretary-General then flew to Geneva where he had brief talks on the Persian Gulf situation with the Foreign Minister of Switzerland, Rene Felber, at the airport. Later, for over an hour, he received pledges of support from the Foreign Ministers of the 12 States members of the European Economic Community (EEC). The meeting was presided over by Foreign Minister Jacques Poos of Luxembourg, current Chairman of the EEC, and the Secretary-General undertook to keep the 12 Governments informed of the results of his mission through Foreign Minister Poos.

The Secretary-General then met with Foreign Minister Budimir Loncar of Yugoslavia in his capacity as Chairman of the Non-Aligned Movement. The Foreign Minister again expressed to the Secretary-General full support of the non-aligned States for his mission.

* *** *

1635P

4-1

0071

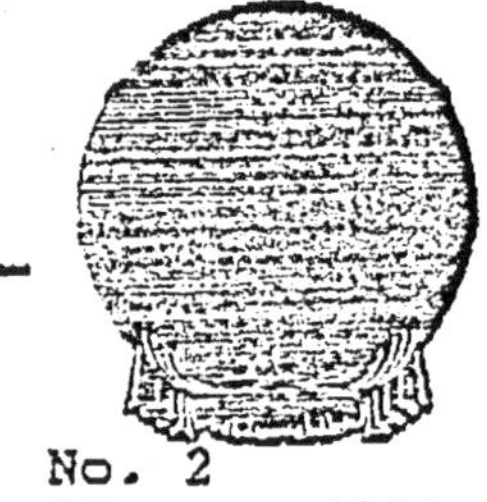

PEOPLE'S REPUBLIC OF CHINA
MISSION TO THE UNITED NATIONS

155 WEST 66th STREET, NEW YORK, N.Y. 10023

PRESS RELEASE

No. 2
10 Jan. 1991

ANSWERS BY THE SPOKESMAN OF THE CHINESE FOREIGN MINISTRY

1. Question: What is your comment on the Geneva talks between US Secretary of State and Iraqi Foreign Minister which made no progress?

Answer: It was reported that the talks held in Geneva on January 9 between US Secretary of State and Iraqi Foreign Minister failed to make any progress. This is not what the international community has been looking forward to.

We urge Iraq to adopt a realistic approach and immediately pull out its troops from Kuwait.

We hope that the international community will continue its efforts to seek a peaceful settlement of the Gulf crisis.

2. Question: Do you have any comment on the question of settling the Gulf crisis as tension keeps mounting in the region?

Answer: We once again urge Iraq to respond to the appeals from the international community by unconditionally withdrawing its troops from Kuwait as soon as possible, so that peace and stability can be restored in the Gulf region.

China supports all dialogues, mediation efforts and other diplomatic activities designed to seek a peaceful settlement of the Gulf crisis, and will continue to work with the international community to this end.

3. Question: The Phnom Penh side has recently indicated once again that the Phnom Penh regime will not dissolve its army, because only the army of Phnom Penh can prevent Khmer Rouge's return to power. What is your comment on it?

Answer: under the pretext of "preventing Khmer Rouge's return to power", the Phnom Penh side is now trying to keep its regime and army intact and legalize them. It is a deliberate attempt to create obstacles to a political settlement of the Cambodian question. This shows that the Phnom Penh side is insincere in bringing about national reconciliation and a fair settlement of the Cambodian question, and has retrogressed from the position of the four Cambodian parties' joint declaration issued in Jakarta, which contravenes the principled spirit of the framework documents on the Cambodian question worked out by the five permanent UN Security Council members and the aspiration of the Cambodian nation. It is an undeniable reality that Cambodia at present has four political and military forces. Exclusion of any party or monopoly of power by any party will run counter to the political reality of Cambodia and will never bring about a comprehensive, fair and reasonable political settlement of the Cambodian question.

4-5

0072

Union of Soviet Socialist Republics

PERMANENT MISSION TO THE UNITED NATIONS
136 EAST 67TH STREET • NEW YORK, NEW YORK 10021

Press Release

No. 7
January 8, 1991

SOVIET FOREIGN MINISTRY WELCOMES BUSH INITIATIVE ON GULF

Moscow, January 4, TASS. The following statement was read out by Soviet Foreign Ministry Spokesman Vitaly Churkin at a briefing on January 4, 1991:

"The Soviet Union is consistently pursuing a peace settlement in the Gulf crisis. In the course of the last few days, the Soviet side exerted active efforts to promote direct dialogue between the United States and Iraq, without which it is hard to imagine the possibility of a peace settlement.

Talks with Iraqi President Saddam Hussein and other Iraqi leaders, held in Baghdad in late December by Soviet Deputy Prime Minister Igor Belousov who headed the Soviet inter-departmental group created on the instruction of the Soviet President, focused on this problem. On the instruction of the Soviet Foreign Minister, head of the Soviet Foreign Ministry's Middle East and Northern Africa Department V.Kolotusha specifically discussed the issue in Baghdad with Iraqi Foreign Minister Tareq Aziz, who is also Deputy Prime Minister.

At the same time, the Soviet side maintained contact with U.S. representatives.

/...

4-7

0073

- 2 -

The Soviet side also exchanged opinions with other countries, particularly the Arab countries and the head of the Non-aligned Movement. Consultations were held in Moscow on December 3 with Co-Chairman of the Soviet Palestinian-Middle East Committee Abu Mazin, who is also a member of the Palestine Liberation Organisation Executive Committee.

The Soviet Union is satisfied with U.S. President George Bush's new initiative to hold a meeting between U.S. Secretary of State James Baker and the Iraqi Foreign Minister in Switzerland on January 7, 8 or 9.

We hope that the U.S. President's proposal will receive a positive response from the Iraqi leadership. Hopes for resolving the Gulf crisis on the basis of U.N. Security Council resolutions are justly pinned on direct U.S.-Iraqi talks. The goodwill pause should end with a victory of common sense. It should bring confidence that justice and stability will be restored in the Gulf".

* * *

4-4

0074

관리 번호	91-93

원 본

외 무 부

종 별 :

번 호 : UNW-0061 일 시 : 91 0111 1700

수 신 : 장관(중근동,국연,기정)

발 신 : 주 유엔 대사

제 목 : 걸프사태관련 동향(안보리)

대:WUN-0055

금 1.11. 권참사관이 유엔 사무국 직원및 관련 대표부등과 접촉, 파악한 표제건 안보리내 동향을 아래와같이 보고함.

1. 유엔 사무총장이 이락 방문을 마치고 1.14(월) 오전 뉴욕에 귀환하는 대로 안보리회의(공식 또는 비공식)를 소집, 동결과를 청취할 예정으로 있음.

2. 예멘은 피점령 아랍영토내 사태를 토의하기 위한 긴급 안보리를 1.9. 요청하여 왔는바, 1.10 및 1.11 간 안보리는 비공식 협의회를 개최, 동건 토의를 계속하고 있음. 비동맹권 국가들은 이스라엘이 팔레스타인인의 보호를 강화하기 위한 제반 안보리 결의를 이행토록 촉구하는 결의안 채택을 요구하는 반면, 미국은 유사한 결의안이 바로 12 월중에 채택된바, 있었으므로 의장 성명으로 하자는입장을 고수하고 있어 쌍방이 현재 협상을 계속중에 있음. 끝

(대사 현홍주-국장)

예고:91.6.30 일반

1991.6.30.에 예고문에 의거 일반문서로 재분류됨

중아국 장관 차관 1차보 2차보 국기국 정문국 안기부

PAGE 1

91.01.12 07:15

외신 2과 통제관 FE

0075

관리 번호 91-56

외 무 부

종 별 :

번 호 : UNW-0062 일 시 : 91 0111 1700

수 신 : 장관(중근동,국연,기정)

발 신 : 주 유엔 대사

제 목 : 걸프사태 관련 동향(주요국동향)

대:WUN-0055

표제건 관련 금 1.11. 권참사관이 JERKIC 유고대표부 참사관과 접촉, 파악한 주요국 동향을 아래보고함.

1. 비동맹권 동향

0. 론차르 유고 외무장관은 90 년 12 월말 이락 방문시 후세인 대통령과 면담, 유엔 결의의 이행을 촉구하고 이락이 쿠웨이트에서 철수하면 비동맹권이 같은 비동맹국인 이락의 친구로서, 이락의 주요 관심사인 중동의 항구적 평화 방안을 강구해 나가기위하여 이행당사자에게 중재노력을 할 용의가 있음을 밝혔음. 후세인 대통령은 이락이 취할 금후 입장에 대해 아무런 언급없이 종전의 주장을 되풀이 하였음.

0. 론차드 유고 외무장관은 1.11. 제네바에서 데 꾸에야르 유엔사무총장과 면담, 상기와같은 비동맹권 입장을 재확인하고 사무총장의 중재노력을 지지한다고 밝혔음.

2. 북구제국의 동향

0. 노르웨이를 중심으로한 북구제국이 이락의 쿠웨이트 철수후 쿠웨이트에 유엔평화 유지군 파견방안을 제의하였음.

0. 동 방안은 이락의 쿠웨이트 철수가 실현된 이후의 PEACE-KEEPING 을 위한 사후조치 방안으로서, 현단계에서 거론은 시기상조 라는것이 사무국등 분위기이며 급선무는 이락의 쿠웨이트 철수를 유도해내기 위한 PEACE-MAKING 방안의 강구임.끝

(대사 현홍주-국장)

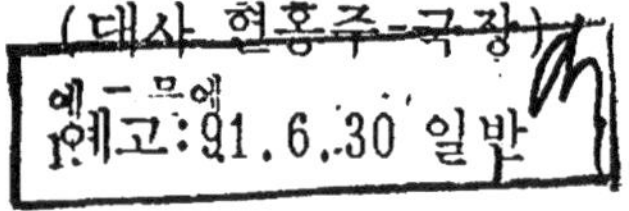
예고:91.6.30 일반

중아국 장관 차관 1차보 2차보 국기국 정문국 안기부

PAGE 1 91.01.12 07:16

외신 2과 통제관 FE

0076

관리 번호	91 -40

외 무 부

종 별 :

번 호 : UNW-0068 일 시 : 91 0111 1800

수 신 : 장관(중근동,국연,해기,기정)

발 신 : 주 유엔 대사

제 목 : 걸프사태관련 동향(유엔외신기자 반응)

1. 유엔사무총장의 바그다드 방문관련 유엔 주요 외신들은 제네바 회담 결렬후 미.이락간 대화채널이 단절단 현 상황하에서 전쟁방지의 돌파구가 마련될런지는 알수없지만 미.이락간 대화를 또한번 마련하는데 기여하는 마지막 외교적 노력으로서 평가하면서 사담 후세인이 미국에 직접 굴복, 철수했다기 보다는 체면을 살리는 방법에 대해 훗세인으로 부터 직접 듣고 그 방법을 미국과 안보리에전달할수 있기를 기대한다고 전망했음.(로이터, 유피아이, 신화등)

2.1.11. 자 NYT 의 이락군의 중동평화 회담 연계 철수시사 관련보도에 대해서는 관계 아랍국가의 수도로부터 확인된 내용이 없으며 인용된 일부 아랍외교관의 WISHFUL THINKING 으로 보인다는 반응을 보임.(AFP 유엔지국장)

3. 전쟁발발 가능성관련 유엔외신은 1.15. 직후 발발 가능성에 대해서는 부정적인 견해가 일반적이며, 유엔헌장 7 장이 규정한 통신두절 또는 외교관계 단절등 추가 제재 조치를 강구한후 무력사용을 결정해야 한다는 의견(CSM 특파원 TED MORELLO), 무력사용의 경우에도 무력사용의 싯점, 구체적 형태등 관련 안보리 이사국간에 또 한차례의 협의가 요청된다는 의견(TASS 지국장 E.MENKES), 안보리 이사국간에도 1.12. 미의회의 결의안 표결 결과에 따라 영향을 받게 될것이라는 의견(AFP 지국장) 등 다양한 견해를 표명함.

4. 유엔 외신대상 정오브리핑에 배포한 사무총장 일정및 중국, 소련 대표부가 배포한 프레스릴리스를 별전송부함.

첨부:관련자료 4 매.:UNW(F)-009

끝

(대사 현홍주-국장, 관장)

예고:91.6.30 일반

중아국 공보처	장관	차관	1차보	2차보	국기국	청와대	총리실	안기부

PAGE 1

91.01.12 08:44

외신 2과 통제관 FE

0077

JAN 11 '91 18:05 KOREAN [illegible] 009 10171 1800

F 첨부물

(중근동. 국연. 해기. 기자)

United Nations

총4054

Press Release

Department of Public Information • News Coverage Service • New York

SG/T/1638
11 January 1991

SECRETARY-GENERAL, ON WAY TO BAGHDAD, HOLDS TALKS WITH PRESIDENT MITTERRAND IN PARIS; EEC AND SWISS FOREIGN MINISTERS, NON-ALIGNED CHAIRMAN IN GENEVA

(Received from a spokesman accompanying the Secretary-General.)

GENEVA, 11 January -- Secretary-General Javier Perez de Cuellar arrived in Geneva Friday on his way to Baghdad following a short stopover in Paris during which he met for half an hour with President François Mitterrand of France.

During the meeting, which took place at the Elysee Palace, President Mitterrand pledged the full support of France for the mission of the Secretary-General. The Secretary-General said he "enormously appreciated this support". They also discussed the situation in the Persian Gulf following the failure of the Geneva talks last Wednesday. French Foreign Minister Roland Dumas accompanied the Secretary-General to the meeting and further discussions were held between them on the same topics.

The Secretary-General then flew to Geneva where he had brief talks on the Persian Gulf situation with the Foreign Minister of Switzerland, Rene Felber, at the airport. Later, for over an hour, he received pledges of support from the Foreign Ministers of the 12 States members of the European Economic Community (EEC). The meeting was presided over by Foreign Minister Jacques Poos of Luxembourg, current Chairman of the EEC, and the Secretary-General undertook to keep the 12 Governments informed of the results of his mission through Foreign Minister Poos.

The Secretary-General then met with Foreign Minister Budimir Loncar of Yugoslavia in his capacity as Chairman of the Non-Aligned Movement. The Foreign Minister again expressed to the Secretary-General full support of the non-aligned States for his mission.

* *** *

1635P

For information media—not an official record

4-1

0078

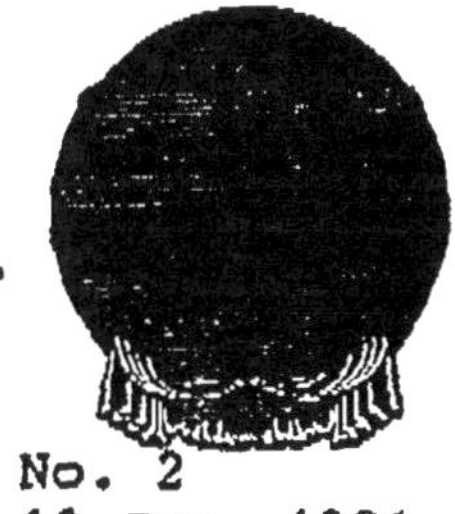

PEOPLE'S REPUBLIC OF CHINA
MISSION TO THE UNITED NATIONS

155 WEST 66th STREET, NEW YORK, N.Y. 10023

PRESS RELEASE

No. 2
10 Jan. 1991

ANSWERS BY THE SPOKESMAN OF THE CHINESE FOREIGN MINISTRY

1. Question: What is your comment on the Geneva talks between US Secretary of State and Iraqi Foreign Minister which made no progress?

Answer: It was reported that the talks held in Geneva on January 9 between US Secretary of State and Iraqi Foreign Minister failed to make any progress. This is not what the international community has been looking forward to.

We urge Iraq to adopt a realistic approach and immediately pull out its troops from Kuwait.

We hope that the international community will continue its efforts to seek a peaceful settlement of the Gulf crisis.

2. Question: Do you have any comment on the question of settling the Gulf crisis as tension keeps mounting in the region?

Answer: We once again urge Iraq to respond to the appeals from the international community by unconditionally withdrawing its troops from Kuwait as soon as possible, so that peace and stability can be restored in the Gulf region.

China supports all dialogues, mediation efforts and other diplomatic activities designed to seek a peaceful settlement of the Gulf crisis, and will continue to work with the international community to this end.

3. Question: The Phnom Penh side has recently indicated once again that the Phnom Penh regime will not dissolve its army, because only the army of Phnom Penh can prevent Khmer Rouge's return to power. What is your comment on it?

Answer: under the pretext of "preventing Khmer Rouge's return to power", the Phnom Penh side is now trying to keep its regime and army intact and legalize them. It is a deliberate attempt to create obstacles to a political settlement of the Cambodian question. This shows that the Phnom Penh side is insincere in bringing about national reconciliation and a fair settlement of the Cambodian question, and has retrogressed from the position of the four Cambodian parties' joint declaration issued in Jakarta, which contravenes the principled spirit of the framework documents on the Cambodian question worked out by the five permanent UN Security Council members and the aspiration of the Cambodian nation. It is an undeniable reality that Cambodia at present has four political and military forces. Exclusion of any party or monopoly of power by any party will run counter to the political reality of Cambodia and will never bring about a comprehensive, fair and reasonable political settlement of the Cambodian question.

4-5

0079

Union of Soviet Socialist Republics
PERMANENT MISSION TO THE UNITED NATIONS
136 EAST 67TH STREET • NEW YORK, NEW YORK 10021

Press Release

No. 7
January 8, 1991

SOVIET FOREIGN MINISTRY WELCOMES BUSH INITIATIVE ON GULF

Moscow. January 4, TASS. The following statement was read out by Soviet Foreign Ministry Spokesman Vitaly Churkin at a briefing on January 4, 1991:

"The Soviet Union is consistently pursuing a peace settlement in the Gulf crisis. In the course of the last few days, the Soviet side exerted active efforts to promote direct dialogue between the United States and Iraq, without which it is hard to imagine the possibility of a peace settlement.

Talks with Iraqi President Saddam Hussein and other Iraqi leaders, held in Baghdad in late December by Soviet Deputy Prime Minister Igor Belousov who headed the Soviet inter-departmental group created on the instruction of the Soviet President, focused on this problem. On the instruction of the Soviet Foreign Minister, head of the Soviet Foreign Ministry's Middle East and Northern Africa Department V.Kolotusha specifically discussed the issue in Baghdad with Iraqi Foreign Minister Tareq Aziz, who is also Deputy Prime Minister.

At the same time, the Soviet side maintained contact with U.S. representatives.

/...

4-3

0080

- 2 -

The Soviet side also exchanged opinions with other countries, particularly the Arab countries and the head of the Non-aligned Movement. Consultations were held in Moscow on December 3 with Co-Chairman of the Soviet Palestinian-Middle East Committee Abu Mazin, who is also a member of the Palestine Liberation Organisation Executive Committee.

The Soviet Union is satisfied with U.S. President George Bush's new initiative to hold a meeting between U.S. Secretary of State James Baker and the Iraqi Foreign Minister in Switzerland on January 7, 8 or 9.

We hope that the U.S. President's proposal will receive a positive response from the Iraqi leadership. Hopes for resolving the Gulf crisis on the basis of U.N. Security Council resolutions are justly pinned on direct U.S.-Iraqi talks. The goodwill pause should end with a victory of common sense. It should bring confidence that justice and stability will be restored in the Gulf".

* * *

4-4

0081

관리번호	91-42

외 무 부

종 별 :

번 호 : UNW-0071 일 시 : 91 0111 1830

수 신 : 장관(중근동,국연,기정)

발 신 : 주 유엔 대사

제 목 : 걸프사태관련 공관보안강화

금 1.11 당관에서 입수한 이락의 테러위협관련 대책 동향을 아래보고함.

1. 대 테러 대책동향

가.1.11. 뉴욕경찰국은 이락테러리스트들에 의한 테러활동에 대비한 안전조치들을 각 예하 경찰에 지시

나.1.14. 16:00 부터 테러정보 접수및 분석을 위한 경찰상황실 운영예정

다.1.10 부터 JFK 공항등 국제공항을 통한 쿠웨이트등 아랍인의 입국검색강화(이락및 쿠웨이트 여권소지자는 입국시 지문채취등 특별관리)

2. 당관으로서도 비상근무체제를 구축하고 보안대책에 필요한 조치를 강구하고 있음. 끝.(대사 현홍주-국장)

예고:91.6.30 일반

중아국 차관 1차보 2차보 국기국 총리실 안기부

PAGE 1

91.01.12 09:07

외신 2과 통제관 FE

0082

원 본

외 무 부

종 별 : 지 급

번 호 : UNW-0076 일 시 : 91 0114 1900

수 신 : 장 관(중근동,국연,기정)

발 신 : 주 유엔 대사

제 목 : 걸프관련 사태

1. 금 1.14. 귀환한 데꾸에야르 유엔사무총장의 이락방문 결과를 청취하기 위한 안보리 비공식 비공개회의(INFORMAL CONSULTATION OF THE WHOLE)가 금 1.14. 21:00 개최될 예정임.

2. 데꾸에야르 사무총장은 금일 오전 JFK 도착시 기자들의 질문에 대해 자신의 후세인대통령과의 회담이 성공적이지 못하였으며, 평화를 향한 진전으로 볼수있는 아무런 제의를 이락으로부터 받지 못하였다고 대답하였음.

동 질의 답변 내용은 별전 FAX 와 같음.

첨부:유엔사무총장 질의답변내용 : UNW(F)-012

끝.

(대사 현홍주-국장)

중아국 1차보 2차보 중아국 국기국 정문국 안기부 미주국

PAGE 1

91.01.15 12:36 FG

외신 1과 통제관

0083

UNW-0076 외 첨부물 UNW(FT)-0126 10114 ... (중근동.국연.기조) 종고 OH

Remarks made by the Secretary-General on Mon[illegible] 14 January at JFK airport at approximately 9.00 a.m.

Q. What are you going to tell the Security Council today?

S-G Be patient, wait until I go to the Council. I cannot go into the details with you, the only thing I can tell you is that unfortunately I have not much in my hands. My visit has been of course interesting but I have not been offered anything from the Iraqi authorities which I can consider a step towards peace.

Q. How would you characterise your talks with Saddam Hussain?

S-G Polite but unfortunately unsuccessful.

Q. Is there any hope left for peace?

S-G As far as I am concerned, I have done what I have to do -- I don't know whether others will do something but it appears to me that it is perhaps a little late for embarking on any other efforts.

Q. What do you expect from the Security Council meeting today?

S-G I will give to the Security Council the details of what I have heard and what I have said to Mr. Saddam Hussain.

Q. Has President Mitterrand offered any alternatives?

S-G No, no, I discussed with the President of France, I was on the telephone with the Prime Minister of the United Kingdom, with the Minister of Luxembourg in his capacity as the Chairman of the Twelve, with the Ambassador of the United States, the Ambassador of the Soviet Union, all of these in less than two hours and I am a little exhausted.

Q. What time will you address the Security Council and how disappointed are you?

S-G It is not for me to decide, but I think it will be around 6:00 in the afternoon so I can have time to draft my (report), because I have slept only two hours.

Q. Have you lost hope?

S-G In some ways, yes.

Q. Mr. Hussain said that you came to Baghdad just to listen that you met with Mr. Bush four times before you came to Baghdad, can you tell me, did you advance any of your own ideas?

2-1

0084

S-G As you know, I was not the messenger of President Bush, I was a messenger of the international community as a whole who wanted peace, a just peace.

Q. Did you advance the idea of a conference on the Palestinian question?

S-G No, this question was not specifically raised.

Q. Diplomacy has succeeded before on that part of the world, why not this time?

S-G You have an expression in English "you need two to tango" and I wanted very much to dance but I didn't find a nice lady to dance with (laughter).

Q. Did Saddam Hussain mention withdrawal at any time?

S-G No, he didn't express any desire to withdraw from Kuwait.

* * *

2-2

0085

관리번호	91/1081

	분류번호	보존기간

발 신 전 보

번 호 : WUS-0131 910114 1646 FC 종별 : 긴급

수 신 : 주 수신처 참조 대사. 총영사

WJA -0173 WUK -0087
WSV -0117 WFR -0062
WUN -0071 WIT -0079
WSB -0084 WCA -0043

발 신 : 장 관 (중근동)

제 목 : 페만사태 비상 대책

연 : WUS-0107

연호와 같이 페만사태 비상 대책 수립에 참고코자 하니 1.13. 케야르 유엔 사무총장의 사담 후세인 대통령 회담, 결과 및 1.14. 이라크 비상의회 소집 기타 유엔이 정한 이라크의 철군 시한을 앞두고 일련의 움직임에 주재국 정부, 언론계, 학계등의 관찰, 정세전망, 입장등을 파악 지급 보고 바람. 끝.

1991. 6. 30. 에 예고문에 의거 일반문서로 재분류됨

(차 관 유 종 하)

예 고 : 91.6.30. 까지

앙고재	91년 1월 14일	중근동과	기안자 성명		과 장		국 장		차 관	장 관

보안통제	

외신과통제

0086

관리 번호 91-60

원 본

외 무 부

종 별 : 지 급

번 호 : UNW-0083　　　　일 시 : 91 0114 2100

수 신 : 장관(국연,중동,기정)

발 신 : 주 유엔 대사

제 목 : 걸프사태

1. 금 1.14.(월) 21:00 개최예정인 안보리 비공식회의에서 불란서는 걸프사태관련, 자국의 구상(안보리 의장 선언문안)을 안보리 회원국의 검토를 위해 문서로 배포할것으로 파악된바, 불란서측 문서를 입수, 별첨 FAX 송부함.(이하 동 선언문안 요지)

가. 유엔사무총장의 이락 방문결과를 청취하고 평화를 수호하기 위한 결의로써, 안보리 이사국들은 이락 당국에 최종 호소를함.(1 항)

나. 안보리는 이락이 계획된 일정에 따라 쿠웨이트에서 즉각 철수하며 이를신속하고도 대규모로 시행할 의사를 지체없이 발표할것으로 촉구함.(2 항)

다. 상기 조치가 취해지는대로 사무총장은 국제감시단 파견및 평화 유지군의 파견을 통해 이락의 철군을 통제 확인토록 협조함.(3 항)

라. 이락에 대해서는 불공격을 보장함.(4 항)

마. 특히 평화적 해결을 확실히 하기 위해 모든 유용한 협상을 추진하는데 있어 아랍국가들과 협력하여 필요한 조치를 취함.(5 항)

바. 이러한 해결이 안보리의 제반 결의에 따라 이루어지고 난후, 안보리 이사국들은 이지역의 기타문제의 해결을 위해 적극 기여할 것인바, 특히 90.12.20 자 안보리 의장 선언에따라 적절한 시기에(또한 적절히 구성된) 국제회의를 개최함으로써 아랍. 이스라엘 문제및 팔레스타인 문제를 해결하는데 기여토록함.

2. 상기 불란서측 제안에대한 당지 언론의코멘트 요청에 대해 PICKERING 주유엔 미국대사는 "TOO LITTLE, TOO LATE" 라는 반응을, 주유엔 쿠웨이트 대사는 철군시한 하루전에 이러한 제의를 하는것이 별로 효과가 없을것이라는 부정적인 반응을 보인것으로 파악됨.

3. 한편, 1.14. 암만발 신화사 통신에 의하면 케야르 사무총장의 후세인 대통령

국기국	장관	차관	1차보	2차보	중아국	청와대	총리실	안기부

PAGE 1　　　　91.01.15 12:52
외신 2과 통제관 BW

0087

면담결과에 대해 언론들이 실패한 것으로 보도하고 있는것과 관련 금일 후세인 대통령이 발트하임 오지리 대통령에게 전화를걸어 케야르 사무총장의 방문이 실패가 아니며 여전히 평화적 해결의 여지가 있음을 유엔및 관계국에 전달해 줄것을 요청하였다고함.(주유엔 신화사 지국제보)

4. 또한 금 18:00 당지 CNN 방송은 바그다드발 BERNARD SHAW 기자 보도를 통해 이락 고위 관계자에 의하면 이락은 여전히 협상의 여지를 배제하지 않고 있는것으로 본다고 보도하였으며, 주유엔 이락대사도 금일 이락의 협상 가능성을 시사하는 발언을 한것으로 파악됨. 반면 상기 CNN 방송은 백악관 출입기자 보도를 통해 백악관측이 상기 보도와는 달리 이락과의 협상 가능성에 대해 매우 비관적인 입장을 취하고 있다고 함.

첨부:상기 FAX:UNW(F)-013

끝

(대사 현홍주-국장)

예고:91.6.30 까지

PAGE 2

0088

JAN 14 '91 20:20 KOREAN MI

UNW(FR)-013 10114 1/00
(국연. 중근동. 기정)

Objet: Golfe - Initiative Francaise pour la Paix

Vous trouverez ci-joint le projet de declaration que la France soumet au conseil de securite comme ultime tentative pour la paix dan le golfe:

1. Ayant entendu le rapport du Secretaire General des Nations Unies au sujet de la mission qu'il a effectuee en Irak les 12 et 13 Janvier 1991 et resolus a ne rien negligent pour sauvegarder la paix, les membres du Conseil de Securite lancent un ultime appel aux dirigeants Irakiens.

2. Ils les invitent a annoncer sans autre delai l'intention de l'Irak de se retirer du Koweit selon un calendrier programme et de commencer des maintenant un retrait rapide et massif.

3. Des que sera pris cet engagement, le Secretaire General des Nations Unies apportera son concours au controle et a la verification du retrait des forces Irakiennes par l'envoi d'observateurs internationaux et la mise en place d'une force de maintien de la paix pour la composition de laquelle il sera fait appel a des pays arabes.

4. Une garantie de non agression pourra etre apportee a l'irak.

5. Par ailleurs, les mesures necessaires seront prises, en liaison avec les pays arabes, pour promouvoir toute les negociations utiles afin de consolider le processus de reglement pacifique.

6. Des lors que ce reglement aura ete obtenu dans le respect des resolutions du Conseil de Securite, les membres de celui-ci apporteront leur contribution active au reglement des autres problemes de la region et, en particulier, du conflit Israelo arabe et du probleme palestinien par la convocation, au moment approprie, d'une conference internationale (dotee d'une structure appropriee), conformement a la declaration du President du Conseil de Securite en date du 20 Decembre 1990, afin d'assurer la securite, la stabilite et le developpement dans cette partie du monde.

1 — 1

0089

원 본

(배부처 확인)

외 무 부

종 별 : 지 급

번 호 : UNW-0084 일 시 : 91 0114 2300

수 신 : 장 관(국연,중동,기정)

발 신 : 주 유엔 대사

제 목 : 걸프사태(안보리 동향)

1.금 1.14(월) 21:00 소집 예정이던 사무총장 귀임보고를 듣기위한 안보리 회의가 22:00 이후로 연기됨.이는 예멘이 이스라엘 점령지내 진상조사 결의안 (안보리결의 681 호 :90.12.20) 의 이행을 촉구하는 결의안 채택을 요청함에 따라 이 문제를 먼저 협의하 기위한것이라고 함.

2.이에 앞서 연호 불란서 구상에 대하여 안보리 상임이사국 간에 비공식 협의가 있었는바, 미국, 영국, 소련은 이싯점에서 안보리 무력사용 결의내용으로 부터 후퇴할 경우, 1.15 철수시한을 포함한 안보리 결의 전체가 무력화 된다는 이유로 반대하였다고 하며, 이에따라 불란서 구상이 받아들여질 전망은 희박한 것으로 파악되고 있음.주유엔 불란서 대표부는 현재 본국정부와 이문제를 협의중에 있다고함.끝 (대사 현홍주-국장)

국기국 1차보 중아국 중아국 정문국 안기부 미주국

PAGE 1

91.01.15 13:27 WG

외신 1과 통제관

0090

원 본

외 무 부

종 별 :

번 호 : UNW-0085 일 시 : 91 0114 2300

수 신 : 장 관(중동,국연,기정)

발 신 : 주 유엔 대사

제 목 : 걸프사태 (PLO 간부 피살)

금 1.14(월) 21:00 경 주유엔 PLO 상주대표는 주유엔출입기자들과 기자 회견을 갖고 PLO 제 2인자를 포함한 고위간부 2명이 금일 튀니스에서 피살 되었는바, 이는 이스라엘의 소행일 가능성이 크다고 언급하면서, 이 문제를 다루기 위하여 명 1.15안보리 소집을 요청할 것이라고 말함.끝

(대사 현홍주-국장)

중아국 1차보 국기국 정문국 안기부

PAGE 1

91.01.15 13:31 WG

외신 1과 통제관

0091

원 본

외 무 부

종 별 : 지 급

번 호 : UNW-0086 일 시 : 91 0115 0010

수 신 : 장관(국연,중동, 기정)

발 신 : 주 유엔대사

제 목 : 걸프사태 (안보리 동향)

1. 께야르 유엔 사무총장의 이락 방문결과 보고를 청취하기 위한 안보리 비공식 협의회가 당지시간 1.14(월) 23:15 개최 되었음.

2. 상기 비공식 협의에 앞서 사무총장은 상임 이사국과사전 협의를 가진바, 금번이락 방문에서 사태 해결을위한 아무런 돌파구 (BREAKTHROUGH)를 마련하지 못하였다고 보고 하였다 하며 이에 비추어 안보리 앞 보고 에서도 특별히 새로운 내용은 없을것으로 보고 있음.

3. 이스라엘 점령 아랍 영토 문제 관련 결의안 시행문제에 관하여는 미국이 연호결의안 상정에 동의하여 현재 문안을 검토하고 있는 것으로 알려짐. 금일 회의시동결의안을 표결할지 여부는 불명이나 표결에 부쳐질 경우 미국은 기권할 것으로예상된다는 것이 안보리 주변의 관측임. 끝

(대사 현홍주-국장)

국기국 1차보 미주국 중아국 정문국 안기부

PAGE 1

91.01.15 14:31 DA

외신 1과 통제관

0092

외 무 부

종 별 :

번 호 : UNW-0087 일 시 : 91 0115 0145

수 신 : 장관(중근동,국연,기정)

발 신 : 주 유엔 대사

제 목 : 걸프관련 사태 (유엔사무총장 및 안보리 동향)

1.15 (화) 01:20 안보리 비공식 회의에 자신의 이락 방문결과를 보고하고 나오면서 케야르 유엔사무총장은 기자들의 질문에대해서 아래요지로 답변하였음.

1.안보리에 본인이 보고한 내용은 안보리에서 비밀로 취급하기로 결정하였으므로 상세히 밝힐수 없어 미안함.

2.본인은 어떠한 새로운 제안을 가지고 이락에 간 것은 아니었음.

3.금일 안보리 회원국들은 최후 순간까지 평화를위해 노력한다는데 전원일치의 의견을 가지고 있었음. 안보리는 불란서의 구상등 평화를 위한 방안을 모색하기 위하여금 1.15중에도 계속 협의 할 것으로 알고있음.끝

(대사 현홍주-국장)

중아국	장관	차관	1차보	2차보	중아국	국기국	정문국	안기부

PAGE 1

91.01.15 16:11 CG

외신 1과 통제관

0093

외 무 부

종 별 :

번 호 : UNW-0088 일 시 : 91 0115 0145

수 신 : 장관(중근동 국연, 해기, 기정)

발 신 : 주유엔대사

제 목 : 걸프관련 사태(안보리 동향)

1. 금 1.14. 예멘 대표부는 예멘 SALEH 대통령이 발표한 걸프사태의 평화적 해결방안을 안보리 문서로 배포하였음.

2. 상기 안보리 문서는 별첨 FAX 와 같음.

첨부: 예멘의 제안 : UNW(F)-014

끝

(대사 현홍주-국장)

중아국	장관	차관	1차보	2차보	중아국	국기국	정문국	안기부
공보처								

PAGE 1

91.01.15 16:13 CG

외신 1과 통제관

0094

JAN 15 '91 01:46 KOREAN MISSION P.1

UNW-0088 의 첨부물

UNW(F)-014 10115 0145

(중근동. 국연. 해기. 기정) 총2매

UNITED NATIONS

S

Security Council

Distr.
GENERAL

S/22068
14 January 1991
ENGLISH
ORIGINAL: ARABIC

LETTER DATED 14 JANUARY 1991 FROM THE PERMANENT REPRESENTATIVE OF YEMEN TO THE UNITED NATIONS ADDRESSED TO THE PRESIDENT OF THE SECURITY COUNCIL

I have the honour to transmit herewith the text of the initiative announced by President Ali Abdullah Saleh, Chairman of the Command Council of the Republic of Yemen, at the meeting of the Council of Representatives held today, Monday, 14 January 1991, with a view to bringing about a peaceful settlement of the current crisis in the Gulf.

I should be grateful if you would have this text circulated as a document of the Security Council.

(Signed) Abdalla Saleh AL-ASHTAL
Ambassador
Permanent Representative

91-01031 2621 E (E) /...

2-1

0095

Ano

S/22068
English
Page 2

Annex

1. Withdrawal of Iraq from Kuwait.

2. Arab and international forces to take up position in the area of the dispute between Iraq and Kuwait, under League of Arab States and United Nations supervision.

3. Foreign forces in the region to withdraw immediately upon Iraq's agreement to withdraw from Kuwait.

4. Pledge by the Security Council to implement its resolutions concerning the Arab-Israeli conflict by hastening the convening of the International Peace Conference on the Middle East.

5. Pledge by those States which have forces in the Gulf and Arabian peninsula region not to use force against Iraq.

6. Cessation of the economic boycott against Iraq immediately after acceptance of these proposals by the parties to the dispute.

-----

2 - 2

0096

외 무 부

종 별 :

번 호 : UNW-0091 일 시 : 91 0115 1500

수 신 : 장 관 (중근동,국연,기정,해기)

발 신 : 주 유엔 대사

제 목 : 걸프관련 사태 (안보리)

연: UNW-0084

1. PICKERING 주유엔 미국대사는 1.15, 오전 언론으로부터 불란서안에 대한 논평을 요청받고 연호 불란서안이 만약 안보리에서 표결에 회부될 경우 미국은 거부권을 행사할것 이라고 대답하였음.

2. 다수의 안보리 회원국들은 유엔 결의안상 시한이 만료되는 1.15.자정 이전 안보리가 마지막으로 이락에 대해 안보리 결의이행을 촉구하는 멧세지를 보내는데 (결의안 또는 의장 성명)동조하는 것으로 파악됨. 끝

(대사 현홍주-국장)

중아국	1차보	중아국	국기국	정문국	안기부	공보처

PAGE 1

91.01.16 09:13 WG

외신 1과 통제관

0097

외 무 부

종 별 :

번 호 : UNW-0092 일 시 : 91 0115 1500

수 신 : 장 관 (중근동,국연,기정,해기)

발 신 : 주 유엔 대사

제 목 : 걸프관련 사태 (안보리 및 사무총장 동향)

1.안보리는 1.15.(화) 10:30 불란서의 안보리 의장성명 초안 토의를 위해 회의 개최예정이었으나, 12:30 현재 동 개최가 지연되고 있는바 영국과 쏘련측이 공동제안중인 초안 내용은 별첨과 같음.

2.데 꾸에야르 사무총장의 1.15. 10:00 기자들과 의문답 내용을 별첨 송부함.

3.또한 1.15. 당지발 신화사 통신 타전 내용도아울러 송부함. 끝

(대사 현홍주-국장)

첨부: FAX (UNW(F)-015)

중아국 1차보 중아국 국기국 정문국 안기부 공보처 2차보 미주국

PAGE 1

91.01.16 09:13 WG

외신 1과 통제관

0098

-0092

첨부 1 UNW(F)-015 10115 1500 P.1 총 매
(중근동. 국연. 기정. 一□1) UK + SU

STATEMENT BY THE PRESIDENT OF THE SECURITY COUNCIL

having heard the report of the Secretary-General on his visit to Baghdad, the members of the Security Council endorse the Secretary-General's efforts to secure peace by making a last urgent and solemn appeal to President Saddam Hussein. Even now, on the day of the deadline set by Security Council Resolution 678, the members of the Security Council appeal to Iraq to display wisdom and responsibility and to make the only necessary step, which is to withdraw unconditionally from Kuwait on the basis of the resolutions of the Security Council and in full compliance with those resolutions. If President Saddam Hussein does this he can still avert war. The Security Council, representing the whole international community, urges him to act accordingly in the interests of his own country and the world.

0099

첨부 2

Remarks of the Secretary-General at approximately 10:00 a.m. on Tuesday 15 January 1991

Q. We were wondering if the French and Arab initiatives can succeed in the face of such stiff US opposition?

S-G You are not in the right place. You should go up and see what the members of the Security Council decide to do. It is not for me to pass any judgement. As you know, it is the pratice of the Secretary-General not to try and influence the members of the Security Council.

Q. Do you think there is any chance for these initiatives?

S-G I think there are many member countries which are interested.

Q. Is it reasonable for Washington to reject the French plan just because it calls for a peace conference?

S-G It is not for me to pass judgement on the positions of member countries.

Q. Belgium is calling for your office to appoint a mediator to resolve the Palestinian issue?

S-G That is first news. The idea of appointing a special representative is an old one. Resolution 242 already asks for an appointment and as you know Ambassador Jarring has resigned and I have to appoint of course a (new) special representative -- but I haven't heard anything about the Belgian initiative so far.

Q. Is the American stance hostile -- in Mr. Pickering's words, "it is inappropriate for Zaire to make the peace offer in the form of a statement"?

S-G I cannot pass judgement on the position of member countries.

Q. Is it late for diplomacy?

S-G Well, it is 10:00 a.m. our time, and we have 14 hours for diplomacy.

* * *

0100

첨부 3

BC1 NYB034 9101150933 (1825) NYZ006 9101150933

.BNY:P:N:YANG YUEHUA:E:91/01/15/09/15
79
UNITED NATIONS AAA011552
IRAQ READY FOR PACKAGE SOLUTION TO GULF CRISIS

UNITED NATIONS, JANUARY 15 (XINHUA) -- U.N. SECRETARY-GENERAL JAVIER PEREZ DE CUELLAR REPORTEDLY SAID DURING HIS REPORT TO THE U.N. SECURITY COUNCIL ON HIS TRIP TO BAGHDAD THAT IRAQ IS READY FOR A PACKAGE COMPREHENSIVE SOLUTION TO THE GULF CRISIS AND READY TO SACRFICE FOR PEACE.

ACCORDING TO SOME ARAB SOURCES, THE SECRETARY-GENERAL, WHO JUST RETURNED YESTERDAY FROM HIS +UNSUCCESSFUL+ PEACE MISSION TO IRAQ, TOLD THE COUNCIL MEMBERS THAT IRAQI PRESIDENT SADDAM HUSSEIN MENTIONED TO HIM THAT SOLVING THE EVERY COMPLICATED ISSUE DURING A SINGLE MEETING WOULD BE VERY DIFFICULT.

AFTER THE BRIEFING, THE U.N. CHIEF TOLD REPORTERS THAT THE COUNCIL MEMBERS UNANIMOUSLY DESIRED FOR A PEACEFUL SOLUTION TO THE CRISIS AND WILL CONTINUE THEIR EFFORTS FOR A WHOLE DAY TODAY TO AVOID THE WORST.

HOWEVER, ACCORDING TO THESE SOURCES, THE U.N. CHIEF REQUESTED THE COUNCIL NOT TO LEAK OUT +THE CONNFIDENTIAL+ CONTENT OF HIS REPORT TO THE NEWS MEDIA FOR FEAR THAT HIS FURTHER PEACE EFFORTS WOULD BE SPOILED.

HE REPORTEDLY SAID THAT THE IRAQI AUTHORITIES INSISTED ON DIRECT TALKS WITH THE U.S., THE EUROPEAN COMMUNITY AND SAUDI ARABIA SO THAT EACH SIDE COULD KNOW WHAT IT WOULD TAKE AND WHAT IT SHOULD GIVE.

HE ALSO TOLD THE COUNCIL MEMBERS THAT IT WAS UP TO THEM TO DECIDE WHETHER THERE IS A DIPLOMATIC CHANGE TO IMPLEMENT THE SECURITY COUNCIL RESOLUTIONS.

THE COUNCIL WILL RESUME ITS CONSULTATIONS AT 10 AM THIS MORNING TO CONSIDER THE FRENCH PROPOSAL FOR A PEACEFUL SETTLEMENT OF THE CRISIS. IT IS SAID THAT THE +CONFIDENTIAL+ DETAILS OF THE U.N. CHIEF'S PEACE PLAN WILL BE POSSIBLY MADE KNOWN TO THE PUBLIC. ENDITEM
(CHECK UPON FILE)

0101

외 무 부

종 별 :

번 호 : UNW-0096 일 시 : 91 0115 1710

수 신 : 장 관(중근동,국연,해기,기정)

발 신 : 주 유엔 대사

제 목 : 페만사태관련 동향

연:UNW-0092

연호관련 1.15. 신화 및 UPI 송고기사를 별전보고함.

첨부:FAX 3매:UNW(F)-016

끝

(대사 현홍주-국장)

중아국 1차보 중아국 국기국 정문국 안기부 공보처

PAGE 1

91.01.16 09:34 WG

외신 1과 통제관

0102

UW-0096 외 ||||W(F)-016 10115 1시 총3매

#25. 국연. 해기. 기26)

북미 Xinhua (Qian Wenrong) - United Nations

"SECURITY COUNCIL HOLD CONSULTATIONS ON GULF CRISIS AGAIN TODAY"

The Security Council began informal consultations on the gulf crisis as only hours away from the UN deadline for Iraq to withdraw from Kuwait or face a military attack to be launched by the US-led multinational forces.

Francois Giuliani, spokesman said that the informal consultations are concentrated on a draft statement of the Security Council President, which would endorse the UN Secretary-General's efforts to secure peace by making a last urgent and solemn appeal to Iraqi President Saddam Hussein for an unconditional withdrawal from Kuwait.

But, the draft does not mention the convening of an international peace conference on the Middle East as it is contained in the French proposal circulated here last night and requested by Saddam Hussein.

British Ambassador to the United Nations, David Hannay, told reporters before the informal consultations began that I hope we will come to an agreement on a political appeal as soon as possible today.

He said that in the report of the UN Secretary-General on his mission to Baghdad submitted to the Security Council last night, there are elements acceptable to the Security Council, but he didn't give any details on the UN chief's report.

He believed that the Security Council will support a larger appeal for peace, regarding the international conference on the Middle East as it is contained in new French peace initiative, the British Ambassador said the idea for a peace conference will be pursued in the Security Council today. He indicated that the Security Council will support the convening of such a conference at an appropriate time . But, he declined to accept any linkage between the gulf crisis and the proposal conference, emphasizing that these are two separate issues.

Soviet Ambassador, Yuriy Vorontsov said any last minute appeal is very good and we will support it. But he didn't say whether the Soviet Union will support the new French peace initiative or not.

The new French proposal calls on the Security Council to issue a final appeal to the Iraqi leader to announce without further delay the intention of Iraq to withdraw from Kuwait according to a programmed time-table and to start a speedy and massive withdrawal.

At the same time, the proposal suggests that the UN will send in international observers and a peace-keeping force composed of arab troops to monitoring and verify the withdrawal of the Iraqi forces. It will also offer Iraq guarantee that it will not be attacked and an international conference will be convened at an appropriate time to deal with the Israel-Arab conflict.

As a usual practice, the Security Council will hold formal consultations after informal consultations and then proceed to a formal meeting to take action on a draft or a statement.

It is still unknown when the formal meeting of the Council will begin. UN Secretary-General said that he expected the Security Council will meet whole day today.

Despite my mission to Baghdad has not given the result as expected, the members of the Security Council unanimously desire a peaceful solution of the gulf situation.

3 - 1

0103

IIII
d ibc-iraq-un sked

Security Council plans to issue last peace appeal to Iraq[
By J.T. NGUYEN[

UNITED NATIONS (UPI) — Members of the U.N. Security Council huddled Tuesday a desperate attempt to work out a last appeal to President Saddam Hussein to his troops out of Kuwait before the withdrawal deadline was to expire.

Government representatives returned to the Security Council chamber for closed-door consultations after spending most of last night to hear Secretary-General Javier Perez de Cuellar on his failed peace mission to Bag Sunday and to discuss what they should do not next.

The adjourned early Tuesday morning without taking and decision any reconve at around 10:30 a.m. for informal discussions. The deadline for Iraq to pull of Kuwait was set at midnight EST Tuesday (0500 GMT Wednesday).

British U.N. Ambassador David Hannay told reporters the council wanted to is a "straightforward" appeal for peace to Saddam without weakening the Securit Council's resolve to implement its 12 resolutions against Iraq.

"For the appeal to be rapid and effective, it needs to be clear and unambiguous," Hannay said. "Hopefully, one would have a positive response fr Iraq."

Soviet U.N. Ambassador Yuliy Vorontsov also said his government supported th idea of issuing the appeal. The diplomats said they hoped the council would agree on the text sometime Tuesday before the midnight deadline.

Hannay proposed that the council endorse Perez de Cuellar's peace efforts by making a "last urgent and solemn" appeal to Saddam.

"Even now, on the day of the deadline set by the Security Council resolutior 678, the members of the council appeal to Iraq to withdraw unconditionally f Kuwait on the basis of the resolutions and in full compliance with those resolutions," the council would say in the appeal, the text of which was advanced by Hannay.

"If President Saddam Hussein does this, he can still avert war," it says. "T Security Council, representing the whole international community, urges him t act accordingly in the interests of his own country and the world."

The 15-nation was also supposed to take up a six-point peace plan proposed b France to avert a war between Iraq and the 28-nation, U.S.-led multinational force in the Persian Gulf.

But France conceded Tuesday that it was unable to overcome U.S. opposition t the plan and indicated that its foreign minister, Roland Dumas, will not try sell it to Saddam. If France decided to withdraw its proposal, the council wo then focus on the peace appeal.

The plan met strong U.S. objection Monday night when U.S. Ambassador Thomas Pickering said the United States was against any linkage, even a superficial one, between the Gulf crisis and the Palestinian issue in the Israeli-occupie West Bank and Gaza strip.

U.N. diplomats believed the French initiative came too late and might cause more confusion during the remaining hours before the expiration of the deadli

In Washington, the White House's press secretary Marlin Fitzwater said the United States had not flatly rejected the plan.

"We have problems with the linkage to the Palestinian question, which we ha discussed in the past," Fitzwater said.

France's last-minute peace plan would have the Security Council call on Iraq begin immediately a "rapid and massive" withdrawal from Kuwait under the supervision of a U.N. observer force.

The plan was handed to the president of the 15-nation council, Zaire's U.N, Ambassador Bagbeni Adeito Nzengeya, within hours after the Paris government announced its intention to initiate a peace bid to salvage the failed weekend mission of Perez de Cuellar.

Under the proposal, the council would call on Iraq to announce "without delay its intention to withdraw from Kuwait according to a timetable and to begin immediately a "rapid and massive" pullout.

3-2

0104

Once the pullout has begun, the U.N. secretary-general would set up the pro of monitoring the withdrawal of the Iraqi forces by sending international observers and a peacekeeping force composed of troops from Arab countries.

Iraq would be guaranteed that it would not be attacked and necessary measur would be taken with the cooperation of Arab countries to promote negotiation toward a peaceful settlement.

Once those measures are carried out, the Security Council would bring its "active contribution" to the resolution of other problems in the region, in particular the Arab-Israeli conflict and the Palestinian problem, by conveni "at an appropriate time" an international conference on Middle East peace, w would conform to a declaration by the council on last Dec. 20 in order to en security, stability and development in that part of the world.

Perez de Cuellar returned to New York Monday morning, sounding dejected for having failed to persuade Saddam to withdraw from Kuwait. He reported to the council Monday night.

Perez de Cuellar said he returned empty-handed and warned other peace-maker that it is "perhaps a little late for embarking on any other (diplomatic) efforts."

"The only thing I can tell you is that, unfortunately, I have not much in m hands," he said when asked what he would tell Security Council members.

"My visit has been of course interesting, but I have not been offered anyth from the Iraqi authorities which I can consider a step towards peace."

He termed his 2 1/2-hour talks Sunday with Saddam in Baghdad "polite, but unfortunately unsuccessful."

Asked whether he had lost hope, Perez de Cuellar said, "In some ways, yes."

3-3

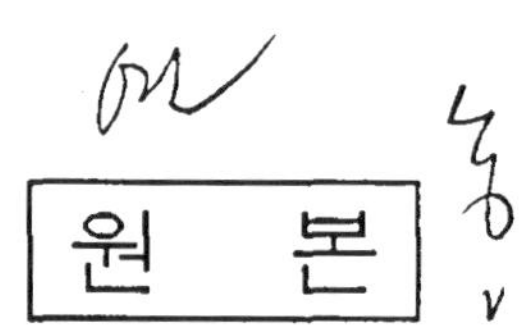

외 무 부

종 별 : 지 급

번 호 : UNW-0101 일 시 : 91 0115 1830

수 신 : 장 관(국연,중근동,기정)

발 신 : 주 유엔 대사

제 목 : 걸프관련사태(안보리, 유엔사무총장 동향)

연:UNW-0091

1.미, 영등 다수 안보리 상임이사국의 반대로 불란서는 연호 제안을 철회하였으며, 연호 영.소의 공동제안에 대해서도 미국이 강하게 반대함으로써 안보리가 이락에 대해 마지막으로 평화를 호소하는 결의안 또는 의장 성명을 채택하는 방안은 사실상 폐기된 것으로 관측되고 있음.

2.상기 상황에 따라 안보리대신 유엔사무총장이 이락에대해 마지막으로 호소하는 성명을 금일저녁발표할 것으로 알려짐.

3.금일 저녁 안보리가 소집되어 인도, 예멘, 자이레등 비동맹 7개국이 공동제안한 피점령 아랍영토내 사태에 관한 별첨 결의안에 표결할 예정임.

첨부:상기 3항 언급 비동맹 결의안초안(FAX):UNW(F)-017 끝

(대사 현홍주-국장)

국기국 1차보 중아국 정문국 안기부 미주국 2차보

PAGE 1

91.01.16 08:49 WG

외신 1과 통제관

0106

P.1

UNW-0101 의 첨부문

UNW(F)-017 101-1830 (국연, 중근동. 기정) 총1매

UNITED NATIONS

Security Council

PROVISIONAL

S/22056
15 January 1991

ORIGINAL: ENGLISH

Côte d'Ivoire, Cuba, Ecuador, India, Yemen, Zaire and Zimbabwe: draft resolution

Reaffirming its resolution 681 (1990), particularly paragraph 3 thereof,

Having learnt with deep concern and consternation that Israel has, in defiance of Security Council resolutions, and in violation of its obligation under the Fourth Geneva Convention of 1949, deported four Palestinian civilians on 8 January 1991,

1. Declares that the action of the Israeli authorities of deporting four Palestinian civilians on 8 January 1991, is in violation of previous Security Council resolutions, in particular Security Council resolution 681 (1990), as well as in violation of the Fourth Geneva Convention of 1949, which is applicable to all the Palestinian territories occupied by Israel since 1967, including Jerusalem;

2. Demands that Israel, the occupying power, refrain from deporting any Palestinian civilians from the occupied territories and to ensure the safe and immediate return of all those deported;

3. Decides to keep the situation under review.

2653E

1-1

0107

외 무 부

종 별 : 긴 급

번 호 : UNW-0108 일 시 : 91 0115 2000

수 신 : 장 관(중근동,국연,해기,기정)

발 신 : 주 유엔 대사

제 목 : 걸프사태(유엔사무총장 발표문)

연:UNW-0101

연호 금 1.15. 안보리에서의 제반노력이 결렬됨에 따라 께야르 유엔사무총장은 금 18:00 별첨성명을 발표하였음.동 성명은 팔레스타인 문제와 관련, '걸프사태가 해결되면 팔레스타인 문제를 포함한 아랍.이스라엘 분쟁을 포괄적으로 해결하기 위해 모든 노력을 경주할 것이라는 보장을 관계정부 최고위층으로 부터 받고있으며, 본인도 최대한 노력할것임을 약속한다' 는 내용을 포함하고 있음.

첨부:상기 성명문 FAX:UNW(F)-018

끝

(대사 현홍주-국장)

중아국	1차보	중아국	국기국	정문국	안기부	공보처	

PAGE 1

91.01.16 10:10 WG

외신 1과 통제관

0108

#UNW-0108 의 첨부물

UNW(FI)-018 10115 2000 총4매
(중근동, 국연, 해기 1과)

Statement by the Secretary-General on 15 January 1991

As 15 January advances,
and the world stands poised between peace and war,
I most sincerely appeal to President Saddam Hussein
to turn the course of events away from catastrophe
and towards a new era of justice and harmony
based on the principles of the United Nations Charter.

All of our efforts in this direction will fail
unless Iraq can signify its readiness
to comply with the relevant resolutions
of the Security Council, beginning with resolution 660.

If this commitment is made,
and clear and substantial steps taken
to implement these resolutions,
a just peace, with all of its benefits, will follow.
I therefore urge President Saddam Hussein to commence,
without delay,
the total withdrawal of Iraqi forces from Kuwait.

4-1

0109

Once this process is well underway,
I wish to assure him,
on the basis of understandings that I have received
from governments at the highest level,
that neither Iraq nor its forces
will be attacked by those arrayed
in the international coalition against his country.

Further, with the commencement of withdrawal,
as Secretary-General of the United Nations,
I would, with the consent of the parties concerned,
and the agreement of the Security Council,
be prepared immediately to deploy United Nations observers and,
if necessary, United Nations forces to certify the withdrawal
and to ensure that hostilities do not erupt on the ground.

In addition, with compliance of the resolutions,
I would urge the Security Council to review its decisions
imposing sanctions against Iraq.

I would also encourage a process
whereby foreign forces deployed in the area would be phased
out.

Peace in the region requires that all of its problems
be resolved justly and equitably,
in accordance with the principles
of the Charter of the United Nations.

4—2

0110

I have every assurance,
once again from the highest levels of government,
that with the resolution of the present crisis,
every effort will be made to address,
in a comprehensive manner,
the Arab-Israeli conflict, including the Palestinian question.
I pledge my every effort to this end.

As I stated to the Council last night,
all of us are aware of the extreme gravity
of the decisions to be made in the period ahead.
No-one and no nation can
- except with a heavy heart -
resort to the other "necessary means"
implied by resolution 678,
knowing in advance that tragic and unpredictable consequences
can follow.

I trust, in the circumstances,
that wisdom and statesmanship will prevail in all quarters
in order to move decisively away from conflict.
In appealing to President Saddam Hussein today,
I wish him to know that I will readily devote my every capacity
to working with him, and with all others concerned,
to this end.

4-3

0111

In the tenth and final year of my tenure
as Secretary-General of the United Nations,
no cause would give me greater satisfaction
than to set the Middle East as a whole
on the road to just and lasting peace.
And no disappointment would be greater and more tragic
than to find the nations of the world engaging in a conflict
that none of their peoples want.

****

4-4

0112

관리 번호	91/288

원 본

외 무 부

종 별 :

번 호 : UNW-0118 일 시 : 91 0116 1900

수 신 : 장관(중근동,국연,기정)

발 신 : 주 유엔 대사

제 목 : 걸프관련사태(안보리동향)

1. 데꾸에야르 유엔사무총장이 자신의 이락방문 결과에 관하여 1.14. 안보리에 보고한 내용을 별전 FAX 보고함.

2. 동 자료는 안보리 회원국에만 비공개로 배포된것임.

첨부:상기 보고서:UNW(F)-019

끝

(대사 현홍주-국장)

예고문: 91. 6. 30에 재분류문에 의거 일반문서로 재 분류됨.

검토필(1991. 6.30.)

중아국 장관 차관 국기국 청와대 안기부

PAGE 1

91.01.17 09:34

외신 2과 통제관 BT

0113

#별첨 UNW(F)-019 10-1 1900 총3매
(중근동. 국연. 기정)

STATEMENT BY THE SECRETARY GENERAL TO THE SECURITY COUNCIL ON 14 JANUARY 1991

1. You will recall that on Thursday, 10 January, I informed you, Mr. President, that I had decided to accept a standing invitation from the Government of Iraq to visit Baghdad in order to have discussions with the authorities, in particular with President Saddam Hussein. I took this decision following the outcome of the meetings that were held in Geneva on 9 January between US Secretary of State James Baker and Iraqi Foreign Minister Tariq Aziz, bearing in mind the provisions of resolution 678. Prior to my departure, I received messages of strong support from a great number of world leaders, including those of many members of the Security Council. All of them expressed the profound hope, that a way be found to obtain the implementation of the relevant Security Council resolutions by peaceful means.

2. En route to Baghdad, I made brief stops in Paris, Geneva and Amman. In Paris, I met with President Mitterrand, and in Geneva, I had the opportunity to review the situation with the Foreign Ministers of the European Community. While there, I also met with Foreign Minister Loncar of Yugoslavia, in his capacity as Chairman of the Movement of Non-Aligned States. In Amman, I met with King Hussein, who was deeply concerned about the impasse and the disastrous consequences for Jordan and the region if hostilities erupted. While in Amman, I also met with Foreign Minister Nastase of Romania, who was travelling in the area.

3. I travelled to Baghdad in the afternoon of 12 january where, upon arrival, I had a three-hour meeting with Foreign Minister Tariq Aziz. On 13 january, prior to my meeting with the Iraqi President, I met with the Chairman of the Palestine Liberation Organization, Mr. Yasser Arafat, at his request. It should be noted in this connection that, like King Hussein, Mr. Arafat was extremely disturbed by the prospects of a military confrontation, the consequences of which would be devastating for the region, not least for the Palestinians.

4. In the evening of 13 January, I was received by President Saddam Hussein for some two and a half hours. At the outset of our meeting, I underlined to him that I had come to Baghdad at my own initiative, but with the widest possible support from the membership of the United Nations. I added that, as Secretary-General of the United Nations, I had responsibilities under the Charter to strive for peace and, accordingly, I urged him to comply fully with the relevant resolutions of the Security Council, starting with resolution 660. I pointed out that I intended to report to the Council upon my return to New York and that, if I were to do so without serious progress having been made, I was duty-bound to reflect this in my report. In emphasizing the importance of the implementation of the resolutions, I stated that progress in this direction would facilitate the undertaking of measures with respect to stability and security in the region. I touched upon possible steps that could be taken in the post-withdrawal phase (such as those related to peace-keeping, assurances of non-attack and the present sanctions). I also referred to possible regional security arrangements. In connection with the broader Middle east peace process, I referred to resolutions already adopted by the General Assembly, my own efforts, and the Presidential Statement of the Security Council of 20 December 1990 which clearly implied that a major effor could soon be made.

3-1

0114

5. In his opening comments, President Saddam Hussain sait that he did not wish to conceal from me his ambivalence about our meeting. On the one hand, he had wanted me to come to Baghdad to discuss the present crisis because I had, through contacts developed during the Iran-Iraq conflict, dealt with his country and knew its "traits".

On the other hand, he expressed concern that, if our meeting were to produce insufficient results, it could be used by those who wished to wage war against Iraq.

Underlining a theme that had been emphasized during my meeting the previous evening with Foreing Minister Tariq Aziz, the President said that it would not be possible, in a single meeting, to find "ready solutions to such a complicated situation". He noted that whereas resolution 598, which Iraq had accepted, set out a comprehensive approach to the issues addressed therein, the Security Council had not, regrettably, adopted a comprehensive approach in dealing with the present crisis.

6. The President dwelt at length on Iraq's claim to Kuwait, and underlined that in the period prior to 2 August 1990, it had become "a base for conspiracy" against Iraq.

He pointed out that although Iraq had never accepted resolution 660, it had agreed, in the early days of the crisis, to attend a mini-summit in Jeddah and had begun to withdraw its troops from Kuwait. But those efforts, which he stated were aimed at achieving "an Arab solution", were undermined by the introcution of foreign forces into the region, which heightened the threat posed to Iraq.

Criticizing what he called "precipitous" actions by the Security Council, he stated that Iraq had been tried in absentia and his Foreign Minister had been denied the facilities he needed to be able to present his case. Further, he stated that on earlier occasions when the Council has called for the withdrawal of troops, this had been accompanied by a call for negotiations between the parties; withdrawal had not been set as a precondition for such negotiations. Moreover, he cited examples of Israeli occupations and annexation, noting that Israel had never been subjected to sanctions or outside military intervention as a means of ensuring compliance with Security Council resolutions. This he stated, was indicative of a double standard that persisted until the present.

It was unfortunate, he said, that his initiatives of 12 and 19 August, which had advocated the application of a single standard and a set of principles in addressing comprenensively the issues of the region, had never been seriously considered.

3-2

0115

7. On the question of withdrawal, the President stated that the Iraqi people today regarded Kuwait as Iraq's "19th province", and "would not even whisper the word withdrawal", as war was looming and such an utterance would give a psychological advantage to Iraq's adversaries.

At the same time, Iraq was prepared for an in-depth dialogue.

In this connection, I should add that in my meeting with the Foreign Minister the previous evening, Mr. Tariq Aziz repeatedly stressed Iraq's desire for dialogue with the United States, the European Community and the Arab states, in particular, Saudi Arabia. The President stated that his Government was prepared to discuss a "package deal" because, in such an arrangement, each parti knew exactly what it would have to give and what it would receive.

The Iraqi people were, he said, "ready to sacrifice for the cause of peace" if others would do the same.

8. On two separate occasions during our meeting, the President called on me to use my good offices, saying that if the other parties were to permit me to play a role in search of a solution, Iraq would facilitate my task and cooperate with me. In response to my comment that this idea would be a non-starter if the position of Iraq was irreversible on the subject of withdrawal from Kuwait, the President reacted by saying that that was not what he meant.

He reiterated that I should try to engage the views of the parties, including Iraq, in order to make proposals that could lead to a solution. I explained to the President that, while I would reflect this suggestion in my report to the Security Council, I felt that any effort of mine would naturally need to be in furtherance of the relevant resolution of the Security Council.

9. Mr. President,

From the foregoing, it must sadly be concluded that a most ominous situation exists at present.

Despite the near universal yearning for peace and the intense efforts of many, includind myself, to secure compliance by Iraq, the relevant resolutions of the Security Council remain unimplemented.

At this solemn hour, with 15 January upon us, members of the Council must once again consider whether there are any diplomatic measures that can still be taken by the Organization, or by its members individually or collectively, to secure full implementation of the Council.s resolutions by peaceful means. All of us are aware of the extreme gravity of the decisions to be made, for no one and no nation can -except with a heavy heart- resort to the other "necessary means" implied by Resolution 678, knowing in advance that tragic and unpredictable consequences can follow.

0116

원 본

외 무 부

종 별 : 지 급

번 호 : UNW-0122 일 시 : 91 0116 2330

수 신 : 장 관(중근동,국연,해기,기정)

발 신 : 주 유엔 대사

제 목 : 페만사태관련 동향

1.금 1.16 19:45 유엔사무총장은 전쟁발발 관련 기자질문에 대해 다음과같이 답변하였 음.

'WHAT CAN I TELL YOU, DEAR FEIENDS ?

AFTER ALL MY EFFORTS, AFTER ALL THE EFFORTS OF SO MANY COUNTRIES AND SO MANY PERSONALITIES THAT WE ARE NOW FACING AWAR.

AT THIS VERY MOMNET , AFTER ONLY ONE HOUR AND HALF OF HOSTILITITES, I AM NOT WELL INFORMED.

I HAVE NOT MANY DETAILS OF WHAT HAPPENED. BUT I THINK IT ISFOR ME TO EXPRESS MY DEEP SORROW.

AS SECRETARY GENERAL OF THE UNITED NATIONS.I CAN ONLY BESADDENED BY THE BEGINING OF THE HOSTILITIES.'

2.큐바는 금일저녁 안보리 소집을 요청하고, 의장국인 자이레와 비공식 협의를 갖고 있으며 한편 PICKERING 미국대사는 23:00 안보리 이사국들에 금번 'OPERATION DESERT STORM' 에 대해 설명예정인 것으로 알려진바, 진전사항 추보하겠음.끝

(대사 현홍주-국장)

중아국 ②	장관	차관	1차보	2차보	국기국	정문국	청와대	총리실
안기부								

PAGE 1

91.01.17 13:25 WG

외신 1과 통제관

0117

국제전화 통화 기록전

1. 일 시 : 91.1.17(목) 13:22-13:25 (3분)

2. 통화자

   - 송화자 : 주유엔대표부 서대원 참사관

   - 수화자 : 국제연합과 이규형 과장

3. 내 용

   - 서 참사관 : 수시간전 발발한 페만전쟁 관련, 유엔사무총장은 기자 질문에 대해 매우 슬픈일(deep sorrow) 이라고 답함. 또한 안보리 이사국간에 bilateral informal consultation 이 진행중인 것으로 알려지고 있으나 안보리 회의 개최에 대해서는 아직 구체적인 사항이 알려지지 않고 있음.

0118

페만 개전관련 안보리 동향 (1)

91.1.17.(목) 14:40

국제연합과

1. 안보리는 1.17.(목) 14:10(한국시간) 페만사태 관련 협의를 위한 안보리 비공식 비공개 회의를 개최중임. (뉴욕시간으로 17일 새벽 00시 10분)

2. 동 회의 개최에 앞서 주유엔 미국대사는 성명을 발표하였는 바, 동 내용은 부쉬 미대통령이 수시간전에 발표한 내용과 대동소이하며 전쟁의 불가피성을 강조하는데 역점을 둠. 한편 주유엔 쿠바대사도 안보리회의 참석에 앞서 미국이 선제 무력공격을 감행한데 대한 비난성명을 발표하고 대이라크 제재 조치의 효과가 나타날때까지 기다려야 했음을 강조함.

3. 안보리회의 개최에 앞서 13:30경 안보리상임이사국간에 비공식 개별협의가 개최된 바 있음.

(출 처 : 주유엔대표부 전화통보)

0119

외 무 부

종 별 : 긴 급

번 호 : UNW-0123 일 시 : 91 0117 0140

수 신 : 장 관(중근동,국연,해기,기정)

발 신 : 주 유엔 대사

제 목 : 페만사태 동향(유엔안보리)

연:UNW-0122

1.연호, 안보리 비공식협의 (양자)가 1.16 23:00 경시작된데 이어 1.17 00:10 부터 전체협의가 개최중임.

2.상기 전체협의시 PICKERING 미국대사 발언문 및 쿠바대사 발언문의 ADVANCE TEXT 를 별첨 확스송부함.

첨부:상기 발언문:UNW(F)-023

(대사 현홍주-국장)

중아국 장관 차관 1차보 2차보 중아국 국기국 정와대 총리실
안기부 공보처

PAGE 1 91.01.17 15:18 WG
외신 1과 통제관

0120

FUNW-0123 의 첨부물 (국연. 중근동. 해기. 기정) 총4매

안보리 협의시 Pickering 대사 발언문 (advance text)

(1. 17. 00:10 회의 시작)

In consultation with key members of the international coalition, the President has ordered U.S. forces to commence military operations against Iraqi forces in Iraq and Kuwait. U.S. and coalition forces have initiated combat operations.

Although coalition forces are striking military and strategic targets in Iraq, our goal is not the destruction, occupation or dismemberment of Iraq. It is the liberation of Kuwait.

The President's decision is pursuant to and in conformity with UN Security Council resolution 678, which authorizes the use of "all necessary means" after January 15 to implement relevant UN Security Council resolutions and to restore international peace and stability in the area.

The President took this step only after exhausting all diplomatic options and after having determined that the Government of Iraq would not comply peacefully with the United Nations Security Council resolutions calling upon it to withdraw from Kuwait.

The Government of Iraq was given every opportunity to withdraw. The United States and its coalition partners took every step possible to leave Iraq in no doubt of the consequence of a failure to comply with the UNSC resolutions by January 15.

The U.S. strongly preferred that Iraq comply peacefully with all UNSC resolutions, and the international community made exhaustive diplomatic efforts to that end. Iraq has rejected or ignored:

--Secretary Baker's direct talks with Foreign Minister Tariq Aziz on January 9 and the President's written letter to Saddam Hussein of January 5;

--The personal efforts of UNSYG Perez de Cuellar during his mission to Baghdad on January 12-13, and his appeal on January 15 to withdraw unconditionally; and

--Supporting efforts by the European Community, the Arab League, the Non-Aligned Movement, and numerous countries and private public individuals.

4 - 1

0121

In the course of these efforts, Iraq was assured that, if it withdrew peacefully: (1) It would not be attacked; (2) It could negotiate a peaceful resolution of its differences with Kuwait after withdrawal as stated in UNSC Resolution 660; (3) Economic sanctions not related to the military establishment would be quickly reviewed; (4) The U.S. sought no permanent ground presence in the region; and (5) The U.S. would continue to seek peaceful resolution of the Arab-Israeli dispute.

All such diplomatic efforts were rejected by Iraq.

Economic sanctions and the UN embargo failed to force Iraqi compliance, and there was no indication that they would do so in the forseeable future.

Iraq was continuing the dismantlement of Kuwait, the strengthening of its fortifications, and the manufacture of additional weapons of mass destruction.

Indeed, Iraq made clear it did not recognize the UNSC Resolutions and would not comply with them.

Further delay would only have prolonged the suffering of the Kuwaiti people and increased risks to the coalition Forces.

U.S. and coalition operations are being carried out in full compliance with applicable international conventions on the laws of armed conflict, including attempting to minimize civilian casualties.

We have warned Iraq to avoid the use of weapons of mass destruction (chemical, biological, and nuclear) and to respect its obligations under the Law of Armed Conflict and the Geneva Protocol of 1924. Use of such tactics and weapons will occasion a dramatic escalation of hostilities and objectives.

We have also made clear that we will hold the Iraqi leadership responsible for any destruction of Kuwait's oil fields and for any acts of terrorism carried out against the U.S. or our allies.

In light of the plans of Iraq and groups acting on its behalf to conduct terrorism against American targets throughout the world, we seek your cooperation in enhancing the security of our citizens and facilities. We are ready to work with you in countering terrorist threats.

4 - 2

0122

We hope to bring hostilities to conclusion as soon as possible, consistent with the full implementation of UNSC resolutions.

Iraq can still avoid further destruction by unconditional, immediate, and complete withdrawal from Kuwait.

Security Council resolution 678 requested all states to provide appropriate support for actions taken by states cooperating with Kuwait to implement the Security Council decisions.

4-3

0123

안보리 회의시 쿠바측 발언 (Advance text)
(1.17. 00:10 회의 시작)

The hegemonic policy of the United States and the intransigence of Iraq are the main elements responsible for the outburst of war in the Gulf. Fidel blamed the United Nations and the politicians of our time for their lack of capacity to avoid the conflict. Everybody is to blame, he expressed, after showing his sentiments of pain and chagrin for these developments and for the loss in human life and material wealth.

The main responsibility lies on the shoulders of he who fired the first shot and of those who supported him, said Fidel visibly worried.

Cuba did all it could in the U.N. Security Council and in direct contacts with Iraq to achieve a political solution. After accusing the United Nations and the United States for their double standard, Fidel asked himself what would have happened if Kuwait has been invaded and occupied by a country that posessed nuclear weapons.

Fidel insisted that the war could have been avcided if sanctions against Iraq would have been given more time. The United Nations still has an arsenal of measures in reserve to comply Iraq to leave Kuwait and restore the sovereignty of that emirate without firin a shot.

The war will have unpredictable consequences for mankind as a whole and particularly for non oil producing Third World countries.

4-4

0124

외 무 부

종 별 : 지 급

번 호 : UNW-0124 일 시 : 91 0117 0140

수 신 : 장관(중근동,국연,해기,기정)

발 신 : 주유엔대사

제 목 : 페만사태 동향

연:UNW-0123

1. 연호 협의는 약 40분간 진행되어 미국,큐바,영국,사우디,쿠웨이트등이 발언한것으로 파악되었으며, 12:50 종료 되었음.

2. 동 협의에서 큐바가 안보리 긴급 이사회 소집을 제의하였으나, 미국이 강력 반대하였다함.끝

(대사 현홍주-국장)

중아국 1차보 2차보 미주국 국기국 청와대 총리실 안기부 공보처

장관 차관

PAGE 1 91.01.17 15:35 BX

외신 1과 통제관

0125

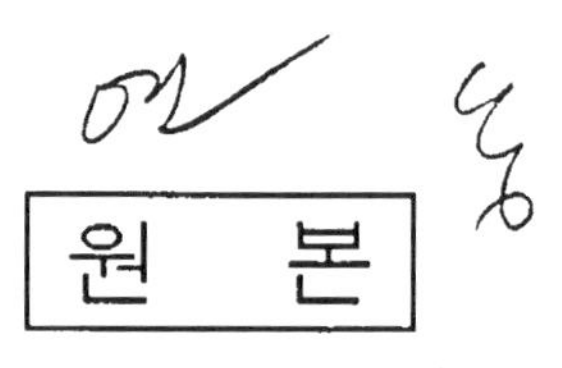

외 무 부

종 별 :

번 호 : GVW-0106 일 시 : 91 0117 1840

수 신 : 장관(국연,중근동,영해)

발 신 : 주제네바대사대리

제 목 : UNDRO 비상전화 통보

1.17 당지 UNDRO (유엔재해구조 조정관실) 사무국은 당관에 걸프사태 관련 24시간통화 가능한 비상전화번호 (41-22-733.20.10) 를 통보하여왔는바, 참고 바람.끝.

(대사대리 박영우-국장)

국기국 장관 차관 1차보 2차보 중아국 중아국 영교국 청와대
총리실 안기부 대책반

PAGE 1

91.01.18 04:28 CG

외신 1과 통제관

0126

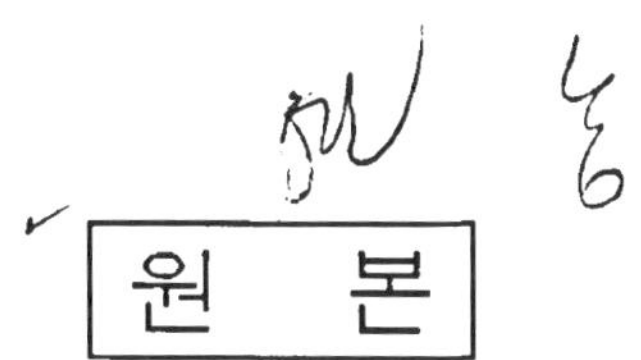

원 본

외 무 부

종 별 :

번 호 : UNW-0127 일 시 : 91 0117 1800

수 신 : 장 관(국연,중근동,해기,기정)

발 신 : 주 유엔 대사

제 목 : 페만사태

1.금 1.17 오전 유엔사무총장은 페만사태관련 기자질문에 대해 아래와 같이 답변함.

Q: MR. SECRETARY, YOUR REACTION, SIR, TO EVENTS OVERNIGHT?

SG:IN VIEW OF THE FAILURE OF DIPLOMACY, WE COULDN,T EXPECT ANYTHING DIFFERENT. AND THEREFORE, FOR THE TIME BEING, I DON'T THINK THAT IT'S TIME FOR DIPLOMACY AT THIS VERY MOMENT, WHICH MEANS THAT THERE'S NOT MUCH I CAN DO.

IT WOULD BE, ANYWAY, FOR THE SECURITY COUNCIL TO ACT. AS YOU KNOW, YESTERDAY THERE WAS A MEETING OF THE SECURITY COUNCIL AT WHICH THREE COUNTRIES-- THE UNITED STATES , FRANCE AND THE UNITED KINGDOM-- INFORMED THE MEMBERS OF THE COUNCIL, BUT THERE WAS NO DECISION BY THE COUNCIL. AND NO DECISION WAS EXPECTED, EITHER.

Q:HAVE YOU HAD ANY CONTACT WITH THE US GOVERNMENT OR THE GOVERNMENT OF IRAQ ?

SG: AS YOU KNOW PRESIDENT BUSH CALLED ME ONE HOUR IN ADVANCE (OF HOSTILITIES).

Q: SIR, DO YOU SEE ANY PROSPECT OF PEACE ANY TIME SOON?

SG:IT DEPENDS ON IRAQ, WHETHER IRAQ CAPITULATES.

2.당지 외신 UPI 에의하면 유엔사무총장은 이란의 RAFSANJANI 대통령이 페만사태관련 중재역활 및 전쟁난민에 대한 인도주의 적원조제공 의향을 표명한데 대해 지금은 시기가 아니라고 하고 모든것은 이락의 항복여부에 달려있다는 반응을 보인것으로 보도됨.

3.한편 당지 소련대사는 기자질문에 대해 유엔이 이락에 대해 45일간의 시간을

국기국	장관	차관	1차보	2차보	중아국	중아국	청와대	총리실
안기부	공보처							

PAGE 1

91.01.18 09:04 WG

외신 1과 통제관

0127

준바 있으나 결과는 불행한것이 되었다고하고 금번사태의 추이는 이락에게 달려있다고 말함.끝

(대사 현홍주-국장)

PAGE 2

0128

관리 번호	91-109

원본

외 무 부

종 별 :

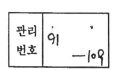

번 호 : UNW-0132　　　　일 시 : 91 0118 1800

수 신 : 장관(국연,중근동,기정)

발 신 : 주 유엔 대사

제 목 : 걸프사태(의료진 사우디파견)

연:UNW-41

1. 헝가리 대표부 BUDAI 참사관은 금 1.18 권참사관에게 헝가리 대표부는 헝가리 의료진 사우디파견 사실을 1.16 안보리 의장에게 문서로 통보하고 동 사본을 데꾸에야르 유엔사무총장에게 송부 했다고 알려 왔음.

2. 동 사본은 별전 FAX 와같음.

첨부:상기서한 사본:UNW(F)-027

끝

(대사 현홍주-국장)

예고:91.6.30 일반

국기국　중아국　안기부

PAGE 1　　　　91.01.19 08:43
외신 2과 통제관 FE

0129

01/18/91 18:48 ☎ 2127346056 HUNG UN NEW YORK

별첨 :

UNW(F)-027 1016 1800
(국연. 중근동. 기조)

총1011

PERMANENT REPRESENTATIVE
OF THE REPUBLIC OF HUNGARY
TO THE UNITED NATIONS

10 EAST 75th STREET, NEW YORK, N.Y. 10021

Son Excellence M. Bagbeni Adeito Nzengeya
Président du Conseil de Sécurité
New York

16 Janvier 1991

Monsieur le Président,

J'ai l'honneur de vous informer que le Gouvernement de la République de Hongrie a décidé d'envoyer en Arabie Séoudite un groupe de personnel militaire médical, aux termes d'un accord établi entre les deux Gouvernements et conformément aux résolutions pertinentes du Conseil de Sécurité.

Je voudrais également vous informer que j'envoie une copie de la présente lettre au Secrétaire Général des Nations Unies.

Je saisis l'occasion pour vous renouveler l'expression de ma plus haute considération.

Erdős András
André Erdos
Ambassadeur

0130

1 - 1

외 무 부

종 별 :

번 호 : UNW-0131 일 시 : 91 0118 1800

수 신 : 장 관(국연,중근동,해기,기정)

발 신 : 주 유엔 대사

제 목 : 걸프사태

금 1.18 유엔사무총장의 이락의 대 이스라엘 공격관련 기자질문에 대한 답변내용을 별첨보고함.

첨부:상기자료:UNW(F)-026

끝

(대사 현홍주-국장)

국기국 1차보 중아국 ~~청와대~~ 공보처

PAGE 1

91.01.19 08:47 WH

외신 1과 통제관

0131

UNW-0131 외
첨부물

UNW(F)-026 10118 1600
(국연, 중근동, 해기. 기정)

총1매

Remarks of the Secretary-General at approximately 9:50 a.m. on Friday 18 January 1991.

Q. What is your reaction to the attacks on Israel?

S-G Well, I must say that I most regret these attacks. Firstly because it helps to spread the conflict, as Israel is not part of the coalition, and secondly because the targets were civilian targets.

Q. What is your message to Israel, do you expect them to respond?

S-G I expect them to be as patient as possible.

Q. What about the attack on the Saudis?

S-G Well, at least the Saudia Arabians are part of the coalition but as Secretary-General of the United Nations, I am not pleased to see hostilities around the world.

Q. What is the UN doing about this right now?

S-G Don't forget that this is something that is done in the framework of the Security Council resolutions. There is not much that the United Nations can do. At any rate, at my level, I have done my best.

Q. Are you still having contacts with the Iraqis?

S-G Not in the last two days. I have not been in contact with the Iraqi ambassador.

Q. What do you expect Israel to do, do you expect them to retaliate?

S-G I don't know, that is for them to decide. My humble advice would be for them to be as patient as possible.

Q. Are you in contact with them?

S-G No, I am not.

* * *

0132

더맑은 마음을, 더밝은 사회를, 더넓은 미래를

분류기호 문서번호	중근동 720 -22	협조문용지 (720-2327)	결재	담 당	과 장	국 장
시행일자	1991. 1. 19.					
수 신	수신처 참조	발 신	걸프사태대책본부장 (서명)			
제 목	폐만사태 명칭 조정					

금후 "폐만사태", "폐만전"은 "걸프사태", "걸프전"으로 조정 지칭키로 하였음을 알려 드립니다.

첨 부 : 관련자료 1부. 끝.

수신처 : 각 실국(과)장, 외교안보연구원장

0133

페만사태 명칭 조정

1. 금후 페만사태, 페만전은 걸프사태, 걸프전으로 조정 지칭키로 함.

2. 명칭 조정 사유

   o 과거 이란(페르시아)이 중동지역의 최강국이었던 관계로 페르시아만(Persian Gulf)으로 호칭

     - 일부 지도에는 아직도 페르시아만으로 표기

   o 아랍 국가들은 "아라비아만"(Arabian Gulf)으로 호칭하며, 페르시아만으로 지칭하는데 거부감을 갖고 있음.

   o 따라서, 중립적인 표현인 걸프(the Gulf)로 지칭하는 것이 타당함.

   o 현재 미국 및 구주 각국은 모두 "걸프"라는 명칭을 사용중이며 (예 : 미 CNN 방송은 War in the Gulf 라는 Headline 사용), 다만 일본은 "灣岸" 이라고 호칭

3. 시행 방안

   o 오랫동안 국내 언론등에서 페만이라는 용어를 사용해와서 급작스러운 명칭 변경에 어려움이 있음을 감안, 명칭 조정은 시간을 두고 서서히 시행, 완결시키도록 함.

   o 금 1.19. 외무장관 기자 간담회에서 상기 명칭 변경 사유를 설명하고 협조를 당부한바 있음.

0134

관리 번호	91 —123

원 본

외 무 부

종 별 :

번 호 : UNW-0142 일 시 : 91 0121 1330

수 신 : 장관(국연,중근동,기정)

발 신 : 주 유엔 대사

제 목 : 걸프사태(의료진 사우디파견)

대:AM-7

연:UNW-41,132

1. 아국 의료진의 사우디 파견 사실을 본직 서한으로 유엔안보리 의장에게 통보하는 문제를 아래사항을 참조, 검토하여 주실것을 건의함.

2. 동 통보시 고려사항

가. 통보이유

0. 안보리 관련 결의상 아국이 동 파견사실을 유엔에 통보토록 요청받지는 않았으나, 다국적 군대의 군사조치가 이락에 의한 안보리 결의의 이행을 보장하기 위한것이므로 아국이 동목적 달성에 기여한다는 사실을 유엔에 정식 통보, 아국이 유엔헌장상 원칙을 확립하고 유엔의 권능과 권위를 제고하기 위한 국제적 노력에 적극 참여한다는 사실을 강조 함으로써 아국 유엔가입 여건 조성을 도모할수있음.

나. 통보대상

0. 쿠웨이트와 협력하는 유엔회원 국가들에 의한 무력사용을 허용한 유엔안보리 결의 678 호는 제 3 항에서 "모든국가" 가 상기 강제조치를 적절히 지원해 줄것을 요청한바 있음.

0. 따라서 아국의 공식 통보대상은 안보리 의장으로 함이 적절함.(헝가리도안보리 의장에게 통보) 동 통고시 아국서한을 안보리 문서로 배포할 것을 요청하지는 않음.

0. 한편 유엔사무총장은 90.12.7. 자 회람서한에서 안보리 결의 678 호의 텍스트를 당관에 송부 해온바 있어 동인에게도 상기 안보리 의장앞 서한 사본을 송부토록함.

다. 서한요지

0. 아국 의료진의 사우디파견 결정사실 언급

0. 동 파견은 안보리관련 제 결의의 규정및 한-사우디 양자간 합의에 따라 파견

국기국 장관 차관 1차보 2차보 중아국 청와대 총리실 안기부

PAGE 1

91.01.22 07:09

외신 2과 통제관 FE

0135

0. 유엔헌장 준수및 국제평화와 안전유지를 위한 유엔의 권능확립에 대한 아국의 COMMITMENT 재확인

끝

(대사 현홍주-차관)

예고:91.12.31. 일반

검토필(1991.6.30.)

PAGE 2

0136

외 무 부

종 별 :

번 호 : UNW-0143 일 시 : 91 0121 1630

수 신 : 장 관(중근동,국연,기정)

발 신 : 주 유엔 대사

제 목 : 걸프사태관련 동향(주요국 동향)

안보리 문서로 배포된 표제건관련 주요국의 동향을 아래보고함. (동관련 문서는 FAX 보고함.)

1.사우디아라비아

- 1.18 안보리 의장에게 안보리 678호에 따라 쿠웨이트 해방을 위한 작전이 사우디시간 1.17 02:50개시되었음을 통보(S/22105)

2.인도

- 1.17 자 수상 성명으로 후세인 이락대통령에게 유엔안보리 결의에 따라 쿠웨이트로 부터 즉각 철수토록 촉구함.동성명은 이락의 쿠웨이트철수에 따른 상호적대행위중지, 평화적 해결방안 모색 노력재개 (동 MODALITY 는 안보리 에서 결정)방안을 제시하고, 고르바쵸프 소련 대통령으로부터도 유사한 제의를 받고 평화를 위해소련과 공동노력할것임을 천명(S/22086)

3.유고

- 1.17자 대통령 성명으로 이락이 쿠웨이트로 부터 즉각 철수하는것만이 현 사태의 추가적인 악화를 막는 유일한 방법임을 밝힘.(S/22088)

4.튜니시아

- 1.17자 각의성명으로 안보리가 현전부 상태를 종식시키기 위한 긴급한 조치를 채택하도록 촉구함(S/22085)

5.알제리아

- 1.17 자 외교부 대변인 성명으로 군사작전의 즉각적인 중지및 이락, 쿠웨이트 , 걸프전지역으로부터 모든 외국군 철수촉구(S/22104)

6.소련

- 1.18 자 외교부 성명을 통하여 이락당국은 쿠웨이트 점령으로 시작된

중아국 장관 차관 1차보 2차보 국기국 정문국 청와대 총리실 안기부

PAGE 1 91.01.22 09:31 WG

외신 1과 통제관

0137

자신의행동이 이락국민에 죽음과 파괴를 초래할 뿐이며 중동지역전체에 불행을 가중시킬뿐임을 이해하여야 한다고 촉구함.끝

첨부:상기 안보리문서(FAX):UNW(F)-030

(대사 현홍주-국장)

PAGE 2

0138

JAN 21 '91 16:09 KOREAN MISSION P.1

#UNW-0143의 첨부물 UNW(F)-030 10171 1630
(중근동. 국연. 기정)
총14매

UNITED NATIONS

S

Security Council

Distr.
GENERAL

S/22111
18 January 1991
ENGLISH
ORIGINAL: RUSSIAN

LETTER DATED 18 JANUARY 1991 FROM THE PERMANENT REPRESENTATIVE OF THE UNION OF SOVIET SOCIALIST REPUBLICS TO THE UNITED NATIONS ADDRESSED TO THE SECRETARY-GENERAL

I have the honour to transmit to you herewith the text of the statement of the Ministry of Foreign Affairs of the USSR concerning the launching of missiles by Iraq against Israel, on 18 January.

I should be grateful if you would have this text circulated as a document of the Security Council.

(*Signed*) Yuliy VORONTSOV

91-01867 2085h (E) /...

14-1

0139

English
Page 2

Annex

Statement of the Ministry of Foreign Affairs of the USSR concerning the launching of missiles by Iraq against Israel

During the night of 17 to 18 January, Iraq launched missiles on sections of Tel Aviv, Haifa and some other Israeli urban centres.

There is absolutely no doubt that the aim of this operation was to try to convert the problem of Kuwait into a regional conflict and to make the war spread like a conflagration to the Middle East as a whole.

The Soviet Union has always taken a firm and unambiguous stand against such a development, particularly in the course of its contacts with the Iraqi authorities. We are convinced that it is impossible to resolve one problem by creating another and that it would be dangerous, above all for the peoples of the region itself, if this conflict were to develop into another, even wider and more complex conflict.

At this critical juncture, we make another appeal to the Iraqi authorities to show that they are realistic and understand that their actions, beginning with the occupation of Kuwait, can bring only death and destruction to the Iraqi people and further misfortune to the region as a whole. The leaders of the Arab States cannot fail to understand this, responsible as they are for the well-being of their people. We hope that the Arabs will not let themselves be dominated by their emotions and will not take part in plans aimed at unleashing a new military confrontation with Israel.

In the Soviet Union, we also certainly hope that, for its part, the Israeli Government will show the necessary restraint and not embark on a path that would result in still greater tension in the Middle East.

Once again, the Soviet Union takes a firm stand in favour of a settlement of the problem of Kuwait on the basis of the resolutions of the United Nations Security Council and in favour of the earliest possible break in the stalemate in other situations of conflict in the Middle East. The peoples of the region must, finally, be able to enjoy peace and live in tranquillity.

0140

// —

UNITED NATIONS

Security Council

Distr.
GENERAL

S/22104
18 January 1991
ENGLISH
ORIGINAL: ARABIC/FRENCH

LETTER DATED 17 JANUARY 1991 FROM THE CHARGE D'AFFAIRES A.I. OF THE PERMANENT MISSION OF ALGERIA TO THE UNITED NATIONS ADDRESSED TO THE SECRETARY-GENERAL

I have the honour to transmit to you herewith the text of a statement issued on 17 January 1991 by the spokesman of the Ministry of Foreign Affairs of the People's Democratic Republic of Algeria. I should be grateful if you would have this letter and its annex circulated as a document of the Security Council.

(Signed) Amar BENDJAMA
Chargé d'affaires a.i.

91-01774 2107e (E) /...

14-3

0141

Annex

Statement issued on 17 January 1991 by the official spokesman of the Ministry of Foreign Affairs of Algeria

Since 2 August 1990, the Arab nation has been confronted with a critical situation and one of the most dangerous in all its history. The tragedy reached its climax with the massive military intervention against fraternal Iraq carried out by an international alliance led by the greatest of the Western military powers. In order to carry out this operation against a third-world country, the greatest mobilization of means of destruction in the history of warfare was carried out in Arab territory over a period of only five months.

This war is an expression of intransigence, of a sense of power and of a desire for hegemony. True power, however, is that which is bestowed by God, and He requires of those upon whom he has conferred it that they should be wise and just. The conceit and sense of power of the parties concerned have left no room for flexibility and compromise. This is also true with respect to the righting of the greatest wrong committed in this century, namely that to which the heroic Palestinian people fell victim more than 40 years ago. This war which has been imposed on the fraternal Iraqi people has been forcefully rejected by Algeria in the past, and it condemns it today in the strongest possible terms.

The destiny of the Arab nation has never before been threatened in the tragic manner in which it is being threatened today.

Motivated by an awareness of the painful consequences that would stem from such a war and mindful of the great dangers that threaten the unity and destiny of the Arab nation, Algeria, together with those vital Arab forces that grasp the higher interest of the Arab nation in achieving a peaceful solution within an Arab framework, has striven for the full mobilization of the Arab nation's lively conscience and its deep awareness of its interests with a view to achieving an Arab solution within an Arab framework.

Algeria has spared no effort to appeal to all those States with which it has relations and to all men of good-will in the world to strive for more understanding and greater flexibility in the search for a solution that will ensure the higher interests of the Arab nation and, at the same time, achieve world peace. Such a solution would be based, on the one hand, on respect for the international rule of law and the restoration of the sovereignty of Kuwait and, on the other, on the preservation of Iraq, whose achievements and capabilities represent a precious acquisition for the Arabs as a whole.

Algeria has acted out of a conviction that this war, aimed as it is at the destruction of Iraq, will necessarily affect Kuwait and other Arab countries, that it will inevitably have an impact on the entire Arab world and that it will benefit only the enemies of the Arab nation, principally a Zionist entity that can only emerge from the war strengthened.

/...

14-4

0142

Since 2 August last, Algeria has constantly affirmed that the Gulf crisis, no matter how recondite and complex its underlying causes and regardless of its grave regional and international consequences, could have been resolved justly and honourably within an Arab framework by means of dialogue and negotiations.

However, the Cairo summit convened on 10 August 1990, at which the Arabs assembled in order to seek an Arab solution precluding direct or indirect foreign intervention, supplanted joint Arab action by resort to foreign forces and thus opened the way to intransigence, a hardening of positions and an irrational yielding to the logic of war.

Algeria has constantly rejected the logic of war. It has always been aware of the devastating impact of an armed conflict, of the instability and insecurity that the Arab world, and indeed the world as a whole, would undergo as a result of the political and economic upheavals that it would cause and of the sense of wrong and humiliation that it would produce in the Arab nation.

The Arab world, which will be afflicted with unprecedented destruction and division, will be the first victim of the end of the cold war and of the new international political order intended to be established on the woes of the Arab world.

The Palestinian cause, that sacred Arab cause which is present in the current conflict just as it is present in all crises which convulse the Middle East, is once more a victim of the interests of power and of a disregard of the international rule of law to which appeal is made by those who bear responsibility for the war.

Algeria has always been against the resort to violence and the forcible annexation of territory, and these are firmly established and deeply held principles that have constantly guided Algeria in its foreign policy.

Algeria further believes that international legitimacy is an indivisible whole, and this means that international legitimacy is to be applied to one and all, in all circumstances and in all places, beginning with the question of Palestine.

Algeria, which strove assiduously up to the last moment in order to avert a catastrophe, charges one and all with their responsibilities towards the Arab peoples and towards history.

The Arab nation is facing the gravest trial of its modern history, and the Algerian people must endure that trial with its well-known courage and determination and in the spirit of responsibility and solidarity with which it is graced.

Closer than ever to the fraternal Iraqi people, Algeria expresses its solidarity with that people in the ordeal that has been imposed upon it. It calls upon all peoples that cherish peace and justice to strive earnestly for an immediate halt to military operations, for the withdrawal of all foreign forces and

/...

S/22104
English
Page 4

fleets from Iraq, from Kuwait and from the entire region, and for an immediate start to be made on a process leading to the peaceful settlement of the Middle East issue through the convening of an international conference.

At this crucial stage in the history of the Arab nation, Algeria commits itself to exerting every effort for the mobilization and utilization of all such forces as may bring about a return to a state of lasting peace and stability in the region.

0144

UNITED NATIONS

Security Council

Distr.
GENERAL

S/22085
17 January 1991
ENGLISH
ORIGINAL: FRENCH

LETTER DATED 17 JANUARY 1991 FROM THE PERMANENT REPRESENTATIVE OF TUNISIA TO THE UNITED NATIONS ADDRESSED TO THE PRESIDENT OF THE SECURITY COUNCIL

I have the honour to transmit herewith the text of a communiqué issued by the Council of Ministers of the Republic of Tunisia on 17 January 1991.

I should be grateful if you would have the text circulated as a document of the Security Council.

(Signed) Ahmed GHEZAL
Ambassador
Permanent Representative

91-01528 2019i (E) /...

14-7

0145

Annex

[Original: Arabic]

The Tunisian Government has received the news of the outbreak of war in the Gulf region with serious concern and profound displeasure.

Tunisia, which upholds the values of dialogue and the principle of solving disputes by peaceful means, expresses its distress at the tragedy being undergone by the Arab community and its sorrow at the ordeal to which the two fraternal peoples of Iraq and Kuwait are subjected. It recalls its appeals and intensive endeavours since the outbreak of the crisis to secure the withdrawal of Iraqi forces, to solve the essence of the conflict by peaceful means in an Arab context and to avoid the internationalization and complication of the issue.

In conformity with these principles, to which it has always adhered, and in order to safeguard international peace and Arab capabilities, Tunisia addresses an appeal to the conscience of the world. It calls upon the Security Council to press ahead with the adoption of urgent decisive measures to put an end to the current fighting and to settle the conflict by peaceful means, in accordance with the requirements of international legitimacy.

0146

UNITED
NATIONS

Security Council

Distr.
GENERAL

S/22088
17 January 1991

ORIGINAL: ENGLISH

LETTER DATED 17 JANUARY 1991 FROM THE PERMANENT REPRESENTATIVE OF YUGOSLAVIA TO THE UNITED NATIONS ADDRESSED TO THE PRESIDENT OF THE SECURITY COUNCIL

I have the honour to transmit herewith the texts of the statements issued on 17 January 1991 by the President of the Presidency of the Socialist Federal Republic of Yugoslavia and by the Federal Executive Council of the Assembly of the Socialist Federal Republic of Yugoslavia regarding the outbreak of war in the Persian Gulf.

I should be grateful if you would arrange for these statements to be circulated as a document of the Security Council.

(Signed) Darko SILOVIC
Ambassador

91-01577 2079h (E) /...

14-9 0147

Annex I

Statement issued at Belgrade on 17 January 1991 by the President of the Presidency of the Socialist Federal Republic of Yugoslavia Dr. Borisav Jovic, regarding the outbreak of war in the Persian Gulf

It is with great disappointment that we must recognize the failure of the efforts undertaken so far by the whole international community to attain a peaceful and political solution and to avoid the outbreak of war in the Persian Gulf, which unfortunately commenced last night.

Our country, as the current Chairman of the Movement of Non-Aligned Countries, did its utmost so that this conflict might be resolved by peaceful means. Until the last moment, we nurtured hope that reason would prevail and that the use of force could be avoided.

Yugoslavia has always founded its international activities on the unyielding position that interference in internal affairs, aggression and occupation cannot be a means of resolving international disputes. This is unacceptable, particularly at this time when the world is on the brink of a new era of peace and co-operation without confrontation, which in the decades behind us was a permanent threat to world peace and security.

Although the armed conflict that we all endeavoured to avoid is under way, it is still not too late to stop it so as to prevent further destruction and new casualties.

That is the reason that even in this hour of great danger we once again appeal to President Saddam Hussein and the Iraqi leadership to comply with the decisions of the United Nations and urgently to commence the withdrawal from Kuwait, the occupation and annexation of which brought about these tragic developments. At this juncture it is the only way of preventing the further escalation of this catastrophe which alas has begun.

The continuation of the war gravely affects all States of the world community in all economic, political and other aspects and therefore presents a real peril to democratic developments in international relations. It is indeed in the interest of all that this situation should be overcome as soon as possible.

/...

0148

1/-10

Annex II

Statement by the Federal Executive Council of the Assembly of the Socialist Federal Republic of Yugoslavia relating to the outbreak of war in the Persian Gulf

As a country committed to peace and to the principles of humanity, democracy and international law of the Charter of the United Nations as well as to the policy of non-alignment, Yugoslavia is deeply saddened by the outbreak of war in the Gulf, with its threat of tragic losses of human life and grave consequences.

Yugoslavia, as the current Chairman of the Movement of Non-Aligned Countries, and in close co-operation with the non-aligned and other countries, has done its utmost to help bring about a political and peaceful resolution of the Gulf crisis.

Even after the deadline set by the Security Council in its resolution 678 (1990) has elapsed, exactly eight hours before the outbreak of war, we made yet another appeal for peace and reason.

To that effect we primarily urged President Saddam Hussein and the Iraqi leadership to act in concert with the principles of law and peace, to withdraw from Kuwait and thus to respond to the expectations of the entire international community and the Movement of Non-Aligned Countries in particular.

Now that the war has begun and the first casualties have been inflicted, we still believe that no efforts should be spared in order to restore peace as soon as possible. The Iraqi compliance with the Security Council resolution 660 (1990) - i.e., the withdrawal from Kuwait - would create conditions to bring the hostilities to conclusion, to avoid further losses and to address peacefully this crisis and the problems of the entire region, in accordance with the principles of the policy of non-alignment and the Charter.

Yugoslavia will continue to endeavour along these lines, in close co-operation with all international factors, the non-aligned countries, the permanent and other members of the Security Council and particularly with the Secretary-General of the United Nations.

14-11 0149

UNITED NATIONS

Security Council

Distr.
GENERAL

S/22086
17 January 1991

ORIGINAL: ENGLISH

LETTER DATED 17 JANUARY 1991 FROM THE PERMANENT REPRESENTATIVE OF INDIA TO THE UNITED NATIONS ADDRESSED TO THE PRESIDENT OF THE SECURITY COUNCIL

I enclose herewith the text of a statement issued today by the Prime Minister of India. I would be grateful if you could have it circulated immediately as a document of the Security Council.

(Signed) C. R. GHAREKHAN

91-01560 2606a (E) /...

14-12 0150

Annex

Statement issued on 17 January 1991 by the Prime Minister of India

I am deeply distressed that hostilities have broken out in the Gulf, in spite of all the efforts made to prevent them. The longer the war lasts, the higher will be the toll in terms of human life and suffering.

I would like to appeal to President Saddam Hussein to announce the commencement of immediate withdrawal from Kuwait, in accordance with the United Nations Security Council resolutions. This should be followed by a cessation of hostilities and the resumption of efforts to find a peaceful solution to the conflict. The modalities for it can be worked out by the United Nations Security Council.

I have a message from President Gorbachev about a Soviet initiative in this regard, and we will join them in a common endeavour for peace. We will co-operate actively within the Movement of Non-Aligned Countries and with all like-minded countries in these joint efforts.

14-13 0151

UNITED NATIONS

Security Council

Distr.
GENERAL

S/22105
18 January 1991

ORIGINAL: ENGLISH

LETTER DATED 16 JANUARY 1991 FROM THE PERMANENT REPRESENTATIVE OF SAUDI ARABIA TO THE UNITED NATIONS ADDRESSED TO THE PRESIDENT OF THE SECURITY COUNCIL

On instructions from my Government, may I convey the following according to operative articles 2, 3 and 4 of Security Council resolution 678 (1990).

An official spokesman in Saudi Arabia has announced today that the operation for the liberation of the State of Kuwait commenced, with God's help and success, at dawn, at 2.50 a.m., the 17th of January 1991 Riyadh time (time difference, already 17th in Riyadh).

The official spokesman further added that in implementation of the Arab and Islamic resolutions as well as of the resolutions of the Security Council which stipulates the necessity for the unconditional withdrawal of the Iraqi invading forces from Kuwait territories and the restoration of legitimacy in the country; and whereas all efforts, initiatives and appeals that had been exerted and addressed to the ruler of Iraq up to the last minute of the deadline that has been set for the withdrawal of Iraqi forces from Kuwait, which is the 15th of January 1991, and what has followed from that up to this morning at dawn; and given that President Saddam Hussein had adamantly rejected all efforts, appeals and endeavours and has also rejected international legality, while it was possible for him to avoid the occurrence of these battles to prevent bloodshed; thus the military operations for the liberation of the State of Kuwait has commenced. Victory is bestowed by God.

I should be grateful if you would circulate this letter as a document of the Security Council.

(Signed) Samir S. SHIHABI
Ambassador
Permanent Representative

91-01803 2237d (E)

14-14 0152

UNITED NATIONS GNW(F)-030 추가 2매

Security Council

Distr.
GENERAL

S/22111
18 January 1991
ENGLISH
ORIGINAL: RUSSIAN

[illegible] THE UNION OF SOVIET SOCIALIST REPUBLICS TO THE UNITED NATIONS ADDRESSED TO THE SECRETARY-GENERAL

I have the honour to transmit to you herewith the text of the statement of the Ministry of Foreign Affairs of the USSR concerning the launching of missiles by Iraq against Israel, on 18 January.

I should be grateful if you would have this text circulated as a document of the Security Council.

(Signed) Yuliy VORONTSOV

91-01867 2085h (E) /...

2-1

0153

Annex

Statement of the Ministry of Foreign Affairs of the USSR concerning the launching of missiles by Iraq against Israel

During the night of 17 to 18 January, Iraq launched missiles on sections of Tel Aviv, Haifa and some other Israeli urban centres.

There is absolutely no doubt that the aim of this operation was to try to convert the problem of Kuwait into a regional conflict and to make the war spread like a conflagration to the Middle East as a whole.

The Soviet Union has always taken a firm and unambiguous stand against such a development, particularly in the course of its contacts with the Iraqi authorities. We are convinced that it is impossible to resolve one problem by creating another and that it would be dangerous, above all for the peoples of the region itself, if this conflict were to develop into another, even wider and more complex conflict.

At this critical juncture, we make another appeal to the Iraqi authorities to show that they are realistic and understand that their actions, beginning with the occupation of Kuwait, can bring only death and destruction to the Iraqi people and further misfortune to the region as a whole. The leaders of the Arab States cannot fail to understand this, responsible as they are for the well-being of their people. We hope that the Arabs will not let themselves be dominated by their emotions and will not take part in plans aimed at unleashing a new military confrontation with Israel.

In the Soviet Union, we also certainly hope that, for its part, the Israeli Government will show the necessary restraint and not embark on a path that would result in still greater tension in the Middle East.

Once again, the Soviet Union takes a firm stand in favour of a settlement of the problem of Kuwait on the basis of the resolutions of the United Nations Security Council and in favour of the earliest possible break in the stalemate in other situations of conflict in the Middle East. The peoples of the region must, finally, be able to enjoy peace and live in tranquillity.

2-2

0154

관리 번호	91-1404

외 무 부

종 별 :

번 호 : UNW-0145 일 시 : 91 0121 1830

수 신 : 장관(국연,중근동,정이,기정)(사본:주미대사:직송필)

발 신 : 주 유엔대사

제 목 : 걸프사태(북한의 안보리문서 배포요청)

연:UNW-1723

1. 금 1.21. 유엔사무국 직원이 권종락 참사관에게 제보한바에 따르면 북한대사 박길연은 안보리 의장앞 (NZENGEYA 자이레대사) 1.19 (토) 자 서한을 통하여 북한이 이락에 대하여 물품을 제공하고있다는 미 국방성 대변인의 언급내용을부인하였음.

2. 북한측 서한요지

0.91.1.16 미 국방성 대변인은 북한이 이락에 물품(SOME COMMODITIES) 을 제공하고 있다고 언급하였음.

0. 북한은 걸프위기 시작단계부터 쿠웨이트의 침공에 반대하여 왔으며 전쟁이 아닌 평화적 해결을 바라왔음.

0. 북한은 동 일관된 입장에따라 이락에 아무것도 제공하지 않고있음. 동 입장은 90.9.1. 북한 외교부장의 유엔사무총장앞 전문에서도 명백히 나타나 있음.

0. 이러한 사실에도 불구하고 미국은 북한의 품위를 손상키 위해 거짓 보고를 날조하였음. 미국은 자신의 정치적 목적을 위해 다른나라를 맹목적으로 "DISGRACE" 하는 서부른 시도를 포기해야함.

91.6.30. 김호덕

0. 동 서한을 안보리 문서로 배포해줄것을 요청함.

3. 북한에서 언급된 90.9.1. 자 외교부장 전문은 연호 보고참조 바람.(북한과 이락관계가 오래전부터 동결되었음을 통보하는 요지임.)

4. 북한측 서한은 별전(FAX) 송부함. 첨부 FAX:UNW(F)-031

(대사 현홍주-국장)

예고:91.12.31. 일반

국기국	장관	차관	1차보	2차보	중아국	정문국	청와대	안기부

PAGE 1

91.01.22 16:38

외신 2과 통제관 BN

0155

#별첨

UNW(F)-031 10121 1830
(국연. 중근동. 기재)
미국: 직송필
총2매

Democratic People's Republic of Korea
Permanent Observer Mission to the United Nations
225 East 86th Street, 14th Floor, New York, N.Y. 10028
Tel. (212) 722-3589 722-3536

New York, January 19, 1991

H.E.Mr. Bagbent Adeito NZENGEYA
President
Security Council
United Nations

I have the honour to clarify the position of the Democratic People's Republic of Korea with reference to the remarks made on January 16, 1991 by the Spokesman of the U.S. Department of Defence, which said the Democratic People's Republic of Korea had provided Iraq with some commodities.

The Democratic People's Republic of Korea has been opposed to the invasion of Kuwait by Iraq from the beginning of the Gulf crisis and wished for its peaceful settlement not by means of war.

The Democratic People's Republic of Korea, out of such a consistent position has provided nothing to Iraq.

This position was clearly indicated in the telegrame (S/21704) sent on September 1, 1990 by the Minister for Foreign Affairs of the Democratic People's Republic of Korea to the Secretary General of the United Nations.

배부처	장관실	차관실	1차보	2차보	기획실	의전장	아주국	미주국	구주국	중아국	국기국	경제국	통상국	정문국	영교국	총무과	감사관	공보관	외연원	청와대	총리실	안기부	문공부
										/20												/	

외어 계

2-1

0156

Notwithstanding the truth, the United States invented a false report in a bid to disgrace the Democratic People's Republic of Korea.

Such an attempt is construed none other than the ill-purposed act to defame the continued peace-loving positions and efforts of the Democratic People's Republic of Korea.

It is urged for the United States to give up such an awkward attempt to blindly disgrace the other for its own political aim.

I request this letter be circulated as a document of the Security Council.

Pak Gil Yon
Ambassador
Permanent Observer

관리 번호	91 -134

	분류번호	보존기간

발 신 전 보

번 호 : WUN-0124 910122 1814 BX 종별 :

수 신 : 주 유엔 대사. ~~총영사~~ (사본: 주미대사) WUS -0254

발 신 : 장 관 (국연)

제 목 : 걸프사태 (의료진 사우디 파견)

대 : UNW-0142

1. 대호, 1.21. 국회동의를 필한 아국의료단의 걸프지역 파견관련, 하기 내용의 서한을 귀직명의로 작성, 유엔사무총장 및 안보리의장에게 각각 전달바람. 또한 귀대표부 명의로 하기 요지의 Press Release 를 작성, 유엔 회원국등에 배포하는 것이 좋을 것으로 사료되니 적의 시행바람.

2. 서한 내용

o 한국정부는 안보리결의 678호 3항과 국제연합헌장 제 7장의 정신을 존중하고 사우디 정부의 요청에 의거, 금번 적절한 규모의 ~~의료단~~ 의료지원단(Medical Support Group)을 사우디지역에 파견하기로 결정하였음을 통보함.

o 유엔헌장 준수 및 국제평화와 안전유지를 위한 유엔의 권능 확립에 대한 아국의 Commitment를 재확인함.

3. Press Release 요지

o 한국정부는 안보리결의 678호 3항과 국제연합헌장 제 7장의 정신을 존중하고 사우디 정부의 요청에 의거, 국군 의료지원단을 사우디에 파견키로 1.21. 국회동의를 거쳐 확정함.(1.23. 본대가 사우디 향발 예정)

/ 계속 /

아중동국장: 전결

보안 통제	(서명)

앙 고 재	91년 1월 22일	유엔과	기안자 성명		과 장		국 장		차 관	장 관
			(서명)		(서명)		전결			(서명)

외신과통제

0158

o 국군의료지원단은 약 150여명 규모로 구성할 예정이며, 다국적군에 대한 의료지원의 임무를 수행하게됨.

o 한국정부는 국제사회에서 무력에 의한 불법적인 침략행위가 용인되어서는 안된다는 국제법과 국제정의에 입각하여 유엔 비회원국임에도 불구하고 안보리의 대이락 제재결의에 적극 참여하여 왔음.

끝.

예 고 : 1991.12.31.일반

(장 관)

검 토 필(1991. 6. 30.)

0159

관리 번호	91 -137

원 본

외 무 부

종 별 :

번 호 : UNW-0157 일 시 : 91 0122 1720

수 신 : 장관 (국연,중근동,해기,기정)

발 신 : 주 유엔 대사

제 목 : 걸프사태 (의료진 사우디 파견)

대: WUN-0124

1. 대호 지시에 따라 의료진 파견 결정사실을 금 1.22. 자 본직 서한으로 안보리 의장, 유엔사무총장에게 통보하였음.

2. 상기 서한 및 당관 프레스릴리스 는 별전(FAX)과 같음. 끝

(대사 현홍주-국장)

예고: 91.12.31. 일반

첨부: FAX (UNW(F)-034)

검 토 필(1991. 6. 30.)

국기국 장관 차관 1차보 2차보 중아국 안기부 공보처

PAGE 1

91.01.23 07:50

외신 2과 통제관 BW

0160

JAN 22 '91 18:48 KOREAN MISSION

UNW(F)-034 10122 1720 검우물 (국연, 중근동, 기정해기)
총 3매

REPUBLIC OF KOREA

PERMANENT OBSERVER MISSION TO THE UNITED NATIONS

OFFICE OF THE AMBASSADOR

22 January 1991

Excellency,

I have the honour to inform you that the Government of the Republic of Korea decided, on 21 January 1991, to deploy in Saudi Arabia a medical group composed of doctors, nurses and other support personnel.

This decision has been made at the request of the Government of Saudi Arabia, in accordance with Security Council Resolution 678, and with respect for the spirit of Chapter 7 of the United Nations Charter.

Taking this opportunity, I wish to reconfirm, on behalf of my Government, the commitment of the Republic of Korea to observe the provisions of the Charter of the United Nations and to uphold the Organization's authority in the maintenance of international peace and security.

Please accept, Excellency, the renewed assurances of my highest consideration.

Hong-choo Hyun
Ambassador

His Excellency
Mr. Bagbeni Adeito Nzengeya
President of the Security Council
United Nations
NEW YORK

3-1

0161

REPUBLIC OF KOREA
PERMANENT OBSERVER MISSION TO THE UNITED NATIONS

OFFICE OF THE AMBASSADOR

22 January 1991

Excellency,

I have the honour to inform you that the Government of the Republic of Korea decided, on 21 January 1991, to deploy in Saudi Arabia a medical group composed of doctors, nurses and other support personnel.

This decision has been made at the request of the Government of Saudi Arabia, in accordance with Security Council Resolution 678, and with respect for the spirit of Chapter 7 of the United Nations Charter.

Taking this opportunity, I wish to reconfirm, on behalf of my Government, the commitment of the Republic of Korea to observe the provisions of the Charter of the United Nations and to uphold the Organization's authority in the maintenance of international peace and security.

Please accept, Excellency, the renewed assurances of my highest consideration.

Hong-choo Hyun
Ambassador

His Excellency
Mr. Javier Perez de Cuellar
Secretary-General
United Nations
NEW YORK

3-2

0162

REPUBLIC OF KOREA

PERMANENT OBSERVER MISSION TO THE UNITED NATIONS
866 UNITED NATIONS PLAZA, SUITE 300, NEW YORK, N.Y. 10017. TEL: 371-1280

No. 02/91 22 January 1991

PRESS RELEASE

THE REPUBLIC OF KOREA SENDS A MEDICAL SUPPORT GROUP TO SAUDI ARABIA

The Government of the Republic of Korea will send a medical support group to Saudi Arabia on Wednesday, 23 January 1991, at the request of the Government of Saudi Arabia and in response to paragraph 3 of the United Nations Security Council Resolution 678.

This decision, which was fully endorsed by the Korean National Assembly on 21 January 1991, further represents the firm commitment of the Government of the Republic of Korea to implement relevant resolutions of the Security Council adopted under the Chapter 7 of the United Nations Charter.

The medical support group is composed of 150 personnel and is expected to provide necessary medical assistance to the multi-national forces deployed in Saudi Arabia to implement the Security Council Resolution 678.

Out of its firm adherence to international law and justice, the Government of the Republic of Korea rejects any unlawful act of aggression in inter-State relations, and will continue to faithfully implement relevant resolutions of the Security Council.

3-3

0163

원 본

외 무 부

종 별 :

번 호 : UNW-0162 일 시 : 91 0122 1830

수 신 : 장 관(국연,중근동,해기,기정)

발 신 : 주 유엔 대사

제 목 : 걸프사태

1.금 1.22. 유엔사무총장의 이락에 대한 유엔결의 이행을 재촉구하는 성명및 미군포로 문제관련 기자질문에 대한 답변내용을 별첨보고함.

2.비동맹의 전쟁종식 노력 (인도, 유고 외상회담)관련 외신보도 내용을 별첨함.

첨부:상기 FAX:UNW(F)-035

끝

(대사 현홍주-국장)

국기국 장관 차관 1차보 2차보 중아국 정문국 청와대 총리실
안기부 공보처

PAGE 1 91.01.23 09:05 WG

외신 1과 통제관

0164

62 외

UNW(F)-035 10122 1830 총 3매
(국연, 중근동, 해기, 기정)

The Secretary-General has witnessed with profound grief and anxiety the increasing severity of the war and the widening of the area of hostilities. To prevent the toll in death and destruction escalating any further and the suffering of the peoples in the region from growing even worse, he appeals most sincerely to the Iraqi authorities to respond positively to his appeal of 15 January, so that efforts may be resumed to find a peaceful solution to this grave and tragic conflict. The Secretary-General is in touch with the main humanitarian agencies of the United Nations system and the ICRC, with a view to ensuring that humanitarian help is provided to those afflicted by this conflict as promptly as circumstances permit.

***

22 January 1991

3-1 0165

Remarks of the Secretary-General at 10:00 a.m. on Tu■■day 22 January 1991.

Q. We are interested in your comments on the condition of the pilots -- how they appeared to you on Iraqi television?

S-G I am extremely concerned because it is something which goes against the Geneva conventions in a very clear manner and I must say that it is a practice which cannot be supported at the United Nations.

Q. One of the judges at the Nuremberg war crime trials suggested that perhaps, should Mr. Saddam be brought to trial, once the Gulf situation is resolved, there might be a role for the UN to preside in his trial?

S-G If the UN is asked to do something, we are always ready to cooperate with any effort but I haven't heard anything about that particular question.

Q. Are you aware of any cease fire proposals that are occurring here at the United Nations?

S-G I think this afternoon perhaps we will see a little clearer because there are some countries which are trying to obtain a cease fire or a pause in hostilities, but we have to think first of a withdrawal if we are consistent with the United Nations Security Council resolutions.

Q. What about Iraq's assertions about civilian casualties?

S-G We have had hardly any information -- you know we have had no information from Kuwait and over the last few days, we have had no contact with the Iraqis, as the ambassador himself has no contact with his Government.

* * *

3-2

0166

r ibc-gulf-nonaligned:1240es 1-22
India, Yugoslavia agree on non-aligned peace effort
BELGRADE (UPI) - India and Yugoslavia agreed Tuesday to press Non-Aligned Movement efforts to end the Persian Gulf war on the basis of U.N. Security Council resolutions that call for an Iraqi withdrawal from Kuwait, the nationa news agency Tanjug said.

Indian Foreign Minister Vidirharan Shukla and his Yugoslav counterpart, Budim Loncar, agreed in talks in Belgrade on the need for "joint activity" with othe non-aligned nations to achieve an end to "the war in the gulf, which is dangerously escalating and threatening with unforeseeable consequences," the agency said.

Shukla arrived in the Yugoslav capital earlier from Moscow, where he held ta with Soviet Foreign Ministry officials on the war and other problems in the Middle East.

India and Yugoslavia were among the 30 developing nations that founded the Non-Aligned Movement in Belgrade in 1961. It now comprises 101 members.

Yugoslavia is the current movement chairman and Loncar had been active in trying to resolve the gulf crisis before war broke out last week, traveling t the gulf three times since December, including a visit to Iraq for talks with President Saddam Hussein.

In a telephone conversation Monday, U.N. Secretary General Perez de Cuellar urged Loncar to pursue the Non-Aligned Movement initiative, which called for Iraq to comply with U.N. resolutions and withdraw from Kuwait. Both Iraq and Kuwait are members of the movement.

3-7

0167

보 도 자 료
외 무 부

91.1.23. 09:30
~~국 제 연 합~~ 과

제 목 : 아국의료단의 걸프지역 파견 결정 유엔 통보

가. 91.1.22. 현홍주 주유엔대사는 Perez de Cuellar 유엔사무총장 및 Bagbeni A. Nzengeya 안보리의장(자이르대사)앞 공한을 통하여 사우디 정부의 요청에 따른 한국의료지원단의 사우디 파견 결정 사실을 통보 하였다.

나. 현홍주 대사는 공한에서,
"한국정부는 안보리 결의 678호 3항과 국제연합 헌장 제7장의 정신을 존중하고 사우디정부의 요청에 의거, 금번 적절한 규모의 의료단을 사우디지역에 파견하기로 결정하였음."을 밝히고 "이는 유엔헌장준수 및 국제평화와 안전유지를 위한 유엔의 권능확립에 대한 아국의 결의를 재확인하는 조치"임을 천명했다.

~~다. 사우디정부에 의료단반을 파견한 국가는 우리나라외에 헝가리, 필리핀이 있는 바, 이들국가도 의료단파견 사실을 유엔에 기통보한 바 있다.~~

양 91년	담 당	과 장	국 장
고 1월			
재 23일	송영완	[서명]	[서명]

0168

(첨부)

1. 안보리 결의 678호

ㅇ 제3항 : 이락이 쿠웨이트로부터 91.1.15.한 철수치 않을 경우 쿠웨이트 정부를 지원중인 국가들이 필요한 모든 조치를 취할 수 있으며 이에 대해 모든국가들이 필요한 지원을 제공할 것을 요청함.

2. 국제연합 헌장 제7장 개요

ㅇ 제7장 : 제39조-51조까지의 규정으로서 평화에 대한 위협, 평화의 파괴 및 침략행위에 관한 조치를 기술함.

0169

관리번호	91 -138

원 본

외 무 부

종 별 :

번 호 : UNW-0160　　　　일 시 : 91 0122 1830

수 신 : 장관(국연,중근동,기정)

발 신 : 주 유엔 대사

제 목 : 일본대사 면담보고

1. 본직은 금 1.22 걸프사태등 관련 HATANO 일본대사 면담한바 주요내용을 아래보고함.

가. 걸프전 전망

금번 전쟁이 공군력만으로 끝나지는 않을것이 확실하게 된이상 일본으로서도 단기전을 예상하고 있지는 않으나 그렇다고 해서 전쟁이 무한정 장기화 되리라고도 보지않기 때문에 최장 6 개월이내에는 끝날것으로 일단 보고있음.

나. 전비등 지원문제

0. 최근 일본 대장성이 G-7 뉴욕회의 참석차 방미중 BRADY 재무장관과 이문제를 논의할 기회를 가졌는바, BRADY 장관은 추가지원요청이 곧 있게될 것이라고하였으나, 동금액 및 시기에 대하여는 구체적으로 언급하지 않았음.

0. 대장성의 견해로는 미국의 요청액수가 일본의 1 차 지원액 40 억불보다 훨씬 더많은 (배이상) 규모가 될것으로 본다함. 일본은 이에 추가하여 물자및 난민수송용 민간항공기 지원 요청을 받고있음.

0.1 차 지원시 40 억불 이상을 제공했음에도 불구하고 지원 발표시기를 실기하여 인색하다는 비판을 받았던 경험에 비추어 일본정부로서는 금번에는 최대한 신속히 지원규모를 결정발표할 생각임.

(이와관련 미측에 대해 지원요구시 대국민, 의회 설명이 용이하도록 액수 산출의 근거를 함께 제시해 주도록 요구하였음.)

0. 일본정부는 전비지원 요구가 2 차로 끝나는 것이 아니라 전황의 진전에 따라 계속 추가 요구가 있을것으로 예상, 이에 대비하고있음.

0. 일본은 그외 ICRC 활동의 일환으로 의료단 20 명을 제네바에 파견중임.

다. 유엔 평화유지 노력 참여문제

국기국　장관　차관　1차보　2차보　중아국　정와대　안기부

PAGE 1　　　　91.01.23　09:25

외신 2과 통제관 BT

0170

0. 자위대가 유엔평화유지군 (BLUE HELMET) 에 참여하는것은 특별법이 제정되지 않는한 현행법상으로 는 불가함.

0. 휴전감시 활동등에의 민간인 참여 가능성 문제를 유엔과 협의 검토한바 있으나 민간인인 경우에도 휴전감시 활동참여를 위하여는 군사문제를 잘 알아야하기 때문에 가능성이 희박한 것으로 봄.

0. 일본의 사회당과 일부 여론은 유엔평화 유지 노력에의 참여를 지지하고 있으나 실질문제는 간단치 않은 것으로 봄.

라. 일본은 200 일 분의 유류를 비축하고 있어 원유공급문제는 크게 우려하고 있지않음.

2. 본직은 아국이 유엔가입 문제를 정부의 금년도 중요 외교목표의 하나로 설정하고 이를 추진중에 있는바 미국의 적극적인 지원태세, 소련의 호의적 자세,중국의 태도변화 가능성 , 등으로 가입추진 여건이 성숙되고 있음에 비추어 일본으로서 배전의 지원을 당부하였음. 끝

(대사 현홍주-장관)

예고:91.12.31. 일반

관리번호	91/1638

외 무 부

종 별 :

번 호 : UNW-0160 일 시 : 91 0122 1830

수 신 : 장관(국연,중근동,기정)

발 신 : 주 유엔 대사

제 목 : 일본대사 면담보고

1. 본직은 금 1.22 걸프사태등 관련 HATANO 일본대사 면담한바 주요내용을 아래보고함.

가. 걸프전 전망

금번 전쟁이 공군력만으로 끝나지는 않을것이 확실하게 된이상 일본으로서도 단기전을 예상하고 있지는 않으나 그렇다고 해서 전쟁이 무한정 장기화 되리라고도 보지않기 때문에 최장 6 개월이내에는 끝날것으로 일단 보고있음.

나. 전비등 지원문제

0. 최근 일본 대장성이 G-7 뉴욕회의 참석차 방미중 BRADY 재무장관과 이문제를 논의할 기회를 가졌는바, BRADY 장관은 추가지원요청이 곧 있게될 것이라고하였으나, 동금액 및 시기에 대하여는 구체적으로 언급하지 않았음.

0. 대장성의 견해로는 미국의 요청액수가 일본의 1 차 지원액 40 억불보다 훨씬 더많은 (배이상) 규모가 될것으로 본다함. 일본은 이에 추가하여 물자및 난민수송용 민간항공기 지원 요청을 받고있음.

0.1 차 지원시 40 억불 이상을 제공했음에도 불구하고 지원 발표시기를 실기하여 인색하다는 비판을 받았던 경험에 비추어 일본정부로서는 금번에는 최대한 신속히 지원규모를 결정발표할 생각임.

(이와관련 미측에 대해 지원요구시 대국민, 의회 설명이 용이하도록 액수 산출의 근거를 함께 제시해 주도록 요구하였음.)

0. 일본정부는 전비지원 요구가 2 차로 끝나는 것이 아니라 전황의 진전에 따라 계속 추가 요구가 있을것으로 예상, 이에 대비하고있음.

0. 일본은 그외 ICRC 활동의 일환으로 의료단 20 명을 제네바에 파견중임.

다. 유엔 평화유지 노력 참여문제

국기국	장관	차관	1차보	2차보	중아국	청와대	안기부

PAGE 1

91.01.23 09:25

외신 2과 통제관 BT

0172

0. 자위대가 유엔평화유지군 (BLUE HELMET) 에 참여하는것은 특별법이 제정되지 않는한 현행법상으로 는 불가함.

0. 휴전감시 활동등에의 민간인 참여 가능성 문제를 유엔과 협의 검토한바 있으나 민간인인 경우에도 휴전감시 활동참여를 위하여는 군사문제를 잘 알아야하기 때문에 가능성이 희박한 것으로 봄.

0. 일본의 사회당과 일부 여론은 유엔평화 유지 노력에의 참여를 지지하고 있으나 실질문제는 간단치 않은 것으로 봄.

라. 일본은 200 일 분의 유류를 비축하고 있어 원유공급문제는 크게 우려하고 있지않음.

2. 본직은 아국이 유엔가입 문제를 정부의 금년도 중요 외교목표의 하나로 설정하고 이를 추진중에 있는바 미국의 적극적인 지원태세, 소련의 호의적 자세,중국의 태도변화 가능성 , 등으로 가입추진 여건이 성숙되고 있음에 비추어 일본으로서 배전의 지원을 당부하였음. 끝

(대사 현홍주-장관)

예고:91.12.31. 일반

THE SECRETARY-GENERAL

23 January 1991

Excellency,

I should like to draw your attention to a communication addressed to me by the President of the Security Council (S/22033) informing me of the recommendations of the Security Council Committee established by resolution 661 (1990) concerning the situation between Iraq and Kuwait (S/22021 and Add.1). Copies of these documents are attached to this letter. These recommendations were formulated by the Security Council in response to requests for assistance received from Bulgaria, Tunisia, Romania, India, Yugoslavia, Lebanon, the Philippines, Sri Lanka, Yemen, Czechoslovakia, Poland, Mauritania, Pakistan, the Sudan, Uruguay, Viet Nam, Bangladesh and the Seychelles, under the provisions of Article 50 of the United Nations Charter.

The Security Council recognized the need for providing assistance to these countries and appealed to all States on an urgent basis to provide immediate technical, financial and material assistance to these States to mitigate the adverse impact on their economy of the application by them of the sanctions against Iraq pursuant to Security Council resolution 661 (1990). I would like to express the strongest possible support for this appeal.

In accordance with the recommendation of the Committee, I would be grateful if you could provide me the relevant information, on a quarterly basis with a first report reaching me by the end of February 1991, on action taken by your Government to alleviate the special economic problems of these States.

Accept, Excellency, the assurances of my highest consideration.

Javier Pérez de Cuéllar

The Minister for Foreign Affairs
of the Republic of Korea

0174

공　　란

(NYT / Jan. 20, 91)

The Weapons

Scud Missiles: An Arsenal of Terror

By ERIC SCHMITT

Special to The New York Times

DHAHRAN, Saudi Arabia, Jan. 19 — Iraq's surface-to-surface Scud missiles have always been more a weapon of terror than of destruction.

Baghdad is reported to have fired 12 Scuds at Israel and one at Saudi Arabia in the last two days. Fearing that the missiles might be carrying chemical or biological warheads, panicky residents and soldiers have scrambled for gas masks and air-raid shelters.

But the missiles so far have carried only conventional explosives that caused relatively minor damage and about 30 injuries.

The second barrage against Israel this morning, however, delivered a far more powerful political blow: bringing Jerusalem to the brink of retaliation, an act that could splinter Arab members of the allied coalition aligned against Iraq.

The Scuds have proven difficult to wipe out, despite the allied forces' overwhelming air supremacy.

The two dozen Scud launchers in fixed sites in southern Iraq are likely to have been destroyed, military analysts said, but scores of other mobile launchers in the same region can elude detection by concealment and by constantly changing location.

"It's like trying to find a needle in a haystack," the commander of American air forces in the Persian Gulf region, Lieut. Gen. Charles A. Horner, said on Friday.

Military analysts estimate that Iraq has stockpiled 300 to 1,000 of the long-range missiles.

Scuds — the term is a NATO code-name for the Soviet-designed SS-1 missile — have rained terror on their targets since Syria fired early versions against Israel in the 1973 Arab-Israeli war.

Range Was Extended

Iraq originally bought Scuds from the Soviet Union and North Korea, Pentagon officials said. In the Iran-Iraq war in the 1980's, Baghdad modified the Scuds to extend their range to up to 560 miles from 190 miles.

But in doing so, Iraq sacrificed punch for propulsion, and drastically reduced the missile's destructiveness. The Scuds, never blessed with pinpoint accuracy, became even harder to control, sometimes drifting 2,000 yards from an intended target.

Although a poor weapon to bomb a specific target like air bases and power plants, the Scuds prove highly effective when fired at large urban areas where a hit of any sort is virtually guaranteed to terrify the population.

After Baghdad and Teheran declared a cease-fire in 1988, the Scuds were trained on Israel when President Saddam Hussein of Iraq stepped up his threats against that nation.

Threat of Chemical Attack

Since the invasion of Kuwait in August, military analysts have debated whether Iraq has the ability to load chemical warheads on the Scuds.

Some experts say Iraq cannot load Scuds with chemical warheads, arguing that the heat generated in the warhead by atmospheric friction would dissipate the chemicals.

But the threat of such a chemical attack put the Scud launchers at the top of the allied hit list.

Reconnaissance satellites spotted Scud launchers, surrounded by antiaircraft batteries, and most of the Sovi-

배	장관실	차관실	1차보	2차보	기획실	의전장	아주국	미주국	구주국	중아국	국기국	경제국	통상국	정문국	영교국	총무과	감사관	공보관	외연원	청와대	총리실	안기부	문공부
부처										10				1								1	

2-1

0176

The Iraqi Scud Missile: An Elusive Target

Use The Soviet-made SS-1 missile, code-named Scud by NATO, is a surface-to-surface missile used to attack targets beyond the range of artillery. It can be fitted with conventional, chemical or nuclear warheads.

Deployment Missiles can be mounted on transporters or in a fixed position. Launchers are accompanied by a command and control vehicle and a meteorological station to calculate the missile trajectories. Exact crew size is unknown. Crew includes drivers and launching [illegible], the tanker vehicle crew and crew of a reloader vehicle with extra missiles.

Accuracy The margin by which a missile may miss its target is said to be anywhere from 1,100 to 3,300 yards. American cruise missiles have a margin of error of only about 30 yards.

Fuel Missiles are propelled by liquid fuel, which requires some time to place in to the missiles, and can launch only five to seven missiles from a single pad before it needs an overhaul to ready it for further firings.

Source: Periscope Database

Range Iraq's modified Scud missiles include the Hussein, with a range of 375 miles, and the Abbas, with a range of 560 miles. Some of these missiles are fitted with booster rockets. The Soviet Scuds have a range of only 190 miles.

Armament The Hussein can carry 1,102 pounds of explosives. The Abbas can carry 661 pounds. Standard Scuds carry about 2,100 pounds. Modifications may reduce accuracy and capacity.

Associated Press

The New York Times

et-made fixed sites were destroyed in the first few waves of F-15E, F-16, Tornado and A-10 attack planes.

Guided by RF-4 reconnaissance planes and OA-10 and TR-1 observation aircraft, American and British fighter bombers continued their assault on the missile sites and other military targets today.

Military analysts said it was unclear why Iraq had abandoned its night strikes and waited until early this morning to fire three more Scuds at Israel, when the firings would be more noticeable.

The answer, in part, may be timing. The mobile launchers take about two hours to set up...

Nor is it clear whether the threat of chemical attack has passed. "Iraq may not have them, or any chemical missiles may have been destroyed on that first day," said a Congressional aide who is familiar with the Iraqi military.

2-2

0177

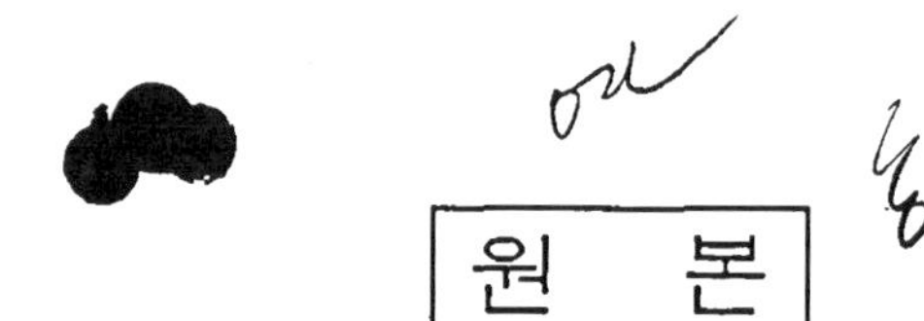

외 무 부

종 별 :

번 호 : UNW-0166 일 시 : 91 0123 1200

수 신 : 장관 (국연,중근동,정이,기정)

발 신 : 주유엔대사

제 목 : 걸프사태 (북한의 안보리문서 배포)

북한의 대이락 물자공급을 부인하는 북한대사의 1.19.자 안보리 의장앞 서한이 1.21.자 안보리문서 (S/22120) 로 금 1.23. 배포되었음. 끝

(대사 현홍주-국장)

국기국 장관 차관 1차보 2차보 미주국 중아국 중아국 정문국
청와대 총리실 안기부

PAGE 1

91.01.24 02:50 CG
외신 1과 통제관

0178

관리번호	91-1488

외 무 부

종 별 :

번 호 : UNW-0169 일 시 : 91 0123 1430

수 신 : 장관(국연,중근동,정이,기정)

발 신 : 주 유엔 대사

제 목 : 걸프사태(북한의 안보리문서)

연:UNW-0164

금 1.23. 본직이 미국대표부 WATSON 차석대사와 면담, 표제건에 관하여 협의한 내용을 아래보고함.

1.WATSON 대사는 국방성에 조회해본결과, 현재까지 파악된 경위를 아래와같이 언급하였음.

0. 조선중앙통신의 보도는 PETER WILLIAMS 국방성 대변인의 이름까지 거명하였으나, 국방성 대변인이 북한이 이락에 물자를 공급하고 있다는 언급을 한적이 없음.

0.1.15. 국방성 정례 브리핑시 한기자가 북한을 포함하여 몇몇 국가가 이락에 대해 물자를 공급하고 있다는 소문이 있는바 사실이냐고 질문한데 대해, 국방성 대변인은 "본인으로서는 확인할 만한 정보를 가지고 있지 않다. 확인되는 사실이 있으면 국방성 기자실용 게시판에 게시하겠다" 라고 대답한적이 있으며, 추후 동 게시판에 "특별한 사항이 없다" 는 메모를 게시한바 있었음.

2. 동 대사는 북한측의 주장이 근거없는 사실이므로 현재까지 국무성과 협의한 결과로는 추후 별다른 사항이 없는한 공식적인 대응을 고려치 않고 있다고 밝히고, 유엔회원국으로 부터 질문이 있을시 상기 1 항 내용을 사실대로 밝히겠다고 하였음.

3. 본직이 걸프사태 관련 최근 동향을 문의한바, WATSON 대사는 인도, 알제리가 현위치에서의 휴전을 주내용으로 하는 평화안을 내고있으나 미국은 이에대해 전혀 호응할수 없는 입장이라고 말하였음. 베이커 국무장관이 인도수상 및 알제리 대통령에게 직접 멧세지를 보내 그러한 방안은 후세인에게 전력을재정비, 강화토록 유예기간을 주는 것이므로 미국등 다국적군의 군사행동의 목적달성에 도움이 되지않는다는 취지의 입장을 밝힌바, 이들국가는 더이상 그러한 평화중재방안을

국기국 장관 차관 1차보 2차보 중아국 정문국 청와대 안기부

PAGE 1 91.01.24 05:47

외신 2과 통제관 FE

0179

추구하지 않겠다고 약속했다함. 미국으로서는 안보리 또는 어느 FORUM 에서든 다국적군의 군사노력을 중화코자 하는 시도를 배격할 방침이라고함. 끝.(대사 현홍주-장관)

예고:91.12.31. 일반

원 본

외 무 부

종 별 :

번 호 : UNW-0175 일 시 : 91 0123 1900

수 신 : 장 관(국연,중근동,기정)

발 신 : 주 유엔 대사

제 목 : 걸프사태(안보리)

1. 1.23. 오후 사무국에 확인한바에 의하면, 마그레브 5개국 (알제리아, 리비아, 모로코, 모리타니아, 튀니지아)은 걸프사태 토의를 위한 안보리회의 소집을 정식 요청하였다함.

2. 안보리의장은 상기 요청관련 안보리 이사국들과 개별적으로 비공식 협의중인 것으로 알려지고 있으나, 미국의 부정적인 입장이 완강하여 안보리가 실제로 소집될런지의 여부는 불투명한 상태임.끝

(대사 현홍주-국장)

국기국	장관	차관	1차보	2차보	중아국	정문국	청와대	총리실
안기부								

PAGE 1

91.01.24 10:15 WG

외신 1과 통제관

0181

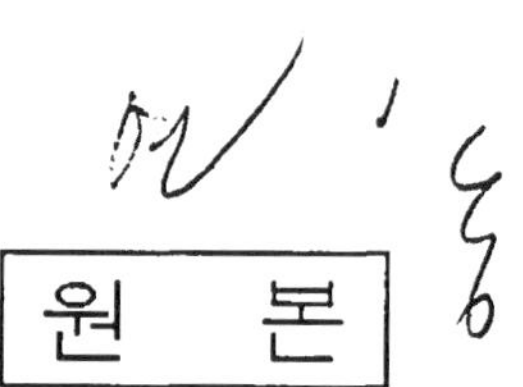

외 무 부

종 별 :

번 호 : UNW-0190 일 시 : 91 0124 2130

수 신 : 장 관(국연,중근동,기정)

발 신 : 주 유엔 대사

제 목 : 걸프사태(안보리 동향)

연: UNW-175

1. 연호 마그레브 5개국과 금 1.24. 예멘의 안보리 긴급회의 소집요청과 관련, 안보리 비공식협의 (전체회의)가 17:00-19:00 간 개최되었음.

2.금일 협의에서는 미국, 영국, 불란서로 부터 걸프사태 진전상황에 관한 설명을 청취한후, 안보리 회의 소집문제를 논의하였다고 하는바, 협의요지는 아래와같음.

가.안보리 공식회의 소집에 관한 국별입장 표명

- 찬성:쿠바,예멘

- 반대:미국,영국,소련, 루마니아

- 중도:인도,오지리 (특히 오지리는 공식회의도 비공식회의도 아닌 PRIVATE MEETING 개최제의)

- 기타 에쿠아돌은 쿠바, 예멘에 다소 동조적인듯한 입장을 표명하였다고 하며, 중국, 짐바브웨, 벨지움, 아이보리코스트는 발언안함.

나.안보리 비공식협의 (전체회의)를 1.28 (월) 다시 갖기로 하고 그때까지 안보리 의장은 안보리 이사국들과 양자 협의를 계속하기 함.

3.안보리 주변 일부 관측통들에 의하면 상기 양자협의 결과에 따라서는 1.28 비공식협의가 당겨질 가능성도 있다고 함.

4.상기 안보리 비공식협의 개시직전 PICKERING주유엔 미국대사는 안보리 회의소집 가능성에 대한 기자들의 질문에 대하여 안보리 결의 678 호 내용을 약화시키는 어떠한 조치에도 반대하며, 따라서 현재로서는 안보리 소집 필요성을 느끼지않는다는 요지로 답변함.(CNN 방송보도)

첨부:안보리 회의 소집요청 문서 2매: UNW(F)-041

끝

국기국 장관 차관 1차보 2차보 중아국 중아국 정문국 청와대
총리실 안기부

PAGE 1 91.01.25 11:57 WG

외신 1과 통제관

0182

JAN 24 '91 21:16 KOREAN MISSION P.1

#UNW-0190 의 첨부물

UNW(F)-041 1012 2130 (국연. 중근동. 기정7) 총2매

UNITED NATIONS

S

Security Council

Distr.
GENERAL

S/22135
23 January 1991
ENGLISH
ORIGINAL: ARABIC

LETTER DATED 23 JANUARY 1991 FROM THE REPRESENTATIVES OF ALGERIA, THE LIBYAN ARAB JAMAHIRIYA, MAURITANIA, MOROCCO AND TUNISIA TO THE UNITED NATIONS ADDRESSED TO THE PRESIDENT OF THE SECURITY COUNCIL

On instructions from our respective Governments, we, the Representatives of the States members of the Arab Maghreb Union, have the honour to request you to convene an urgent meeting of the Security Council to consider the grave situation in the Gulf region.

(Signed) Ali SKALLI
Permanent Representative of Morocco to the United Nations

(Signed) Ahmed GHEZAL
Permanent Representative of Tunisia to the United Nations

(Signed) Amar BENDJAMA
Chargé d'affaires a.i. of the Permanent Mission of Algeria to the United Nations

(Signed) Mohamedou OULD MOHAMED MAHMOUD
Permanent Representative of Mauritania to the United Nations

(Signed) Ali A. TREIKI
Permanent Representative of the Libyan Arab Jamahiriya to the United Nations

배부처	장관실	차관실	一차보	二차보	기획실	의전장	아주국	미주국	구주국	중아국	국기국	경제국	통상국	정문국	영교국	총무과	감사관	공보관	외연원	청와대	총리실	안기부	공보처

91-02299 2212j (E)

2-1

0183

UNITED NATIONS

Security Council

PROVISIONAL

S/22144
24 January 1991

ORIGINAL: ENGLISH

LETTER DATED 24 JANUARY 1991 FROM THE PERMANENT REPRESENTATIVE OF YEMEN TO THE UNITED NATIONS ADDRESSED TO THE PRESIDENT OF THE SECURITY COUNCIL

I have the honour to request an immediate meeting of the Security Council to examine the grave situation in the Gulf region.

(Signed) Abdalla S. AL-ASHTAL
Ambassador
Representative to the
Security Council

2729E

2-2

0184

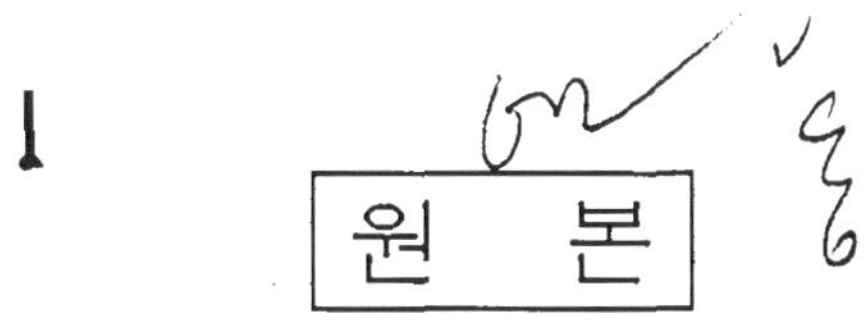

외 무 부

종 별 :

번 호 : UNW-0191 일 시 : 91 0124 2300

수 신 : 장 관(국연,중근동,기정)

발 신 : 주 유엔 대사

제 목 : 걸프사태(안보리 동향)

연: UNW-0190

1. 연호 안보리 비공식 협의 종료후 BAGBENI안보리 의장 (자이레) 은 안보리 협의결과 및 공식회의 소집전망에 대한 기자들의 질문에 대해 직접적인 답변을 피하면서 현재로서는 이락이 안보리 결의에 따라 쿠웨이트에서 즉각 철수하는 것만이 유일한 사태 해결책이라고 답변함. 반면, 주유엔 쿠바대사는 안보리에서 걸프사태를 '협의' 하자고 하는것 자체를 반대한다는 것은 납득할수 없는 처사라고 언급함. (이상 CNN 방송보도)

2. 연호 마그레브 국가들은 안보리 공식회의가 개최될경우 교전행위 즉각중지 및 외교적 해결방한 모색을 촉구할 것으로 알려짐. 끝

(대사 현홍주-국장)

국기국	장관	차관	1차보	2차보	중아국	정문국	청와대	총리실
안기부								

PAGE 1

91.01.25 13:54 WG

외신 1과 통제관

0185

외 무 부

종 별 :

번 호 : UNW-0192 일 시 : 91 0124 2300

수 신 : 장 관(중근동,국연,기정)

발 신 : 주 유엔 대사

제 목 : 걸프사태 관련동향(주요국 동향)

금 1.24. 안보리 문서로 배포된 표제건 관련 주요국 동향을 아래보고함.(별침 FAX참 조)

1.미국(S/22130 : 1.22 자)

- 안브리 결의 678호에 따라 미국이 취한 군사적.외교적 조치설명 (1.21.자 이락정부앞미국무부 공한포함)

2.예멘(S/22127: 1.22 자):대통령 위원회의 1.21.자 성명

- 미국및 연합국의 대 이락침략 행위, 특히 민간인 및 산업시설 공격을 규탄하며, 지체없이 침략행위를 중지할 것을 요청함.

- 안보리가 (1) 모든 군사작전 즉각중지, (2)외군철수, (3) 대 이락 경제제재 철회등을 촉구하는 결의안을 각각 채택하고, 아랍.이스라엘 분쟁에 관한 유엔 결의안을 즉각 시행할 것으로 서약해야 함.

3.요르단(S/22099:1.22 자):1.17 자 정부대변인성명

- 요르단 정부 및 국민은 형제 회교국인 이락에 대한 잔인한 공격을 규탄함.

4.비율빈(S/22139 :1.23 자)

- 1.21. 마닐라 문화센터에 대한 이락국직 테러범의 폭파미수 사건 관련 비율빈 주재 이락대사관 1등서기관 1명을 비엔나 외교관계 협약에 따른 비우호적 인물 (PNG)로 규정,출국토록 조치함.

첨부:상기 문서: UNW(F)-042

끝

(대사 현홍주-국장)

중아국	장관	차관	1차보	2차보	중아국	국기국	정문국	정와대
총리실	안기부							

PAGE 1 91.01.25 13:55 WG

외신 1과 통제관

0186

JAN 24 '91 22:55 KOREAN MISSION P.1

#UNW-0192 -1 첨부물

UNW(R)-042 10124 2300 (중근동. 국연. 기정) 총 11 매

UNITED NATIONS

Security Council

Distr. GENERAL

S/22130
22 January 1991

ORIGINAL: ENGLISH

LETTER DATED 22 JANUARY 1991 FROM THE PERMANENT REPRESENTATIVE OF THE UNITED STATES OF AMERICA TO THE UNITED NATIONS ADDRESSED TO THE PRESIDENT OF THE SECURITY COUNCIL

In accordance with paragraph 4 of resolution 678, I wish, on behalf of my Government, to submit the following report on actions undertaken pursuant to paragraphs 2 and 3 of that resolution, to follow the initial report submitted on 18 January.

Since that report, military forces of the coalition, including United States military forces, acting in accordance with UNSCR 678, have continued their air action against Iraq's military targets, including Iraqi biological and chemical warfare facilities, mobile and fixed surface-to-surface missile sites, and occupation forces in Kuwait and southern Iraq, as well as command and control centers, supply lines and the air defense networks that protect these facilities. Over 8,100 coalition air sorties have been carried out since hostilities began 16 January.

As of the morning of 21 January, United States forces have lost ten aircraft. Other coalition forces have also suffered losses. In addition, fifteen U.S. military personnel have been reported as missing.

The naval forces of the United States have also engaged Iraq's naval forces in the northern Gulf. These attacks have been on Iraqi units that are engaged in operations against coalition forces.

On 17 January, a brief episode of artillery fire was initiated by Iraqi forces, causing some damage to an oil installation in Northern Saudi Arabia. Coalition forces responded to this attack and suppressed any further action from those Iraqi artillery positions.

On 17 January, Iraq launched one surface-to-surface missile at Saudi Arabia. Coalition forces destroyed that missile in mid-air.

배부	장관실	차관실	一차보	二차보	기획실	의전장	아주국	미주국	구주국	중아국	국기국	경제국	통상국	정문국	영교국	총무과	감사관	공보관	외연원	청와대	총리실	안기부	문공부
처																							

91-02235 2063f (E) /...

11 - 1

0187

In the early evening of 17 January (Eastern Standard Time), Iraqi forces also launched a number of surface-to-surface missiles in an unprovoked attack on another UN Member, Israel. Another such unprovoked attack occurred against Israel the following day. This unlawful use of force against the territorial integrity of a UN Member State that is not a party to the conflict was obviously not directed at specific military targets, but rather at civilian targets resulting in civilian casualties.

Late 20 January and early on the morning of 21 January, the Iraqi forces launched ten surface-to-surface missiles against the Saudi Arabian cities of Dhahran and Riyadh. As of today, we have no reports of casualties resulting from these attacks.

On 19 January, the United States provided notification to the ICRC and the Government of Iraq of the presence of two U.S. military hospital ships in the waters off the Arabian peninsula, earlier notification of which had been provided to States party to the Geneva Conventions.

On 19 January, the Government of the United States in a diplomatic note informed the Government of Iraq that it intends to treat captured members of the Iraqi armed forces fully in accordance with the Third Geneva Convention Relative to the Protection of Prisoners of War, and that the United States expected Iraq also to comply fully with this humanitarian convention. United States forces have captured 23 members of the Iraqi armed forces and have told the ICRC we are prepared to facilitate access to those POWs.

Following Iraqi broadcasts 20 January of taped interviews with several coalition prisoners of war, the Department of State called in the Iraqi Chargé d'affaires in Washington to protest the apparent treatment of members of the United States armed forces and other coalition forces held by the Government of Iraq. In a diplomatic note, the United States protested Iraq's apparent treatment of U.S. prisoners of war as contrary to the Third Geneva Convention of 1949 Relative to the Protection of Prisoners of War. The U.S. Department of State reminded Iraq that the mistreatment of prisoners of war is a war crime, demanded full Iraqi compliance with the convention and requested immediate access for the ICRC to any prisoners of war held by Iraq.

Baghdad radio has subsequently reported that the Government of Iraq intends to locate United States and other coalition POWs at strategic sites that may be subject to attack. This is a violation of the Geneva Conventions for which the United States will also hold the Government of Iraq and individual Iraqi officers responsible. Under the Third Geneva Convention, POWs may not be unnecessarily exposed to danger, and must be evacuated to camps in safe areas as soon as possible after capture. The Department of State 21 January therefore called in the Iraqi Chargé d'affaires in Washington to protest strongly such action and to reiterate the protest delivered on 20 January regarding Iraqi treatment of United States and other coalition POWs. The Department of State reaffirmed the above in diplomatic notes to the Government of Iraq.

/...

11 - 2

0188

On 21 January the U.S., British and Kuwaiti Ambassadors in Geneva met with ICRC President Sommaruga to bring officially to his attention Iraqi violations of the Geneva Conventions and to request the ICRC to take appropriate action.

A copy of the 21 January diplomatic note to the Government of Iraq is attached. I have already requested that you distribute as documents of the Security Council the two preceding notes of 19 and 20 January, as well as a circular note dated 19 January 1991 to the States party to the Geneva Conventions on the presence of hospital ships (S/22122).

I should be grateful if you would circulate this letter and its attachment as a document of the Security Council.

(Signed) Thomas R. PICKERING

/...

11-3

0189

Annex

Baghdad radio has reported that the Government of Iraq intends to locate United States and other coalition POWs in Iraq at likely strategic targets of coalition forces. The United States strongly protests the Government of Iraq's threat to so endanger POWs.

Under Article 19 of the Third Geneva Convention, prisoners of war are to be evacuated as soon as possible after their capture to camps situated in an area away from the combat zone, so that they will be out of danger. Under Article 23 of the Third Geneva Convention, no prisoner of war may be sent to, or detained in, areas where he may be exposed to the fire of the combat zone, nor may his presence be used to render certain points or areas immune from military operations. Moreover, prisoners of war are to have shelters against air bombardment and other hazards of war to the same extent as the local civilian population. Iraqi POWs captured by the United States will be accorded these protections.

The United States and other coalition forces are only attacking targets of military value in Iraq; the civilian population, as such, is not the object of attack. Consequently the Government of Iraq is capable of placing coalition POWs in areas where military attacks will not occur.

If the Government of Iraq places coalition POWs at military targets in Iraq, then the Government of Iraq will be in violation of the Third Geneva Convention, and Iraqi officials - whether members of the Iraqi Armed Forces or civilian government personnel - will have committed a serious war crime. The Government of the United States reminds the Government of Iraq that Iraqi individuals who are guilty of such war crimes, as well as other war crimes such as the exposure of POWs to mistreatment, coerced statements, public curiosity and insult, are personally liable and subject to prosecution at any time.

Department of State,
Washington, 21 January 1991.

11-4

0190

UNITED
NATIONS

Security Council

Distr.
GENERAL

S/22127
22 January 1991
ENGLISH
ORIGINAL: ARABIC

LETTER DATED 22 JANUARY 1991 FROM THE PERMANENT REPRESENTATIVE OF YEMEN TO THE UNITED NATIONS ADDRESSED TO THE PRESIDENT OF THE SECURITY COUNCIL

I have the honour to enclose the text of the Declaration regarding the tragic developments in the situation in the Arabian Gulf region issued on Monday, 21 January 1991 by the Presidential Council of the Republic of Yemen.

I should be grateful if you would have the text of this letter and its annex circulated as an official document of the Security Council.

(Signed) Abdalla Saleh AL-ASHTAL
Ambassador
Permanent Representative

91-02192 2024c (E) /...

11-5

0191

Annex

Declaration regarding the tragic developments in the situation in the Arabian Gulf region issued on 21 January 1991 by the Presidential Council of the Republic of Yemen

In the Name of God, the Merciful, the Compassionate

The Presidential Council of the Republic of Yemen is following with extreme grief the tragic developments in the situation created by the cruel and continuing aggression the United States and Allied forces are committing against the fraternal Iraqi people and against its scientific, industrial, economic and military potential and installations, which reveals the true dimensions of the sinister plan for aggression against the fraternal Arab and Muslim people of Iraq.

The Presidential Council considers that the cruel aggression the United States and Allied forces are perpetrating is not aimed at ensuring the implementation of the Security Council resolutions and liberating Kuwait - which continues to be an inter-Arab problem that can be settled only by Arabs, for Kuwait forms an integral part of the Arab Islamic nation and its people is our brother in Arabism and Islam - but has much broader objectives which comprise destroying the capabilities and potential of an Arab Muslim country and subjecting its population to genocide. This is apparent from the ongoing aggressive operations being conducted against civilians and civilian installations and against the economic and development infrastructures of fraternal Iraq. These operations reveal in fact the true scope of a dangerous plot directed not solely against fraternal Iraq, but against the entire Arab and Islamic nation, aimed at controlling its interests, potential and wealth and at endangering its security, independence and sovereignty.

The Presidential Council condemns the cruel aggression being perpetrated against Iraq, and appeals to all States of the world, and in the first place to the fraternal Arab and Islamic countries, to take the position that their national, religious and human obligations dictate towards the iniquitous aggression being perpetrated against the fraternal Arab and Muslim people of Iraq, and urges the international community to bring pressure to bear on the United States of America and its allies to put an end to this aggression without delay and thus give the parties the opportunity of engaging in peaceful dialogue to settle all pending problems so that a global, lasting and just peace can be achieved in the region which will guarantee peaceful coexistence among its peoples, safe from any foreign interference or from a military escalation which would drag the region as a whole towards a devastating conflagration and a terrifying catastrophe which would be difficult to control, and whose destructive effects would be difficult to foresee and would have dangerous repercussions for international peace and security.

In conformity with the firm position of principle of the Republic of Yemen and with the efforts it has made since the beginning of the crisis to ensure a peaceful settlement within the overall Arab context in order to spare the region catastrophic war and destruction, the Presidential Council affirms its intention to continue its efforts to put an end to the bloodshed and achieve peace in the

/...

11 - 6

0192

region. At this crucial juncture and in these extremely serious circumstances the region and the world are experiencing, the Presidential Council urges the international community to take the following steps:

1. Adoption by the Security Council of a resolution calling for an immediate halt to all military operations;

2. Facilitation of Arab and Islamic efforts at peace and mediation designed to put an end to the causes of the dispute between Iraq and Kuwait;

3. Adoption by the Security Council of a resolution calling for the withdrawal of the foreign forces deployed in the region;

4. A commitment by the Security Council to implement immediately and without delay the resolutions of the United Nations relating to the Arab-Israeli conflict;

5. The adoption by the Security Council of a resolution rescinding its resolution 661 (1990) on the imposition of a total embargo against Iraq;

6. The conclusion of a general agreement aimed at eliminating all weapons of mass destruction in the possession of all States in the region and instituting a rigorous control system to ensure respect for this agreement. The conclusion of this agreement would take place after all forms of conflict in the region, including the Arab-Israeli conflict, have come to an end.

The Presidential Council urges the leaders and peoples of the Arab and Islamic nation to assume their historic responsibility in the face of this challenge with which their nation is confronted and to put an end to the aggression being perpetrated against a fraternal Arab and Muslim country, and reaffirms that it is motivated by the desire to halt the bloodshed, preserve the potential and capabilities of the Arab and Islamic nation and save it from the clutches of its enemies and those who have designs on it.

11-7

0193

UNITED NATIONS

Security Council

Distr.
GENERAL

S/22099*
22 January 1991
ENGLISH
ORIGINAL: ARABIC

LETTER DATED 17 JANUARY 1991 FROM THE PERMANENT REPRESENTATIVE OF JORDAN TO THE UNITED NATIONS ADDRESSED TO THE SECRETARY-GENERAL

I have the honour to transmit to you herewith the text of a statement concerning ongoing events in the Gulf region, as issued on 17 January 1991 by the official Jordanian spokesman.

I should be grateful if you would have this letter and its annex circulated as a document of the Security Council.

(Signed) Abdullah SALAH
Permanent Representative

---

* Reissued for technical reasons.

91-02078 2027i (E) /...

11-8

0194

Annex

Text of a statement issued on 17 January 1991 by the official Jordanian spokesman

Since the outbreak of the Gulf crisis, Jordan has been doing its utmost to address its causes and its consequences within an Arab framework. In the first days of the crisis, its leadership was able to obtain an Iraqi commitment to withdraw from Kuwait, and a time was established for that withdrawal to begin. Jordan also obtained Iraq's agreement to attend a mini-summit meeting at Jeddah in order to address the underlying causes that had led to the eruption of the crisis. However, the insistence on the adoption of a resolution by the Arab League, represented by the Arab Ministers of Foreign Affairs, as well as the emergence of extreme and inflexible positions among certain Arab parties, both facilitated the adoption by the Security Council of successive resolutions on the crisis.

This was followed by the arrival of foreign forces in the region, which obstructed the withdrawal from Kuwait at its very outset and aborted the hoped-for mini-summit meeting at Jeddah.

Jordan continued to strive for a peaceful solution, but its repeated attempts encountered obstacles from a number of parties which were clearly determined, from the outset, on the war option and buying time to complete the mobilization of their forces in preparation for aggression against Iraq under the guise of implementing United Nations Security Council resolutions.

Jordan, which has always respected the resolutions of the Security Council and is committed to their implementation, regrets that a similar crisis in the region was not met with an accelerated adoption of resolutions, economic boycott and the threat of hostile action despite the lapse of a long period of time since the inception of that crisis and despite the fact that it gives rise to occupation and the expulsion of an Arab people from its homeland.

The leadership, Government and people of Jordan condemn the brutal assault in the early hours of today on a Moslem, Arab country and people - one that has always hastened to the assistance of its Arab brethren and unhesitatingly paid its due in terms of blood and sacrifice in all of the battles that have been imposed on the Arab nation - by an attack on its capital city in such massive force and with the possibility of continued strikes against it. All of those who took part in this attack will bear responsibility for it before Allah, man and history, for having set out to destroy an Arab military, scientific and human power and a proud and fraternal Arab and Moslem people which is part and parcel of our nation. May Allah guide and safeguard our nation, and enable us to protect the integrity of generations to come after us. It is from Allah that we seek succour.

-----

11 - 9

0195

UNITED
NATIONS

A S

General Assembly Security Council

Distr.
GENERAL

A/45/939
S/22139
23 January 1991

ORIGINAL: ENGLISH

GENERAL ASSEMBLY
Forty-fifth session
Agenda item 153
IRAQI AGGRESSION AND THE CONTINUED OCCUPATION OF KUWAIT IN FLAGRANT VIOLATION OF THE CHARTER OF THE UNITED NATIONS

SECURITY COUNCIL
Forty-sixth year

Letter dated 22 January 1991 from the Permanent Representative of the Philippines to the United Nations addressed to the Secretary-General

I have the honour to bring to your attention certain events which occurred only days ago in the Philippines and which bear an unmistakable connection to the present conflict in the Middle East.

I regret to have to inform you that an Iraqi national was killed and another wounded in Makati, Metro Manila, last Saturday night (19 January 1991), when a bomb they intended to plant in the Thomas Jefferson Cultural Center exploded prematurely. The dead Iraqi was identified as a member of an international terrorist organization. The two were carrying 200 lbs. of explosives and were then 100 yards from their target.

In a related development, Philippine Secretary of Foreign Affairs, Raul S. Manglapus, announced that the Government of the Philippines had declared Mr. Muwafak A-Ani, First Secretary of the Iraqi Embassy in Manila, as persona non-grata in accordance with the 1961 Vienna Convention on Diplomatic Relations. He was given 72 hours from 21 January 1991 to leave the country. Philippine intelligence and security authorities asserted that they had unearthed strong evidence linking him to the failed bombing of the Cultural Center.

Secretary Manglapus said that the decision "should not be looked at as an action against the Government of Iraq and certainly not against the people of Iraq, but directed against the person for acts beyond his diplomatic functions and violation of local laws and regulations".

91-02341 2252b (E) /...

11-10

0196

A/45/939
S/22139
English
Page 2

I should be grateful if you would arrange to have the text of the present letter circulated as a document of the General Assembly, under agenda item 153, and of the Security Council.

(Signed) Sedfrey A. ORDONEZ
Ambassador,
Permanent Representative

11-11

0197

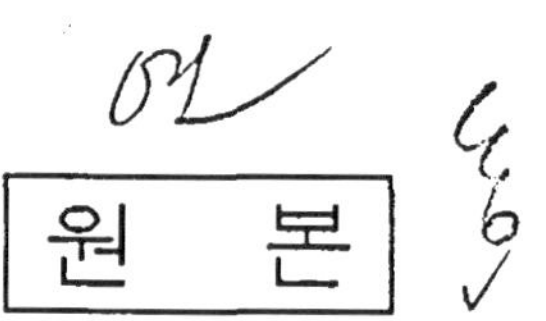

외 무 부

종 별 :

번 호 : UNW-0205 일 시 : 91 0128 1400

수 신 : 장관 (국연,중근동,기정)

발 신 : 주 유엔대사

제 목 : 걸프사태 (안보리 동향)

연: UNW-0190

연호 마그레브 5국에 이어 예멘, 요르단 등이 표제건 안보리 소집을 지지하였음. 금 1.28. 16:00 표제건 토의를 위한 안보리 비공식 협의회가 개최될 예정임. 상임이사국 4개국이 동 소집을 반대하고 있고, 중국은 소집, 비소집 어느쪽이든 무방하다는 피동적인 입장을 취하고 있어 유엔내 일반적인 관측은 뚜렷한 사태 변화가없는한 조만간 표제건 토의를 위한 안보리 공식회의가 소집될 가능성은 적은것으로 보고있음.

끝

(대사 현홍주-국장)

국기국	장관	차관	1차보	2차보	미주국	중아국	청와대	총리실
안기부	대책반							

PAGE 1 91.01.29 06:46 DA

외신 1과 통제관

0198

원 본

외 무 부

종 별 :

번 호 : UNW-0207 일 시 : 91 0128 1900

수 신 : 장 관(국연,중근동,기정)

발 신 : 주 유엔 대사

제 목 : 걸프사태(안보리 동향)

연: UNW-0205

1. 연호 안보리 비공식 협의회가 금 17:00-18:00개최되었으나, 표제건 관련 안보리 소집여부에 대한 결론없이 종결되었음.1.31. 비공식 협의가 속개될 예정으로 알려짐.

2.한편 비동맹은 유고외상의 초청으로 걸프사태 관련 긴급 각료회의를 2.1.(금) 벨그라드에서 개최할 예정으로 알려짐.끝

(대사 현홍주-국장)

국기국 안기부	장관	차관	1차보	2차보	중아국	정문국	청와대	총리실

PAGE 1

91.01.29 09:26 WG

외신 1과 통제관

0199

관리 번호	91 —200

원 본

외 무 부

종 별 :

번 호 : UNW-0218 일 시 : 91 0129 1630

수 신 : 장관(국연,중근동,기정)

발 신 : 주 유엔 대사

제 목 : 걸프사태(안보리 동향)

연:UNW-0207

1. 금 1.29 한. 미 양 대표부간 오찬 협의회시 권참사관이 RUSSEL 미국 대표부 아시아 담당관 에게 표제 동향을 확인한바, 연호 1.31. 로 예정된 안보리 비공식 협의회는 걸프사태와 관련 안보리내 각국이 취하고 있는 조치에 관한 보고를 청취 하기위한 것이며, 걸프사태 관련 안보리 소집 여부를 토의하기 위한것이 아니라함. 특별한 사정이 없는한 단시일내 안보리 공식 회합은 예견되지 않는다함.

2.RUSSEL 담당관은 또한 짐바브웨가 예상외로 표제건 토의를 위한 안보리소집에 반대하는 입장을 금 1.29 발표 하므로써, 코트디브와르, 자이레와 함께안보리내 아프리카 3 국이 모두 친서방 입장을 취하게 되었다함. 짐바브웨의 이러한 친서방적 입장에 대해 미측은 전혀 예측치 못하였으며, 매우 놀랄만한 (STUNNING) 사태로 본다함.(짐바뷔, 코트디브와르, 자이레의 친서방적 입장은 아국유엔가입 추진과 관련하여도 주목되는 사항으로 보임.)

3. 큐바는 1.28 자 안보리 의장앞 서한에서 안보리 잠정의사규칙 제 2 조 및 제 3 조를 원용, 표제건 토의를 위한 안보리를 조속히 소집할것을 요청하였음.끝

(대사 현홍주-국장)

예고:91.12.31. 일반

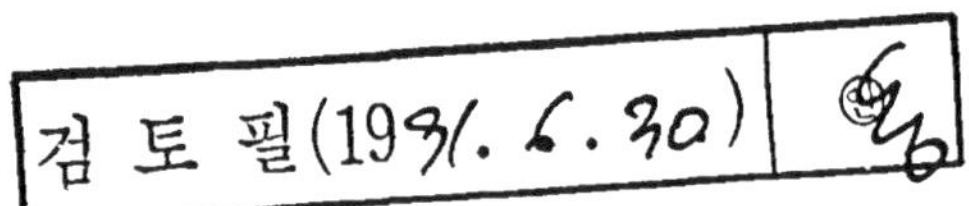

국기국 차관 1차보 2차보 중아국 안기부

PAGE 1 91.01.30 07:08

외신 2과 통제관 FE

0200

분류번호	보존기간

발 신 전 보

번 호 : AM-0030 910130 2351 DP 종별 :

수 신 : 주 전재외 공관장 ■■■■ 대사 총영사

발 신 : 장 관 (미북)

제 목 : 걸프전 관련 아국의 추가 지원

정부는 걸프사태와 관련 다국적군 특히 미국에 대하여 2억8천만불의 추가 지원을 제공키로 결정하고 이를 1991.1.30(수) 18:15(서울시간) 다음과 같이 공식발표 하였음.

1. 정부는 지난해 8.2. 걸프 사태가 발생한 이래 무력에 의한 침략은 용인될 수 없다는 국제 정의와 국제법 원칙에 따라 유엔 안보 이사회 결의를 지지하고 이의 이행을 위한 국제적 노력을 지원하여 왔음. 이러한 입장에서 정부는 지난해 9.24. 다국적군 및 주변국 경제 지원을 위해 2억2천만불의 지원을 발표한 바 있으며 또한 지난 1.24. 사우디에 군 의료 지원단을 파견한 바 있음.

2. 그러나 유엔을 비롯한 전세계 평화 우호국들의 노력에도 불구하고 지난 1.17. 걸프 전쟁이 발발하여 중동 지역은 물론 전세계의 평화 및 안정에도 큰 위협이 되고 있으며, 더우기 이번 전쟁이 예상보다 오래 계속될 조짐이 나타남에 따라 다국적군은 이에 따른 막대한 전비와 재정 수요에 직면하게 되었음.

/계속/

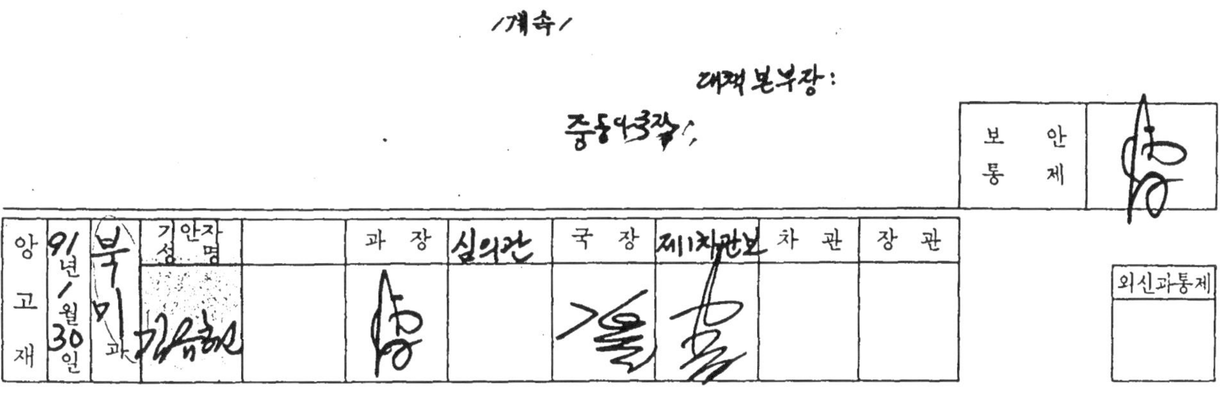

대책본부장:
중동아국장
보 안 통 제
앙 고 재
91년 1월 30일
북미 과
기안자 성 명
과 장
심의관
국 장
제1차관보
차 관
장 관
외신과통제

0201

3. 이에 따라 정부는 다음과 같은 추가 지원을 제공키로 결정하였음.

o 추가 지원 규모는 2억8천만불로함.

- 이중 1억7천만불 상당은 국방부 재고 군수물자 및 장비 제공으로 하고 나머지 1억1천만불은 현금 및 수송 지원으로 함.

(구체적 집행 용도 및 내역은 한.미 양국간 협의를 거쳐 결정 예정)

- 금번 추가 지원은 다국적군 특히 미국을 위한 것이며 주변국 경제 지원은 불포함.

- 아국의 총 지원 규모는 금번 추가 지원으로 작년 약속액 2억2천만불을 포함, 총 5억불이됨.

o 상기 지원과는 별도로 국회의 동의를 받아 후방 수송 지원 목적을 위하여 군 수송기(C-130) 5대를 파견키로 원칙적으로 결정하였으며, 이를 위한 기술적인 사항은 아국 국방부와 주한 미군간에 협의 예정임. 끝.

(장 관)

0202

관리 번호	91 -212

원 본

외 무 부

종 별 :

번 호 : UNW-0233 일 시 : 91 0130 1720

수 신 : 장관 (국연,미북,기정)

발 신 : 주 유엔 대사

제 목 : 걸프사태 관련 추가지원

대: AM-0030

연: UNW-0142

대호 걸프사태 관련 아국 추가지원 내역 (추가경비 지원 및 수송단 파견)도 연호 고려에 비추어 유엔사무총장 및 안보리 의장에게 본직 서한으로 통보코자하는바 별도 본부지침 있을시 지급 회시바람. 끝

(대사 현홍주-국장)

예고:91.6.30. 일반

1991. 6. 30 에 예고문에 의거 일반문서로 재분류됨

국기국 장관 차관 미주국 청와대 안기부

PAGE 1

91.01.31 07:34

외신 2과 통제관 BT

0203

원 본

외 무 부

종 별 :

번 호 : UNW-0234 일 시 : 91 0130 1800

수 신 : 장 관(국연,중근동,기정)

발 신 : 주 유엔 대사

제 목 : 걸프사태 관련 동향

1.주유엔 이란대사는 1.29 자 유엔사무총장앞 서한에서 이란의 중립입장을 재강조하고 교전당사자중 어느쪽의 항공기든 이란에 긴급착륙시는 적대행위가 종료될때까지 억류할 예정임을 통보하였음.이란은 또한 이락정부에 대해 이락 항공기의 이란내 긴급 착륙에 대해엄중 항의 하였음을 언급하였음.

2.상기 서한 별전 송부함.

첨부:상기 서한: UNW(F)-051

끝

(대사 현홍주-국장)

국기국 장관 차관 1차보 2차보 중아국 정문국 청와대 총리실
안기부

PAGE 1

91.01.31 09:01 WG

외신 1과 통제관

0204

UNITED NATIONS

UNW(F)-051 10130 1800

(국연, 중근동 기정_ 총1매

Security Council

Distr.
GENERAL

S/22163
28 January 1991

ORIGINAL: ENGLISH

LETTER DATED 28 JANUARY 1991 FROM THE PERMANENT REPRESENTATIVE OF THE ISLAMIC REPUBLIC OF IRAN TO THE UNITED NATIONS ADDRESSED TO THE SECRETARY-GENERAL

Upon instructions from my Government, I have the honour to inform that a number of Iraqi military aircrafts have made emergency landing in the Islamic Republic of Iran.

The National Security Council of the Islamic Republic, reiterating the position of the Islamic Republic of Iran concerning non-engagement in present hostilities, warned the belligerent parties to refrain from any use of Iranian airspace. It further decided that in the event of emergency landing of any aircraft of either side in the territory of the Islamic Republic of Iran, the aircraft would be seized and held until the termination of hostilities.

In this connection, the Islamic Republic of Iran has registered to the government of Iraq its strong protest at the emergency landing of the above-mentioned aircrafts. Furthermore, reiterating the position of non-engagement of the Islamic Republic of Iran in the hostilities in the Persian Gulf and its commitment to resolutions of the Security Council, the Foreign Ministry of the Islamic Republic of Iran has informed the government of Iraq that, in line with relevant rules of international law, the Islamic Republic of Iran will not allow the use of military vessels and personnel who have entered the territory of the Islamic Republic of Iran to any of the belligerent parties until the termination of hostilities.

It would be highly appreciated if this letter were circulated as a document of the Security Council.

(Signed) Kamal KHARRAZI
Ambassador
Permanent Representative

91-02745 2079f (E)

1 — 1

0205

외 무 부

종 별 :

번 호 : UNW-0235 일 시 : 91 0130 1800

수 신 : 장 관(미북,국연,해기,기정)

발 신 : 주 유엔 대사

제 목 : 걸프전 관련 추가지원

대: AM-0030

당대표부는 1.30 대호 내용을 프레스 릴리스로작성, 각국대표부, 유엔사무국 및 외신기자 대상배포한바, 동자료 별전 송부함.

첨부: FAX 1 매: UNW(F)-052

끝

(대사 현홍주-국장,관장)

미주국	장관	차관	1차보	2차보	국기국	정문국	청와대	총리실
안기부	공보처							

PAGE 1

91.01.31 09:02 WG

외신 1과 통제관

0206

UNW-0255 외
협조문

UNW(F)-052 10130 1800
(미북, 국연, 해기, 기획)

총 1011

REPUBLIC OF KOREA

PERMANENT OBSERVER MISSION TO THE UNITED NATIONS
866 UNITED NATIONS PLAZA, SUITE 300, NEW YORK, N.Y. 10017. TEL: 371-1280

No. 04/91 30 January 1991

PRESS RELEASE

KOREA PROVIDES ADDITIONAL CONTRIBUTION OF 280 MILLION US DOLLARS AND TRANSPORTATION AIRCRAFTS TO MULTINATIONAL FORCES

The Government of the Republic of Korea announced, on 30 January 1991, that it will make an additional contribution of US$ 280 million in financial and material support to the multinational coalition forces in the Persian Gulf region.

Together with the initial contribution of US$ 220 million, which was announced on 24 September 1990, the Republic of Korea's contribution to date totals US$ 500 million. In addition, the Republic of Korea sent, on 24 January 1991, a 154-member medical support group to Saudi Arabia.

The Republic of Korea has also decided to dispatch five transportation aircrafts (C-130) to Saudi Arabia, by mid-February, to be used for transport of supplies inside Saudi Arabia. This decision is subject to the approval of the National Assembly.

These measures further represent the firm and sincere commitment of the Government of the Republic of Korea to help implement the resolutions of the Security Council.

1 - 1

0207

관리 번호	91 -261

	분류번호	보존기간

발 신 전 보

번 호 : WUN-0198 910131 1900 AO 종별 : 지급

수 신 : 주 유엔 대사. ~~총영사~~

발 신 : 장 관 (국연)

제 목 : 걸프사태 관련 추가지원

대 : UNW-0233

연 : AM-0030

대호, 귀건의대로 조치바람. 끝.

예고 : 91. 6.30. 일반

(장관)

1991. 6. 30. 에 예고문에 의거 일반문서로 재분류됨

미주국장: (서명)

	보 안 통 제	(서명)

앙 고 재	91 년 1 월 31 일	UN 과	기안자 성 명		과 장		국 장	차관보	차 관	장 관
			(서명)		(서명)		(서명)	(서명)	(서명)	

외신과통제

0208

관리 번호	91 -245

원 본

외 무 부

종 별 :

번 호 : UNW-0249 일 시 : 91 0131 1730

수 신 : 장관(국연,중근동,기정)

발 신 : 주 유엔 대사

제 목 : 걸프사태(추가지원)

대:WUN-0198

1. 안보리의장 및 유엔사무총장에게 금 1.31. 자 본직 서한으로 대호 아국의추가지원 내역을 통보하였음.

2. 상기서한은 별전 송부함.

첨부:상기서한 2 매:UNW(F)-054

끝

(대사 현홍주-국장)

예고:91.6.30 일반

1991.6.30에 예고문에 의거 일반문서로 재분류됨

국기국 장관 차관 중아국 청와대 안기부

PAGE 1

91.02.01 08:23

외신 2과 통제관 BT

0209

JAN 31 '91 17:31 KOREAN MISSION P.3

#번천 UNW(FI)-054 10131 · 3ㅡ 총2에
(국연 · 중근동 기정)

REPUBLIC OF KOREA

PERMANENT OBSERVER MISSION TO THE UNITED NATIONS

OFFICE OF THE AMBASSADOR

31 January 1991

Excellency,

I have the honour to inform you that the Government of the Republic of Korea announced, on 30 January 1991, that it will make an additional contribution of US $280 million in financial and material support to the multinational coalition forces in the Persian Gulf region.

Together with the initial contribution, which was announced on 24 September 1990, the Republic of Korea's contribution to date totals US $500 million.

The Republic of Korea has also decided to dispatch a squad of five transportation aircraft (C-130) to Saudi Arabia by mid-February, to be used for transport of supplies inside Saudi Arabia. This decision is subject to the approval of the National Assembly.

Please accept, Excellency, the renewed assurances of my highest consideration.

Hong-choo Hyun
Ambassador

His Excellency
Mr. Bagbeni Adeito Nzengeya
President of the Security Council
United Nations
NEW YORK

2 - 1

0210

REPUBLIC OF KOREA

PERMANENT OBSERVER MISSION TO THE UNITED NATIONS

OFFICE OF THE AMBASSADOR

31 January 1991

Excellency,

I have the honour to inform you that the Government of the Republic of Korea announced, on 30 January 1991, that it will make an additional contribution of US $280 million in financial and material support to the multinational coalition forces in the Persian Gulf region.

Together with the initial contribution, which was announced on 24 September 1990, the Republic of Korea's contribution to date totals US $500 million.

The Republic of Korea has also decided to dispatch a squad of five transportation aircraft (C-130) to Saudi Arabia by mid-February, to be used for transport of supplies inside Saudi Arabia. This decision is subject to the approval of the National Assembly.

Please accept, Excellency, the renewed assurances of my highest consideration.

Hong-choo Hyun
Ambassador

His Excellency
Mr. Javier Perez de Cuellar
Secretary-General
of the United Nations
NEW YORK

2-2

0211

외 무 부

종 별 :

번 호 : UNW-0248 일 시 : 91 0131 1730

수 신 : 장 관 (중근동,국연,기정)

발 신 : 주 유엔 대사

제 목 : 걸프사태 관련 동향

1.이락 외무장관앞 유엔사무총장의 1.30 자 서한이동일 안보리 문서로 배포되었음.(S/22172)

2. 상기 서한은 이락이 안보리 관련 결의를 준수토록 촉구한 유엔사무총장의 1.15.자 호소를 반복하는 요지임.동 텍스트는 별전 참고바람.

첨부:상기 텍스트 : UNW(F)-053

끝

(대사 현홍주-국장)

중아국 1차보 국기국 정문국 안기부 2차보 장관 차관 청와대 총리실

PAGE 1

91.02.01 08:56 WG

외신 1과 통제관

0212

UNITED NATIONS

S

Security Council

Distr.
GENERAL

S/22172
30 January 1991

ORIGINAL: ENGLISH

LETTER DATED 30 JANUARY 1991 FROM THE SECRETARY-GENERAL
ADDRESSED TO THE PRESIDENT OF THE SECURITY COUNCIL

I would be grateful if you could bring to the attention of the members of the Security Council the letter I have sent today to His Excellency, Mr. Tariq Aziz. A copy of the letter is attached.

(*Signed*) Javier PEREZ de CUELLAR

91-02996 2099g (E) /...

2-1

0213

Annex

Letter dated 30 January 1991 from the Secretary-General addressed to the Deputy Prime Minister and Minister for Foreign Affairs of Iraq

I have read your letter of 24 January 1991 (S/22154) with regret and cannot but reject its connotations.

When we met at Amman on 31 August 1990 and at Baghdad on 12 January 1991, and again when I met President Saddam Hussein on 13 January 1991, I stated that our efforts to avert the unfolding tragedy would fail unless Iraq could signify its readiness to comply with the relevant resolutions of the Security Council, beginning with resolution 660 (1990). On each occasion, after returning to New York, I reported the views of your Government to the Security Council.

As you know, on 15 January 1991 (see S/22091), I appealed again to President Saddam Hussein to indicate his readiness to proceed in the manner I had suggested to him, so that the course of events could be turned away from catastrophe and towards a new era of justice and harmony, based on the principles of the Charter of the United Nations. I pledged, in such circumstances, to work with him, and with all others concerned, to bring just and lasting peace to the Middle East as a whole.

Today, I reiterate my 15 January appeal, as I did on 22 January 1991, when I also expressed my profound grief and anxiety at the increasing severity of the war, the widening of the area of hostilities and my fear that the toll in death and destruction would escalate unless my appeal received a positive response. I continue to believe that such a response is needed in order to find a peaceful solution to this grave and tragic conflict and to save human lives. In the mean time, in order to alleviate the present suffering which is causing me deep anguish, I have already asked the main humanitarian agencies of the United Nations system to co-ordinate their efforts with a view to ensuring that help is provided to those afflicted by the conflict as soon as circumstances permit.

You will recall, Mr. Minister, that when speaking in the formal meeting of the Security Council after the adoption of resolution 678 (1990), I stressed that, in requiring compliance with the resolutions of the Council, the United Nations sought not surrender but the most honourable way of resolving a crisis in a manner that respected all legitimate interests and was conducive to the wider peace and the rule of law. I also underlined that the actions of the United Nations in the present crisis must be perceived as part of the larger endeavour of the Organization to establish peace through justice, whenever the one was imperiled and the other denied.

That remains my view today and I would therefore urge your Government to make a serious effort to put this tragic situation on the road to a peaceful solution.

(Signed) Javier PEREZ de CUELLAR

-----

2 - 2

0214

원 본

외 무 부

종 별 :

번 호 : UNW-0258 일 시 : 91 0201 1700

수 신 : 장 관(국연,중근동,기정)

발 신 : 주 유엔 대사

제 목 : 걸프사태(안보리동향)

1. 1.31. 21:30 안보리가 속개되어 91.1.31.임기만료되는 UNIIMOG (UN IRAN-IRAQ MILITARY OBSERVERGROUP) 의 임기를 1개월 연장하는 결의안 685호를 전원일치의 찬성으로 채택함.

2.상기건 의제 (UNIIMOG 의 활동과 관련한 유엔사무총장의 보고서) 채택 직전 큐바가 걸프사태와 관련한 안보리 소집문제를 제기하고있는중에, 미국대표는 의사진행에 관한발언권 (POINT OF ORDER) 을 얻어 큐바가 상기의제 채택과 관련한 제안을 하는것이 아닌한 큐바가 제기하는 문제는 동 안보리 의사일정과 무관한 것이라고 주장하였음.이에 예멘대표는 안보리가 의제를 채택하기전 어떠한 안보리 회원국도 발언할 권리가 있다고 주장함.안보리 의장은 안보리 잠정 의사규칙 9조에 따라 매안보리가 다룰 첫 의제는 의제채택이며, 동의사규칙 에 의제채택 이전 발언을 할수있는 규정이 없다고 주장하고 큐바와 예멘이 의사규칙 9조에 도전하였다고 선언하였음. 상기에따라 큐바, 예멘의 의제가 채택된후 발언하겠다고 하였음.

3.상기 1항 결의안 685 호가 채택된후 예멘은 걸프사태 관련 안보리 소집요청이 거부되고 있음을 유감이라고 말하고, 현재 진행되고 있는 대이락 군사작전은 안보리 결의 678호의 범위를 넘었으며, 쿠웨이트 해방이 아니라 이락의군사, 과학 기반을 파괴하기 위한 시도와 같다고 주장하였음.이에 예멘은 안보리 1월의장과 2월의장이 동건관련 안보리 소집요청을 검토해줄것을 촉구하였음.큐바대표는 자신이제기하는 문제가 금일 안보리 의제와 상당부분 관련되어 있음을 아무도 부정할수 없다고 주장하고, 아울러 안보리가 자신의 활동을 규정하는 규범을 무시하는 상황에 놓여서는 안된다고 주장하였음.

4.금일 안보리 종료직전 안보리의장은 안보리 소집과 관련한 잠정 의사규칙 제2조가 정당히 적용되고 있으며, 자신이 모든 안보리 회원국으로부터 동 공식회의

국기국 장관 차관 1차보 2차보 중아국 중아국 청와대 총리실
안기부

PAGE 1 91.02.02 10:02 WG

외신 1과 통제관

0215

소집문제에 관한 협의를 진행하라는 위임을 받았다고 밝혔음.이어 공식회의를 소집해야한다는 원칙에 대해서는 안보리 회원국의 의견이 일치되고 있다고 말하고, 동 회의 소집일자에 합의하기 위하여 비공식 협의회를 진행해 나갈 권한을 위임받았다고 부언하였음. 이에따라 2월의장이 동 비공식 협의를 계속해 나갈것이라고 언급하였음.끝

(대사 현홍주-국장)

0216

원 본

외 무 부

종 별 :

번 호 : UNW-0305 일 시 : 91 0208 1900

수 신 : 장 관(국연,중근동,미북,해기,기정)

발 신 : 주 유엔 대사

제 목 : 걸프사태

1.금 2.8. 오후 안보리는 표제사태 관련 비공식협의회를 개최, 유엔사무총장으로부터 별전 FAX성명을 청취하였음.

2.상기 성명요지

0.안보리 결의 666 호 제3, 제 4항 (유엔사무총장에게 이락및 쿠웨인트내 식품상황을 정기적으로 안보리 제제위에 통고토록요청)에 따라 민간인의 식품수요, 공급상황을 조사하기위해 WHO/UNICEF 합동조사단 파견을 결정하였음.

0.군사적 대결이 진행중이나 동위기를 해소하기 위한 외교적 노력이 중단되어서는 안됨.

0.쿠웨이트및 이라크내 민간인의 고통이 가중되고 있으며, 식수, 전기공급의 중단으로 인한 공공위생상 위협이 심각해지고 있음.

0.이와관련 2.1.자 국제적십자사 의 인도법적용호소에 주목함.모든 전쟁당사국들이 제네바 협약상 의무를 준수토록 촉구함.

0.유엔 시스템은 민간인 및 난민에게 가능한한 모든 인도적 지원을 제공해야 한다고 느끼고 있음.이락내 주거지역에 대한 파괴와 민간인 사상자가 증가하고 있다는 각종 보고를 듣고 당혹하게 느낌.쿠웨이트내 민간인이 당면하고있는 상황에 대해서는 사실상 아무런 정보도 없는바 이문제에도 큰 우려를 표명함.

0. WHO/UNICEF 합동조사단은 아동및 어머니들을 돕기위한 긴급의료 보급품을 전달할것임.이들은 내주말경 바그다드 도착희망함.

첨부:상기성명전문: UNW(F)-060

끝

(대사 현홍주-국장)

국기국 장관 1차보 2차보 미주국 중아국 청와대 총리실 안기부
공보처

PAGE 1 91.02.09 10:00 WG

외신 1과 통제관

0217

#UNW-0305 의 첨부물 UNW(F)-060 10208 1900 (국연. 중근동. 미북. 해기. 기정) 총9매

Statement by the Secretary-General to the Security Council in Informal Consultations on 8 February 1991

The Members of the Council will be aware that I yesterday sent a letter to the Chairman of the Committee established by Security Council Resolution 661 in which I drew attention to the humanitarian situation in Iraq and Kuwait, to my responsibilities under paragraphs 3 and 4 of Resolution 666, and my efforts to ascertain the needs of the civilian populations there. I informed the Committee of the decision that had been taken to send a joint WHO/UNICEF mission to the area. I would like, at this time, to take the opportunity to share with you some reflections regarding my deepening concern with respect to the humanitarian situation arising from the conflict.

9-1

0218

Over three weeks have passed
since a large scale military action began,
stemming from resolution 678.
I have watched the developments of the past 23 days
with anguish and regret.
With anguish because, as Secretary-General of the United Nations,
I cannot but be saddened by the failure of diplomatic efforts,
including my own,
and the consequent necessity to resort to force.
And with regret because, like all of you,
I had, until the last moment,
fervently hoped that the situation between Iraq and Kuwait
could be resolved peacefully.
It was in a final effort to avert hostilities,
and at an ominous moment, that I appealed publically on 15 January
to President Saddam Hussein
to signify his readiness to comply
with the relevant resolutions of the Security Council
and thereby turn the course of events away from catastrophe
and towards a new era of justice and harmony
based on the principles of the Charter of the United Nations.

There is no indication as yet
that Iraq has reconsidered its position.
As you know, I have received two letters,
dated 24 January and 2 February, from the Foreign Minister of Iraq,
to the first of which I replied on 30 January.

9-2

In my letter I reiterated my appeal of 15 January,
stating that I continued to believe that a positive response to it
was needed in order to find a peaceful solution
to this grave and tragic conflict, and to save human lives.
No response has been received.
The hostilities thus rage on, despite the diplomatic efforts
of a number of governments and my own.
The tragic consequences are apparent to all.
A massive military confrontation is underway in the region,
with immense implications for Iraq, Kuwait and,
more widely, the world as a whole.
This should not, however,
mean that diplomatic efforts to solve the crisis be put on hold.
On the contrary, they need to be intensified.

Having said this,
I cannot but
- in the present circumstances -
draw attention to the steadily worsening plight
of the civilian population of Kuwait,
whose suffering has been mounting since 2 August
and of the civilian population in Iraq,
which for three weeks now
has been exposed to aerial action.

9-3

0220

The physical dangers caused by such a situation
are obvious to all.
They are compounded by the hazards to public health
that are daily growing more acute in the absence of electricity
and the increasing shortage of clean water.
The implications for vulnerable groups,
such as women, children and the elderly
are particularly disturbing.

I would like, in this connection,
to draw attention to the solemn appeal
that was issued on 1 February
by the International Committee of the Red Cross,
which highlights the applicability of humanitarian law
to all aspects of the present conflict.
The appeal points out
that millions of civilians have been caught up in the violence,
without shelter or protection against occupation and bombing, and
that growing numbers of combatants are being taken as prisoners.
The appeal states:
"One of the most disquieting aspects of this conflict
is the possibility that the law of war, which is the expression
of the most basic and universal principles of humanity
and of the dictates of the public conscience,
might be swept aside
by the political, military or propaganda demands of the moment.
The right to choose methods or means of warfare is not unlimited.

9-4

0221

Weapons having indiscriminate effects
and those likely to cause disproportionate suffering
and damage to the environment are prohibited.
The wounded, whether civilian or military, and prisoners
must receive special consideration and protection
in compliance with specific rules
which the entire international community has undertaken
to respect."
The ICRC solemnly appealed to all belligerents,
in the name of all civilian and military victims,
to have due regard for humanitarian considerations.
I share the concerns expressed in this appeal,
and trust that the parties to the conflict
will abide by their obligations under the Geneva Conventions.
In particular, I would hope that this conflict
will not result in the use of chemical weapons
and other weapons of mass destruction.

The members of the Council are aware that I have,
ever since 2 August, been deeply concerned
about the humanitarian implications of the situation
arising from Iraq's invasion of Kuwait.
During the subsequent months,
I made continuous efforts to obtain
the agreement of the Iraqi authorities
to send a personal representative to the area.
Regrettably, my efforts were not successful.

9-5

With the crisis having entered a new phase,
and the lives of millions of civilians endangered
by a confrontation that,
for the moment, shows no sign of abating,
I increasingly feel that the UN system
should provide whatever humanitarian assistance it can,
both to refugees and displaced persons
who are fleeing the conflict area
and the civilian populations that remain there.
In this connection, it is disturbing to hear,
from various reports, that civilian casualties are mounting
and that damage to residential areas throughout Iraq
has been widespread.
Of grave and continuing concern, of course,
is the situation facing civilians in Kuwait,
about which there is virtually no information.

With these considerations in mind,
I sent my Executive Assistant, Mr. Jean-Claude Aimé,
to Geneva on 26 - 28 January where,
together with the Executive Director of UNICEF, Mr. James Grant,
they consulted with the President of the ICRC
and the heads of other humanitarian agencies
on the humanitarian needs arising from the conflict.
Furthermore, Mr. Grant had extensive discussions
with the Director-General of the World Health Organization,
Dr. Hiroshi Nakajima.

9-6

0223

On 4 February, I discussed these humanitarian questions
with Mr. Grant,
who drew my attention to a statement issued in Geneva on 30 January
by the National Committees of UNICEF.
The Committees expressed unanimously
their deep and legitimate concern for the plight of the children
in the countries affected by the outbreak of armed conflict
in the region of the Persian Gulf.
They cited inter alia provisions
of the UN Convention on the Rights of the Child
and the Declaration of the World Summit on Children
which provide that care and protection of children
affected by armed conflict must be ensured.
The National Committees urged the Executive Director of UNICEF
to ask me to undertake,
together with the main humanitarian agencies,
all efforts within my power to ensure
that these provisions were respected
and to extend humanitarian help to all those afflicted
by the conflict.

9-7

0224

In light of my discussion with Mr. Grant,
a decision was taken to send a joint WHO/UNICEF mission to the area
which would deliver a shipment of emergency medical supplies
to assist in the care of children and mothers
and ascertain essential health needs.
The dispatch of such supplies
would be within the spirit of the provisions
of the Geneva Conventions of 1949,
the United Nations Convention on the Rights of the Child,
and the Declaration of the World Summit for Children.
Subject to finalisation of the arrangements,
it is hoped that the mission could arrive in Baghdad
by the end of next week.

* * * * *

In making these reflections,
I must also mention my deep concern about the public perception,
-- in all continents and cultures -- of this Organization,
and how important it is for the United Nations
to retain the trust of all the peoples of the world,
whom it is meant to serve.

9-8

0225

I would be less than honest were I to conceal from you
the diverse and numerous expressions of despair --
whether in letters, press editorials, appeals --
that have been sent to me regarding the tragic dimensions
and incalculable consequences of the conflict.
This is a testing moment for the Organization.

9-9

0226

0226

원 본

외 무 부

종 별 :

번 호 : UNW-0340 일 시 : 91 0213 2100

수 신 : 장 관(국연,중근동,해기,기정)

발 신 : 주 유엔 대사

제 목 : 걸프사태(안보리)

1.금 2.13. 17:00 표제건 안보리가 속개됨. 동 안보리회의를 안보리잠정 의사규칙 48조에 따라 비공개로 하자는 영국대표부의 제안이 표결에 회부된바, 찬 9, 반2 (예멘, 쿠바), 기권4 (중국, 인도, 에쿠아돌, 짐바브웨) 로 가결되었음.동 안보리는 명 2.14. 11:00 비공개로 공식회합을 속개키로 하였음.영국측 제안에따라 회의는 비공개이나 회의록은 VERBATIM 으로 배포키로 하였음.

2.금일 주요국 발언요지

0.영국: 1975 년 서부사하라건 토의시 선례도 있는바 공개토의시 이락에대해 잘못된 신호를 보내지않도록 비공개로 개최됨이 바람직함.

0.예멘: 모든 회원국의 관심사인 동사태는 공개적으로 개최되어야함.그간 걸프사태에 관한 안보리 회의는 예외없이 공개적으로 개최되었음.

0.큐바: 안보리의 12개 결의안이 모두 공개회의에서 채택되었음.비공개회의는 위험한 선례를 남기게됨.

0.소련: 공개토의는 이락에 대해 부정확한 멧세지를 보낼 우려가 있음.

0.미국: 안보리 토의는 이락의 쿠웨이트 철수를 촉진하는 방안강구에 촛점을 두어야함.

0.인도, 에쿠아돌: 비공개회의시 타회원국의 의구심을 불러일으키게 됨.그러나 다수 의사에 따르겠음.

0.프랑스, 벨지움: 안보리 소집요청이 있을시 안보리는 언제든지 공식회의를 개최해 야함. 영국안도 안보리내 의견차이를 타협시키는 좋은 방안임.

0.오지리: 안보리 소집여부에 관한 상반된 입장을 조정하기 위한 타협안으로 오지리가 안보리 비공식회합시 동 비공개 공식회의 소집 방안을 제시하였던것임.끝

(대사 현홍주-국장)

국기국 장관 차관 1차보 2차보 중아국 정문국 청와대 총리실
안기부 공보처

PAGE 1 91.02.14 12:40 WG

외신 1과 통제관

0227

UNITED NATIONS

S

Security Council

PROVISIONAL

S/PV.2977 (Part I)
13 February 1991

ENGLISH

PROVISIONAL VERBATIM RECORD OF THE TWO THOUSAND NINE HUNDRED AND SEVENTY-SEVENTH MEETING (PART I)

Held at Headquarters, New York, on Wednesday, 13 February 1991, at 3.30 p.m.

President:	Mr. MUMBENGEGWI	(Zimbabwe)
Members:	Austria	Mr. HOHENFELLNER
	Belgium	Mr. NOTERDAEME
	China	Mr. LI Daoyu
	Côte d'Ivoire	Mr. ANET
	Cuba	Mr. ALARCON de QUESADA
	Ecuador	Mr. AYALA LASSO
	France	Mr. BLANC
	India	Mr. GHAREKHAN
	Romania	Mr. MUNTEANU
	Union of Soviet Socialist Republics	Mr. VORONTSOV
	United Kingdom of Great Britain and Northern Ireland	Sir David HANNAY
	United States of America	Mr. PICKERING
	Yemen	Mr. AL-ASHTAL
	Zaire	Mr. BAGBENI ADEITO NZENGEYA

This record contains the original text of speeches delivered in English and interpretations of speeches in the other languages. The final text will be printed in the Official Records of the Security Council.

Corrections should be submitted to original speeches only. They should be sent under the signature of a member of the delegation concerned, within one week, to the Chief, Official Records Editing Section, Department of Conference Services, room DC2-750, 2 United Nations Plaza, and incorporated in a copy of the record.

91-60354/A 4426V (E)

0228

The meeting was called to order at 5 p.m.

EXPRESSION OF THANKS TO THE RETIRING PRESIDENT

The PRESIDENT: As this is the first meeting of the Security Council for the month of February, I should like to take this opportunity to pay a tribute, on behalf of the Council, to His Excellency Mr. Bagbeni Adeito Nzengeya, Permanent Representative of Zaire to the United Nations, for his service as President of the Council for the month of January 1991. I am sure I speak for all members of the Security Council in expressing deep appreciation to Ambassador Bagbeni Adeito Nzengeya for the great diplomatic skill and unfailing courtesy with which he conducted the Council's business last month.

ADOPTION OF THE AGENDA

The agenda was adopted.

THE SITUATION BETWEEN IRAQ AND KUWAIT

LETTER DATED 23 JANUARY 1991 FROM THE REPRESENTATIVES OF ALGERIA, THE LIBYAN ARAB JAMAHIRIYA, MAURITANIA, MOROCCO AND TUNISIA TO THE UNITED NATIONS ADDRESSED TO THE PRESIDENT OF THE SECURITY COUNCIL (S/22135)

LETTER DATED 24 JANUARY 1991 FROM THE PERMANENT REPRESENTATIVE OF YEMEN TO THE UNITED NATIONS ADDRESSED TO THE PRESIDENT OF THE SECURITY COUNCIL (S/22144)

LETTER DATED 28 JANUARY 1991 FROM THE PERMANENT REPRESENTATIVE OF CUBA TO THE UNITED NATIONS ADDRESSED TO THE PRESIDENT OF THE SECURITY COUNCIL (S/22157)

Sir David HANNAY (United Kingdom): Let me begin by congratulating you, Sir, on your assumption of the presidency and by saying how much we have benefited from the way in which you have handled the informal meetings of the Council; we look forward to your presiding over formal meetings, such as the present one.

I wish also to congratulate your predecessor in that role on the extremely able way in which he chaired the Council during the month of January.

I have asked to speak because I wish to propose, in accordance with rule 48 of the provisional rules of procedure, that the Council decide now to meet in private to consider the item on the agenda which we have just adopted. This proposal, as

(Sir David Hannay, United Kingdom)

members know, has as its inspiration some thoughts put forward by the representative of Austria in our earlier informal contacts. I wish to take those thoughts up and put them forward as a formal proposal now.

It is clearly right, as the provisional rules of procedure envisage, that as a general rule the Council should meet in public with open attendance and coverage by the media. But the rules of procedure also provide for private meetings in exceptional circumstances. In the view of my delegation, these circumstances are exceptional.

First, the Council has adopted a series of resolutions in response to Iraq's invasion of Kuwait, culminating in resolution 678 (1990), authorizing the use of all necessary means to uphold and implement the earlier resolutions. Military action has been undertaken by a number of Member States cooperating with the Government of Kuwait and has the backing of the Council. It has as its sole purpose the upholding of the Council's decisions.

At the same time, diplomacy is actively under way, as it has been ever since 2 August 1990, to see if there is any way to bring about a peaceful settlement of the conflict on the basis of the Council's resolutions.

The Council therefore has grave and particular responsibilities which it must take into account when deciding how it should act in the context of the present requests for a meeting. We should do nothing which could detract from the Council's unity of purpose or blur the signal that is sent to the outside world. In our view, we cannot afford to send mixed signals when that might only delay the realization that a peaceful solution to this crisis has to begin with Iraqi withdrawal from Kuwait.

This occasion here today calls for serious and careful consideration of all developments away from the glare of immediate publicity. If members or non-members of the Council have proposals to make which they believe could lead to

(Sir David Hannay, United Kingdom)

implementation of the Council's resolutions and the liberation of Kuwait, it is right that they should be heard here. But, in our view, members ought to be able to explore carefully with them how those proposals will assist the Council's objectives and, above all, how they have been received by Iraq, which currently constitutes the sole obstacle to peace. All that discussion is better handled in a private meeting.

On past occasions, in the context of Western Sahara in 1975, Council members decided that the format of private meetings would best assist such exploratory discussion designed to clarify ideas and identify possible ways forward. They chose a format which enabled them to enter into a dialogue with those who participated, to ask questions and to receive answers. We believe that that format offers the right model for today's meeting.

In making this proposal, my delegation has no intention of trying to limit participation or restrict knowledge of the proceedings. We recognize that the issues are of universal interest to all Members of the United Nations. It is right that all should be free to attend the debate if they wish to do so and request to do so, and to participate. It is right too that the normal verbatim record should be taken and circulated; I have no intention of limiting and am not proposing to limit that by the use of rule 51. But we do believe that on this occasion the Council will carry out its functions better if the public aspect of the meeting - the presence of the media - does not influence or even distort the course and nature of our debate. That is the reason for the proposal I have made.

The PRESIDENT: I thank the representative of the United Kingdom for the kind words he addressed to me.

Mr. AL-ASHTAL (Yemen) (interpretation from Arabic): There is no doubt, Sir, that your are presiding over the work of the Security Council at a critical time. Nobody can envy you your position. This is a critical stage in the life of

(Mr. Al-Ashtal, Yemen)

the Council and in international relations, and your presence in the Chair - as we have seen in our informal meetings - assures us that our business will be conducted wisely and in accordance with the rules and regulations that govern the work of the Security Council. I congratulate you most sincerely on your assumption of the presidency of the Security Council. I wish you all success during this difficult time.

I cannot fail to express my thanks to my colleague and neighbour at this table, Ambassador Bagbeni Adeito Nzengeya, who conducted the business of the Security Council during what was also a critical time, last month. His skill and wisdom testified to his great ability and rich diplomatic experience, which were evident in the way in which he conducted the Council's business.

I have asked to speak in opposition to the proposal put forward by the representative of the United Kingdom. I do so as the Council member who requested the convening of this meeting in the first place; that request was made on 24 January. I oppose the proposal also on behalf of the representatives of the Arab Maghreb States, who, in a letter dated 23 January 1991 addressed to the President of the Security Council, had also requested the convening of a meeting: the representatives of Algeria, the Libyan Arab Jamahiriya, Mauritania, Morocco and Tunisia to the United Nations. That letter was followed by letters from the delegations of Jordan and the Sudan supporting the request for a meeting. On 28 January the delegation of Cuba, a member of the Security Council, made a similar request.

My objection to the proposal that this meeting be held in private is based on the position we adopted in calling for the convening of a meeting in the first place.

(Mr. Al-Ashtal, Yemen)

Allow me to explain clearly why we oppose the Council's holding a private meeting to consider the deteriorating situation in the Gulf under the agenda item "The situation between Iraq and Kuwait".

The delegation of Yemen, as a member of the Security Council, acts consistently in accordance with the great responsibility it assumed upon becoming a member of the Council. It is in keeping with that sense of responsibility that I shall attempt to explain my delegation's opposition to transforming this meeting into a private one.

The United Nations is a democratic Organization. If there is anything that distinguished the Organization from others, it is its transparency. The Organization has no secrets. Its Charter is clear and its rules and regulations are equally so; all of its proceedings take place in public. This may have resulted from the concern felt by the founding fathers with regard to secret meetings that do not reflect public opinion - meetings in which certain agreements may be hatched in a manner inconsistent with general understanding and, in some cases, even counter to public opinion, to which we must show the deepest respect.

The first words of the Charter are "We the peoples of the United Nations." We are not just the representatives of States. The Security Council does not represent only 15 States: it represents the entire membership of the United Nations and all the peoples of the world. Hence - save in exceptional circumstances to which I shall refer later - everyone expects the Council to meet in public and in a clear and transparent manner.

The exceptions to this established United Nations tradition have been three in number. Members of the Council are familiar with them, as are, I am sure, other representatives here. In 1973 a private meeting was held to consider a draft resolution submitted by States not members of the Council, and during that meeting a statement was heard in explanation of vote, after which the meeting was adjourned.

(Mr. Al-Ashtal, Yemen)

That meeting was attended only by members of the Security Council. A second private meeting was held in 1974 concerning the situation in Cyprus. At that meeting the present Secretary-General of the United Nations, Mr. Javier Perez de Cuellar, was presiding as his country's representative to the United Nations. It was a very short meeting, during which information was submitted by the representative of Turkey; the meeting was then adjourned. In 1975 a third private meeting of the Council was held to hear the representatives of Spain, the Western Sahara and Algeria and to address questions to those representatives on a matter pertaining to the Western Sahara at that time. As I recall, the subject was the so-called Green March. After those questions had been disposed of, the meeting was adjourned.

Today, the representative of the United Kingdom has proposed that this meeting of the Council be transformed into a private one - not for the purpose of putting questions to a delegation on the events in the Gulf or on the situation in the region in general, nor to listen to the parties concerned on any specific question in the Gulf, nor indeed to hear new information from any quarter on the situation in the region, but solely to exclude the media and to begin a series of discussions in which more than 16 Member States have so far inscribed their names to participate. Additional Members may be inscribed on the list of speakers later on. Do we need a private meeting to listen to statements by delegations that represent Members of the United Nations? Do we need a private meeting, particularly since verbatim records of the meeting will be published the following day?

Why do we need a private meeting at all? It has been said that the Council must not appear to be divided and that a public meeting might give the impression that division exists in the Council. No problem is created by difference of

(Mr. Al-Ashtal, Yemen)

opinion. I respect all the members of the Council and the positions taken by their States, and that respect is, I am sure, reciprocated. My delegation voted against one of the resolutions adopted by the Council. What more are we therefore going to do? What is there to conceal, and from whom would we be concealing it?

We are told that a public meeting would serve propaganda purposes: to enable the media to listen to us. I would ask: Why should the media not listen while we discuss a war that is threatening international peace and security? Why can we not express what we want to express before the whole world? Have we not been doing exactly that for six months now? Have we not debated and considered questions pertaining to the Gulf on 12 occasions? Have we not adopted 12 resolutions, the last of which - one of the most important resolutions ever adopted by the Council - was discussed when this Chamber was filled with spectators and in the presence of our foreign ministers?

It is also said that we want a public meeting for domestic consumption in our own countries. Why not? Why can we not speak so that people in our countries can hear what we say?

(Mr. Al-Ashtal, Yemen)

It is well known that there is great concern in Yemen. It is well known that massive demonstrations are going on in the whole region. As officials and responsible people, we are called upon to express our point of view on this war, to seek by all means possible to contain the war and to do our utmost for the restoration of peace. Why should we not inform public opinion in our countries? Why does public opinion in the West have its value while ours is regarded as having absolutely no value? Maybe public opinion has no value when freedom is not exercised; there are a number of States where we hear of no popular reaction. But for us, when public opinion calls upon the State to do something, while we are members of the Council are we supposed to remain silent, to speak in a private meeting, just among ourselves?

It is enough to look at what is happening in the States of the Arab Maghreb, which have requested that the Council meet, to appreciate the sensitivity of the subject, the seriousness of this request and the position of others. I am speaking now, naturally, on behalf of Yemen, but I am also expressing the feelings of millions of Arabs, millions of Muslims and millions of other people the world over, who every day see on their television screens the tragedies of war and who hope that this war will cease. They hope that the problem will be solved peacefully, in a manner that ensures the independence of Kuwait, the withdrawal of the Iraqi forces from Kuwait and the restoration of Kuwait's sovereignty.

From the very first day we have said that although we are a small country we cannot tolerate the occupation or invasion of another State. We still adhere to that position, because it is in that way that we, all the small countries, defend ourselves. But we also want the crisis to be resolved by peaceful means. We have done a great deal to bring about its solution by peaceful means and in an Arab framework.

(Mr. Al-Ashtal, Yemen)

A number of questions are being asked, not only by us but by public opinion and the media. There is nothing secret about these questions and inquiries. People ask what are the objectives of the war currently raging on the basis of resolution 678 (1990). That is a legitimate question. When we look at what is happening, when we read of the plans being made, when we see the way in which operations are taking place and when we hear the declarations and statements made by public officials, do we not have the right to ask what the objectives of those military operations are?

The Security Council has authorized the use of all means for the implementation of its resolutions. Do the words "all ... means" exclude peaceful means? Since the phrase was interpreted as meaning the use of force, does not the Council have the right to determine the framework within which force may be used? It is easy to start wars, but it is difficult to control their extent. Sometimes military commanders do not look too intently at the political objectives. The Security Council has one political objective: Iraq's withdrawal from Kuwait, the restoration of Kuwait's sovereignty and the solution of the crisis between Iraq and Kuwait and in the whole region by peaceful means.

When we see on television the military operations taking place in northern Iraq, with civilian areas being targeted, do we not have the right to ask what the objective is? Does not the Council, which adopted the resolution concerned, have the right to ask that in public? Is it not in the interest of the Council and the United Nations that the Council should be constantly scrutinized by the other Members of the United Nations and public opinion?

There are many questions about the way in which the war is being conducted and about the weapons being used. Do we not have the right to ask those questions?

Why are places so remote from Kuwait being bombed? We read in the newspapers of civilian casualties. There was an example of such a report in the

0237

(Mr. Al-Ashtal, Yemen)

Washington Post the day before yesterday. It was based on a Kurdish source, not an Iraqi source, because, most regrettably, there seems to be a policy in Iraq not to publicize the civilian casualties. These massive military operations cannot but lead to rampant destruction and widespread innocent civilian casualties. Therefore, I was not surprised to read in the Washington Post that Mr. Barazani had said there had been 3,000 casualties - dead and wounded - in certain parts of Sulaymaniyah alone. I was not surprised when he spoke of a bombing raid on a cement factory and a spinning and weaving mill. How does that assist in the liberation of Kuwait?

There are many questions. The event that took place today shakes the conscience of every human being. I do not believe that even the pilots who bombed the shelter, with a reported toll of 500 people, are happy with such results. No human being, on any side of the war, can fail to be disgusted at the use of force in a manner that targets the innocent and the weak and civilian installations.

There is a problem in the Gulf. An error was made by Iraq in its occupation of Kuwait. Are we to allow another error to rectify the first? Are we to allow a third-world country to be destroyed by massive forces? Where is the proportionality in that? There is no proportion in such a reaction, nor in the equipment and the power being used. Is there no other way to solve this crisis?

(Mr. Al-Ashtal, Yemen)

Do we not have the right to call upon the Security Council to have recourse to all means to arrive at a solution? I agree with Mr. Brzezinski, who in an article published in The New York Times said that there seemed to be an insistence on the failure of diplomatic efforts. We now demand that new action be taken through diplomatic means, as is happening currently through Mr. Primakov's visit to Baghdad yesterday. We view with satisfaction that a major Power should be making such an effort in such a situation. We do not feel at all happy when the Council is relaxed, waiting for the results of this war.

I have objected to the convening of a private meeting because nothing beyond what I have just said will be said at such a meeting. We might hear an account from another side, but it will not be any more important or any clearer than what I have just stated. We believe that the Council must not remain remote from the rest of the membership of the United Nations, that no dangerous precedent be set in the history of the United Nations, while we are on the threshold of the so-called new world order, so that this Council is transformed into a secret institution.

This new world order cannot but embrace the entire world, and it cannot be installed except through the United Nations and its Charter, as well as this Council. Short of that, it will only be schemes making use of the United Nations to serve particular purposes.

We are now witnessing the United Nations and this Council giving a blank cheque for the use of force, without attempting to interpret the objectives of the law or without reviewing how the war is conducted or without follow-up on the work for peaceful efforts.

For all the above, we call for this meeting to remain a public meeting. If a private meeting is held, do I then not have the right to wonder why such a private meeting should be held and as to the intention of those who requested it. Those who requested this current meeting do not want a private meeting. What

(Mr. Al-Ashtal, Yemen)

justification is there for a private meeting? Is there a new State member asking for the convening of such a meeting, or do we not need such a meeting and, therefore, perhaps we have to wait until agreement is reached on the convening of a public meeting?

Had it been within our power to participate even in the simplest way possible in putting forward a new idea and making a new effort towards peace through this meeting, we would have done it.

I should like to reaffirm that Yemen is constantly seeking peace in our region. It was with deep sadness that we have witnessed formations, the logic of war, the logic of confrontation, which will lead to nothing but further destruction and deprive our Arab countries of their massive wealth, which is right now being used to attack their children.

The PRESIDENT: I thank the representative of Yemen for the kind words he addressed to me.

Mr. ALARCON de QUESADA (Cuba) (interpretation from Spanish): I should like first of all to express my delegation's great pleasure at seeing you, Mr. President, guiding the meetings of our Council. You very ably represent a country - Zimbabwe - which, for various reasons, occupies a very important part in the hearts of all the people of the third world. Your assumption of the presidency, and the fair, equitable and brilliant manner in which you are discharging this responsibility, are additional evidence of the reasons why all the countries of the third world, and in particular the non-aligned countries, are happy to see Zimbabwe and President Mugabe playing a fundamental role in the promotion of the common struggle for justice. We also wish to extend our congratulations to your predecessor, who last month once again showed his talent and his long diplomatic experience.

(Mr. Alarcon de Quesada, Cuba)

My delegation too wishes to oppose the proposal put forward by the representative of the United Kingdom. I should like at the outset to point out that he referred to certain past situations in which the Council decided to meet in private. But I did not hear anything about the first such precedent, which, I believe, was also a British initiative. In 1956, at the 735th meeting of the Security Council, the Council considered the situation regarding the conflict that had arisen in connection with the Suez Canal as a result of its nationalization, to which the Egyptian Government had proceeded in exercise of its sovereign right, its being a fundamental national resource of that country.

The representative of the United Kingdom at the time spoke in the Council and explained his country's position in connection with the substance of the item that was then under consideration, and he made a similar, but not identical, proposal to the one we have heard today. I shall now quote from the official records of the Council:

> "I have been thinking, during the last day or two, of the best way for us to organize our deliberations with regard to this matter, and perhaps it may be convenient if I indicate my thoughts at this stage to my colleagues.
>
> "It seems to me that, after there has been a chance for those who wish to state their views in public session, it might be a good thing for this Council to move into private session. I would hope that we might reach that point some time on Tuesday, 9 October, perhaps. That would give us an opportunity to consider the next steps in a less formal atmosphere." (735th meeting, paras. 94 and 95)

0241

(Mr. Alarcon de Quesada, Cuba)

The representative of the United Kingdom put this idea forward on 5 October 1956. During the following four days the Security Council continued to meet and heard all those who wished to speak in public meetings, before the Council proceeded to hold a private meeting.

In that connection, I should like to say, first, that it is regrettable that on this occasion the United Kingdom representative has not pointed to that very valuable precedent. At the very least, that would have served as a kind of courteous apology to a group of non-members of the Council that quite some time ago asked for a meeting of the Council.

It has been said that we should try to avoid giving the impression that we are divided or that there is a lack of cohesiveness in the Council. But how can we avoid giving that impression when we have just adopted an agenda that could not be more revealing? It reads: "The situation between Iraq and Kuwait", and it refers to three letters: the letter of 23 January 1991 from the representatives of the Maghreb States, the letter of 24 January 1991 from the representative of Yemen, and the letter of 28 January 1991 which I addressed to the President of the Security Council.

In any event, what is said at this meeting will inevitably remain in the records of the Security Council. No matter how much anyone may wish to disregard the facts, it will be obvious to all that for the past three weeks the Security Council has been confronted by a situation which, to say the least, is very unusual.

In this respect, I should like to recall at this meeting of the Council the view expressed by the United States Government on 21 April 1966, in regard to a situation that does not even remotely relate to this inexplicable delay in convening the Security Council. The then representative of the United States, Ambassador Arthur Goldberg, deemed it necessary to send an official letter to the

0242

(Mr. Alarcon de Quesada, Cuba)

President of the Security Council and to ask that it be circulated as an official document of the Council. That is why I have a copy of it before me. I think that, as a colophon to this story about the Council's inability to meet in the midst of a war that is of concern to everyone - at least to everyone except, it would appear, the Security Council, so far - it is important to recall what Ambassador Goldberg said on that occasion, when the Security Council, in the opinion of the United States, was not being convened as quickly as it should have been to consider a question that it should have been considering and that, I repeat, did not even remotely resemble the one before us now. This is what Ambassador Goldberg said in his letter of 21 April 1966:

"The Security Council is given primary responsibility for the maintenance of international peace and security, according to Article 24 of the United Nations Charter, 'in order to ensure prompt and effective action'. It is required by Article 28 to be 'so organized as to be able to function continuously'. These two Articles established the responsibility of the Council to be available for emergency action to maintain peace and security. The provisional rules of procedure of the Security Council are designed and must be interpreted so as to ensure that the Council can fulfil the responsibilities these Articles place upon it.

"The dominant paragraph of the provisional rules of procedure of the Security Council accordingly is rule 2, which states that 'The President shall call a meeting of the Security Council at the request of any member of the Security Council'. The rule is mandatory and does not give the President the choice of convening or not convening the Council when a member so requests. This has been made clear on numerous occasions. ...

"Even if a majority of Council members are opposed to a meeting, the meeting must be held. Those members opposed to the meeting may express their

0243

(Mr. Alarcon de Quesada, Cuba)

views on the agenda when the meeting is convened, may seek to adjourn the meeting, or to defeat proposals submitted to it, but the President is bound to convene the Council on a request under rule 2, unless that request is not pressed.

"Subject to rule 2, the President is given, under rule 1, the authority and responsibility to set the time of a meeting. In so doing, the President acts not as a representative of his country but as a servant of the Council, and he does not exercise an arbitrary or unfettered discretion. His decision must be related to the requirements of Articles 24 and 28 of the Charter and of rule 2 of the provisional rules of procedure, and to the urgency of the request and situation. A request for an urgent meeting must be respected and decided upon on an urgent basis, and the timing established responsive to the urgency of the situation." (S/7261, paras. 1, 2 and 3)

The letter is of course much longer. I recommend it to anyone wishing to know more about how the major Powers interpreted the Charter and our rules of procedure in other circumstances.

The fact of the matter is that, for reasons I do not need to go into now, on the twenty-eighth day of the war the Council is meeting for the first time - despite the efforts that have been made and the specific requests that have been put forward for some time not only by members of the Security Council but by other Members of the United Nations, on whose behalf it is to be assumed the members of the Council act.

I am sure that, like me, all representatives have received not one, not two, not three but many letters from persons who do not represent Governments, who do not represent States but who are part of the "peoples of the United Nations". Of course I shall not cite all the letters I have received. I shall mention only

0244

(Mr. Alarcon de Quesada, Cuba)

those from four religious organizations of this country and other countries, as well as international religious organizations, that I have received today. They all remind us of the same thing: that the Security Council has certain obligations *vis-à-vis* world peace; that the Security Council has obligations *vis-à-vis* the children and women, the civilians who are losing their lives now; that the Security Council has an unshirkable responsibility under the Charter to act in order to restore peace, and to do so as a matter of the greatest urgency.

(Mr. Alarcon de Quesada, Cuba)

I should like briefly to quote from a letter from a person who represents no one, no church, no government. She says:

(spoke in English)

"I hold no political office, I seek no recognition, advocate no particular religion. I am but a simple mother with a simple request."

(spoke in Spanish)

Her letter is very simple, very brief:

(spoke in English)

"I ask of you, Sir, to please do as much as you can, as quickly as you can, to end the violence. Please put yourself in the place of a mother. A mother will protect her children in every way she knows how. We are all someone's child."

(spoke in Spanish)

Mrs. Kath Emelianoff of South Carolina, in the United States, wrote this letter. I think the language is very simple. She has certainly reminded us all that we do not have the right to ignore certain of our elementary obligations, such as to act in response to such demands.

Of course, a State has the right to ask that this organ meet as a matter of urgency; it does not have the right to shirk such a request. But this body also has an obligation to show a certain sensitivity to requests that may come from anywhere. And now, finally, thanks above all to your leadership, Mr. President, and to the manner in which you have conducted the proceedings of the Council, which deserves the gratitude and appreciation of all the Members of the United Nations, the Security Council seems to remember that rule 2 exists. But even now, having reached this stage, the principal problem is that this kind of shameful outcome of our unshirkable obligation to meet is taking place without anyone knowing about it, without there being any witnesses, without representatives of other Governments

(Mr. Alarcon de Quesada, Cuba)

being able to participate, without representatives of the press being present - and they are, after all, those who can convey to this lady from South Carolina, for example, or the many others writing to us every day, a message of encouragement, such as "Well, at least the Security Council is considering the possibility of restoring peace."

My delegation is categorically opposed to the idea of this meeting's taking place in these circumstances, behind closed doors, simply because the Security Council has for six-and-a-half months been considering the same subject with all the publicity one could possibly imagine. We have met here on 12 occasions to adopt 12 resolutions in front of the television cameras, before live radio microphones, in the presence of dozens of newspapermen, and on every occasion in response to those who had asked for a meeting of the Council.

Before the press, with all the publicity required, the Council adopted resolution 660 (1990), which had the full support of my delegation. It was a resolution that did reflect the unanimous opinion of the members of the Council, and I would say expressed a universally supported view that the independence and sovereignty of Kuwait should be respected and restored, and that the occupation of that territory should cease as soon as possible.

Resolution 661 (1990) was also adopted with full publicity. But let us not be deceived. That resolution did not receive the endorsement of all delegations. Quite clearly it did not. Before the same cameras, which were at that time not considered an obstacle, we put forward our views. At that time we did not believe - and indeed we still hold the same view - that such action was justified. We thought the Council acted over-hastily at a time when the Iraqi authorities were saying they would initiate the withdrawal of their troops from Kuwaiti territory. The representative of Iraq confirmed that here because an important meeting of Heads of Arab States was about to take place. The economic sanctions imposed by

(Mr. Alarcon de Quesada, Cuba)

resolution 661 (1990) were unparalleled in the history of the United Nations. They were so all-encompassing, so complete, that in effect they represented a double standard from the Security Council. Throughout its history, the Council had never done anything similar, even when there were invasions of small countries by major powerful neighbours or when foreign territories had been occupied through the use of force. Territories occupied by Israel can continue to be occupied without the Council's feeling obliged even to consider Chapter VII. Panama and Grenada can be invaded by a powerful neighbour without the Council's even considering any kind of sanctions. Southern Lebanon can continue to be occupied. Many other such cases might come to anyone's mind.

The Council's inconsistency and its hasty action - we made this point cogently at the time - indicated the will of one particular Power and its determination to use the conflict that had been created with the occupation of Kuwait by Iraq for purposes having nothing to do with the restoration of Kuwaiti independence but rather to create the basis for military intervention in the region.

In the full glare of publicity, two weeks later the Council adopted resolution 665 (1990). Have we forgotten that before its adoption there was a debate? We did not all say the same thing. In that debate my delegation drew attention to the fact that the Council had not even waited to receive the first report of the Secretary-General on the manner in which the economic sanctions in resolution 661 (1990) were being implemented.

I wondered whether my colleagues had forgotten that in resolution 661 (1990), which Cuba did not vote in favour of, *inter alia*, the Secretary-General had been requested to present his first report on the manner in which the sanctions were being implemented one month after the adoption of resolution 661 (1990). This Council, with all the television cameras running, without any justification, had to adopt a resolution two weeks before the date on which the Secretary-General was to

0248

(Mr. Alarcon de Quesada, Cuba)

submit his report! My delegation criticized that resolution most harshly because it implied authorization of the use of naval forces already deployed in the region without this Council's having discussed that. But the naval units could not interrupt their exercise in the area and carry out an economic embargo, the strict fulfilment of which had not been questioned by anyone. In respect of the resolution's implementation, we had requested the Secretary-General to submit a report two weeks later. But no one was courteous enough to wait for our Secretary-General's assessment before allowing the use of military units for the alleged implementation of the embargo.

(Mr. Alarcon de Quesada, Cuba)

My delegation detected a clear violation of the Charter of our Organization in that resolution. Seeds were sown in that moment that have now borne bitter fruit. Two principles have apparently taken hold in the work of the Council - principles now in vogue in a few countries and which some Governments seem to admire: "deregulation" and "privatization". The Council very quickly forgot that in order to authorize the use of military force in accordance with the Charter, there is a specific procedure that must be followed. The Council must also assume authority when that is done and a certain monitoring must take place. The rules were set aside and certain States were empowered to act on their own initiative. In other words, they were authorized by the United Nations to "privatize" the use of armed force. Finally, in the full glare of publicity, with all the television cameras of the world rolling, the Security Council adopted resolution 678 (1990), which was a culmination of the process of deregulating and privatizing the Council's essential activities.

Resolution 678 (1990) authorized some to use whatever means they felt necessary without the Council taking the steps clearly laid down in the Charter regarding the use of military force. But at least the final paragraph of that resolution states that the Council will remain seized of the matter.

Some day, one of my colleagues who have so eagerly supported these 12 Security Council resolutions should kindly explain to the representatives of public opinion, of the peoples of the United Nations, the strange phenomenon of this body being used on 12 occasions to lay the foundations of so serious a thing as war, as scores of people throughout the world remind us every day - of this war supposedly being conducted pursuant to the Council's resolutions, and of this august body, in a majestic display of its sense of responsibility, remaining aloof ever since the war began.

(Mr. Alarcon de Quesada, Cuba)

I believe that mankind requires some sort of explanation of this curious phenomenon.

The Security Council has been used as a kind of glove. When it so suits us, we put it on and use it for certain purposes; when it becomes a bother we simply take it off and throw it away. That will be the unfortunate plight of the Security Council unless it confronts the specific situation that has been created in the Gulf, unless it deals with the war's development in the way only it can do: in the same manner as it discussed and adopted all past resolutions - in public, in the full view of all of those who represent the peoples of the United Nations. Just as in similar public circumstances in the past, we would not all be saying the same thing or taking the same approach, but at least some Members of the Organization would have an opportunity to exercise their right to speak out - to speak to world public opinion and express whatever concerns, anxieties and ideas they might have.

In my delegation's opinion, this meeting is finally beginning, though at a time too far removed from when it was first requested and at the risk of being immediately diverted from the public light, as is preferable to some. Yet my delegation believes that it is our obligation and duty to continue to follow this problem as we have done in the past, especially now that war has broken out in the region. We have every obligation in the world to consider the extent to which events in the military arena truly correspond to the authorization of the United Nations or whether they far exceed it. We must consider - as churches, cultural institutions, individuals and simple citizens of the world request us to do - the tragedy that is being imposed on thousands of civilians, particularly women and children, who are being subjected to the most ferocious and relentless bombing. We must consider, for example, to what extent Security Council resolution 678 (1990)

(Mr. Alarcon de Quesada, Cuba)

is in line with certain other resolutions, not those of the Security Council but of a body that some may feel lacks a certain importance: the General Assembly of the United Nations.

The General Assembly, on 4 December 1990 - six days after the adoption of Security Council resolution 678 (1990) - adopted a resolution that is very pertinent to our current discussion. The resolution refers to armed attacks that could take place on nuclear facilities. One hundred and forty-one Members of the United Nations voted in favour of that resolution. One Member voted against it - I will let members of the Council check the records to see who it was, though I do not believe it will be difficult for anyone here to guess. Among the 141, there were many States belonging to the so-called coalition that is at present waging war against Iraq, as well as all the States in the Gulf region and a number of members of the Security Council, including some who voted in favour of resolution 678 (1990) and even some who co-sponsored it.

What does General Assembly resolution 45/58 J say? In operative paragraph 1, it says that the General Assembly:

(spoke in English)

> "Recognizes that an armed attack or a threat of armed attack on a safeguarded nuclear facility, operational or under construction, would create a situation in which the Security Council would have to act immediately in accordance with the provisions of the Charter of the United Nations, including measures under Chapter VII" (General Assembly resolution 45/58 J).

(continued in Spanish)

I infer from that decision that when my colleagues the coalition members of the Council adopted resolution 678 (1990) a week before the adoption of

0252

(Mr. Alarcon de Quesada, Cuba)

resolution 45/58 J they were voting in favour of the use of all necessary means against Iraq, but ruling out any attack on nuclear facilities, operational or in construction. That must have been their intent or they would not have voted in favour of that resolution, as did the overwhelming majority of Members of the Organization.

0253

(Mr. Alarcon de Quesada, Cuba)

Another document, conveyed to the President of the Council by the representative of the United States, contains the transcript of a 23 January press conference given by the United States Secretary of Defense and the Chairman of the United States Joint Chiefs of Staff. At that press conference, General Powell said:

"We have targeted that nuclear facility they have very carefully. I have looked at the bomb damage assessment myself with trained analysts, and I think I can confirm for you that the two operating reactors they had are both gone, they're down, they're finished." (S/22168, annex, p. 10)

It is obvious that a State has informed the Council that it has done something in clear and direct violation of the resolution adopted by the General Assembly subsequent to the Council's adoption of resolution 678 (1990). One can only assume that when the General Assembly resolution was adopted - with affirmative votes of many present around this table who voted also in favour of the Council's resolution - it was because members had decided such things ought not to be done. The International Atomic Energy Agency had clearly enunciated the same position some time earlier.

Is not the Security Council obligated to consider the extent to which there have been violations of those parameters for the use of force authorized in this case by the Council? Is not the Council obligated to meet to consider any measure or idea put forward by any State, even if it does not necessarily pertain to the continuation of the war? It seems to us that "all necessary means" need not be interpreted only as the use of missiles, bombs and bullets. Members may have other views; they may share the opinion we have openly and forthrightly expressed: that the war must stop, that the bombing must stop immediately, and that the Security Council has the obligation to explore other ways and means of resolving the conflict.

(Mr. Alarcon de Quesada, Cuba)

We believe the Council must meet in public, in keeping with the requests made by a number of sovereign States Members of the Organization. It must meet in public also because the war is not the property of the 15 representatives seated at this table; it is of legitimate concern and interest to all States Members of the Organization and a source of legitimate concern and anguish for the peoples of the entire world, which have the right to know the views of the Council - which have the right to follow our deliberations and to see that our consideration of this important subject is taking place not in the dark but in the light of day.

The PRESIDENT: I thank the representative of Cuba for the kind words he addressed to me, my Head of State and my country.

The representative of the United Kingdom has proposed that this meeting be held in private, with the understanding that rule 51 of the provisional rules of procedure of the Security Council will not be invoked on this occasion and that the verbatim record of this meeting of the Security Council will be circulated in all the working languages as an unrestricted document in accordance with rule 49, and that attendance and requests for participation will be treated in the usual manner.

We have also heard statements by the representatives of Yemen and Cuba.

The representative of the United Kingdom has proposed that the meeting be held in private. I shall therefore put that proposal to the vote.

I call first on members wishing to make statements before the voting.

Mr. VORONTSOV (Union of Soviet Socialist Republics) (interpretation from Russian): Permit me first of all to congratulate you, Sir, on your assumption of the presidency of the Security Council for the month of February and to state my conviction that under your leadership the Council's work this month will be effective.

0255

(Mr. Vorontsov, USSR)

I wish also to thank your predecessor, the Permanent Representative of Zaire, for his important work as President of the Security Council for the month of January.

The Soviet delegation supports the proposal that the Security Council meet in private to discuss the situation between Iraq and Kuwait. At the request of a number of States Members of the United Nations, this meeting is taking place at a dramatic moment. The Iraqi leadership persists in its refusal to comply with the resolutions of the Security Council calling for the unconditional and immediate withdrawal of Iraqi troops from Kuwait, despite the hostilities undertaken in accordance with Security Council resolution 678 (1990) to ensure the implementation of the world community's demand.

The Soviet Union is firm in its loyalty to the Council's resolutions and insists on their full and unconditional implementation. That was reaffirmed in the statement made on 9 February by the President of the Soviet Union, Mikhail Sergeiyevich Gorbachev; it is contained in document S/22215, which all members have had an opportunity to see.

The Soviet Union continues to see it as its political and moral duty to do everything it can to ensure the early implementation of Security Council resolutions and an end to the bloodshed. The settlement of the conflict by peaceful means requires that Iraq immediately withdraw its troops from Kuwait. That is precisely the aim of the political efforts of the Soviet Union and a number of other States. Those efforts continue.

Following the personal meeting between Evgeny Primakov and the President of Iraq, held in Baghdad on 12 February, the Iraqi Foreign Minister, Mr. Tariq Aziz, will visit Moscow in a few days' time.

(Mr. Vorontsov, USSR)

In these circumstances, the present meeting of the Security Council, convened at the request of a number of States, should promote Iraq's unconditional compliance with the relevant decisions of the Council. It should serve as a lever of joint influence on Baghdad to come to the only correct solution: a statement that it will withdraw from Kuwait.

(Mr. Vorontsov, USSR)

In our view public debate in the Security Council may be incorrectly interpreted in Baghdad and may thus make more difficult the intensive efforts being made by the Soviet Union and other countries to achieve a peaceful settlement. At the same time we do not exclude the possibility that comprehensive and businesslike discussion of the question of how to arrive at a solution to the Kuwaiti crisis on the basis of the Security Council resolutions in a private meeting of the Council may provide the necessary additional impetus to the diplomatic and political efforts already under way. In tranquil circumstances and free from the public presence, we must attempt to analyse all the questions and ideas in the minds of those who have called for this meeting. We must also raise pertinent questions and have a comprehensive discussion of possible ideas and proposals as to how to begin an intensive search for some peaceful way in which the Council's resolutions can be complied with - that is, Iraq's immediate and unconditional withdrawal from Kuwait - and from that discussion we must then draw the necessary conclusions.

On the basis of the foregoing points, my delegation will vote in favour of the proposal that the Council's further work take place in a businesslike atmosphere in private.

The PRESIDENT: I thank the representative of the Soviet Union for his kind words addressed to me.

Mr. PICKERING (United States of America): First, permit me to congratulate you, Sir, on your assumption of the presidency of the Council and on the leadership you have provided and will, I know, continue to provide to the work of the Council. Let me also thank your predecessor, Ambassador Bagbeni Adeito Nzengeya of Zaire, for his leadership of the Council during the month of January.

0258

(Mr. Pickering, United States)

We are discussing today an important procedural question about how the Council deals seriously with one of the most important issues it has ever had before it. We have been grappling with the question of what next steps the Council should take regarding the Gulf crisis. A wide variety of concerns have been expressed about the need to maintain the integrity of the Council's decisions, the impact of the war, the failure of Iraq to respond to diplomatic overtures and the need for the Council to remain engaged. We have listened carefully, for my Government shares many of the concerns which have been expressed, even if we do not always agree with all of the conclusions.

After having weighed the pros and cons of a variety of options, we have concluded that the interests of all of the members of the Council, and of the Members of the United Nations, can best be served now by a proposal advanced by the Austrian delegation some days ago: the holding of a formal but private meeting of the Security Council. We believe this will enable all who wish to do so to express their views and to exchange ideas in an appropriate setting. At the same time this proposal will enable delegations to get statements on the record if they believe it desirable. But, most of all, I hope that it will offer the opportunity for a serious and constructive discussion, free from the glare of instantaneous publicity and the misinterpretation and misuse to which this meeting might be subject. We have no wish or intent to stifle debate. Indeed, we support this proposal because it will encourage genuine and effective give and take.

We meet at a time of considerable gravity. The Security Council has acted to ensure full Iraqi compliance with its resolutions. It has taken the most difficult of decisions for Member States of the United Nations: to authorize the use of force to confront unprovoked aggression and to achieve a return to international legitimacy and legality. It was compelled to make this decision. A few nations

(Mr. Pickering, United States)

still find it all too easy to turn to violence and aggression to achieve their ends, counting on the acquiescence of others. Unfortunately, Iraq has given the world no reason to believe that it ever intended to comply with the resolutions of the Security Council and the will of the international community.

No one likes the fact that we have been compelled by Saddam Hussein to respond to force with force. There are no greater advocates of peace than those who are called upon to pay the price for defending the principles of international law and conduct contained in the United Nations Charter. Again, we call upon Iraq to withdraw immediately from Kuwait and to comply with the 12 relevant Security Council resolutions. By doing so - and only by doing so - Iraq could end the bloodshed right now, today.

The objectives of the United States and the coalition effort are clear and limited and are set out in the Security Council resolutions. They are: the withdrawal of Iraq from Kuwait, the restoration of Kuwait's legitimate Government and the restoration of international peace and security in the area. Our aims are no broader than to compel Iraq's compliance with the resolutions.

President Bush stated at the outset of coalition activities that we seek neither the destruction of Iraq nor its dismemberment, nor to punish its people for the policy of their leaders. And, despite the propaganda charges to the contrary, never in history have military forces been engaged in battle with so much concern for the limitation of damage to the civilian population. Warfare is indeed a terrible thing. All coalition members are making the maximum effort to avoid civilian casualties. This often means increased risk to our own forces, a cost we are willing to bear. I cannot help but note that this is in stark contrast to Iraq's own policy of deliberately targeting civilian populations for uncertain missile terror attacks. It has also deliberately increased the exposure of its own

0260

(Mr. Pickering, United States)

population by moving military equipment and facilities into civilian areas with the purpose of using innocent Iraqi civilians and their homes as shields against attack.

As President Bush sombrely observed several weeks ago, Americans fight in anger only because we have to fight at all. We did everything we could to avoid this conflict, and we will do our best to bring it to the earliest possible conclusion. Despite the invective to the contrary - some of which we have been subjected to today - this is not a war of hegemony, not a grab for the control of oil reserves and not an attempt to impose an American order on the Arab world. Such foolishness ignores the realities of both Iraqi behaviour and the overwhelming rejection by the Members of the United Nations of that very behaviour. We are in the Gulf, as are the other 30 members of the coalition, to ensure that naked aggression does not succeed. We want to give meaning to the only principles on which a peaceful and prosperous world community can be based. We will stay not one day longer than necessary.

Looking ahead, Secretary Baker outlined on 7 February the expectation of the United States leadership that following hostilities the States of the Gulf themselves and regional organizations such as the Gulf Co-operation Council will take the lead in rebuilding the war-ravaged region and in building a network of new and stronger security ties. No regional State should be excluded from such arrangements.

But what we must discuss today is how the Council will conduct further serious and important discussions on the Gulf crisis. My Government brings one fundamental criterion to this debate: How can we promote the earliest possible withdrawal of Iraq from Kuwait and how can we strengthen the Council's role in achieving this objective? My mathematics may be deficient, but I would like to remind the representative of Cuba that this is something like the 195th day of the war, which began with the Iraqi aggression on 2 August, not the 28th day, as he claims.

(Mr. Pickering, United States)

All of us in this room, and literally thousands and millions of people throughout the world, in dozens and scores of ministries and institutions, have exerted every effort to avoid this conflict. All want it ended as soon as possible, and all agree on one thing: Iraq must leave Kuwait. Iraq's refusal to accept it and its many deeds in contravention of international law make it in a literal sense an outlaw State.

(Mr. Pickering, United States)

Iraq continues to reject every proposal from every envoy seeking peace, including, most recently, Iran and Pakistan. It had already spurned the efforts of the United Nations Secretary-General, the Arab League, the Gulf Co-operation Council and the Organization of African Unity and innumerable bilateral initiatives at the highest levels. Iraq's reaction to the latest Soviet envoy regrettably contains nothing new, and it still refuses to consider or countenance withdrawal. Although efforts will continue, Radio Baghdad on 10 February declared that Iraq rejects the idea of a cease-fire and still insists that the independent nation of Kuwait is an integral part of Iraq. With this as prologue, what, then, is the purpose of this meeting?

With only a few exceptions, no member of the Council is suggesting that it back away from resolution 678 (1990). No one is suggesting that there be a cease-fire without concrete evidence that Iraq will withdraw and comply fully with the Council's resolutions. And all of us, I believe, sincerely seek peace. President Bush has made it clear that he welcomes any mediation effort to convince Iraq to comply fully with the Security Council resolutions and to withdraw its forces from Kuwait.

But there are some States, including Iraq, which are trying to call into question the clear, legal obligations the Council has imposed upon it, and the clear, legal authority granted to the coalition military effort, pursuant to resolution 678 (1990). The Council has acted, and the coalition effort has been undertaken, in keeping with the United Nations Charter. The Council continues to monitor the situation. The United States has submitted frequent, full reports to the Council, as required under resolution 678 (1990).

My country holds that the Council should meet when it is in a position to advance its objectives, and to take action. That is what the international community looks to us for. And, given the continuing refusal of Iraq to

(Mr. Pickering, United States)

acknowledge the validity of the Council's demands, that does not now seem to be the case.

We have yet to have defined for us the purpose of a public debate this afternoon. Is it to explore a cease-fire? Iraq has just made it clear that it is not interested in a cease-fire that is accompanied by withdrawal. A cease-fire without withdrawal is not acceptable. We have no intention of offering Saddam Hussein breathing space in which to regroup his military forces. Nor does he have any need of a pause in the fighting to make the decision that he already needs to make.

Is the purpose of this meeting to exchange information on the military effort? Open scrutiny of coalition efforts occurs every day, with thousands of journalists in the Middle East. The exposure to scrutiny of military operations in the Gulf is indeed unprecedented in history.

At the present juncture, when Iraq remains intransigent and it is not clear what additional steps the Council might take to ensure compliance with its resolutions, our concern is that a meeting will be subject either to misinterpretation or to exploitation. Above all else, we must not do anything which will prolong the conflict, and that, most particularly, includes sending signals, which Iraq will misuse or misperceive, that the Council is not firm in its decisions and is not intent on seeing them implemented.

The signal we must send instead, and keep on sending, is that this body and the international community are resolute and united, as they have been since 2 August. We will not tolerate the unprovoked seizure and attempted obliteration of a Member State of the United Nations. We will not tolerate the outrageous behaviour of Iraqi occupying forces in Kuwait, in contravention of international law. We will not accept the obliteration of Kuwait or the terrorizing or torturing of its people. We will not tolerate indiscriminate terror attacks against

0264

(Mr. Pickering, United States)

civilians in Saudi Arabia and Israel. We will not tolerate flagrant violation of the Geneva Conventions relative to the treatment of prisoners of war. And we will not tolerate mindless attacks on the environment. The Council must make it clear that the international community is prepared to do what is necessary to make sure that this aggression, this lawlessness, is not rewarded.

Given the evident and earnest desire on the part of a number of nations for the Council to meet to discuss the Gulf crisis, and notwithstanding our reservations about the genuine usefulness of such a meeting, we shall join with a majority in the Council. We believe that the form of such a meeting should be in keeping with the purpose, which in this case I take to be a serious discussion and exchange of views, commensurate with the importance and sensitivity of the subject. This will also respond to the appeal of a member of the Council that we do nothing now which would endanger its continuing diplomatic efforts to get Iraq to implement the Council's resolutions.

For the reasons I have indicated, we support the Austrian suggestion that we move to a formal private meeting. This will allow non-members of the Council to share their views, while permitting the exchange and circulation of prepared statements that nations may wish to deliver and to make public. It has become clear in recent days that Iraq is fighting a major campaign to discredit this Council, its resolutions, the United Nations and the person and institution of the Secretary-General. Its disregard for the truth is as obvious as its disregard for its neighbours. It is our earnest belief that this formula will meet the concerns which have been expressed in this Chamber, without providing Iraq an opportunity to exploit our debate or to twist the truth.

We again urge Iraq's leadership to turn away from its destructive course and to bring an end to the needless suffering it has inflicted on the people of Kuwait,

(Mr. Pickering, United States)

the people of the international community, and now on its own population. We hope that all States will join us in affirming support for the enforcement of the resolutions of the Security Council, in confirming their support for the Secretary-General and in renewing the call upon Iraq to bring an end to the conflict in the Gulf.

The PRESIDENT: I thank the representative of the United States for his kind words addressed to me.

Mr. GHAREKHAN (India): I should like first, Sir, to express my delegation's deep satisfaction at your assumption of the presidency of the Council for the month of February. Zimbabwe and India have traditionally enjoyed close, friendly relations. In the short space of 13 days you have already made a deep impression on your colleagues by your wisdom and intelligence and by your prompt actions.

I also wish to pay a tribute to His Excellency Ambassador Bagbeni Adeito Nzengeya, Permanent Representative of Zaire, for the exemplary manner in which he presided over the Council during January.

I should also like to take this opportunity to express my delegation's appreciation of the welcome extended to it by the other members of the Council. We shall strive to the utmost to contribute to the promotion of the objectives of the United Nations Charter in the tradition of the foreign policy and principles that India has consistently followed.

Ever since the outbreak of the armed hostilities in the Persian Gulf my delegation has consistently maintained that it is incumbent on the Security Council to remain seized of the matter and continuously to monitor the situation as it develops. That is the Council's generic responsibility, which it specifically assumed under paragraph 5 of resolution 678 (1990).

0266

(Mr. Gharekhan, India)

The war in the Gulf has aroused tremendous concern in the international community. The human and material destruction being suffered by the people of Kuwait and Iraq, the ever-present danger of the war's escalating to higher levels of intensity and engulfing other countries, the ecological disaster that is threatening countries beyond the immediate theatre of operations - all these factors greatly exercise the minds of the Government and people of India.

0267

(Mr. Gharekhan, India)

We are particularly concerned at the possible use of weapons of mass destruction - chemical, biological, nuclear. The use of chemical weapons would be reprehensible and is prohibited by international law; the use of nuclear weapons would threaten the very survival of mankind and has been declared by the General Assembly a violation of the United Nations Charter and a crime against humanity.

My delegation therefore favours the holding of meetings of the Council, on a regular basis, to provide an opportunity for members to review the situation. Indeed, the international community expects no less of the Council. I do not wish to suggest that the Council has been totally inactive during the past four weeks. The Council has tried to keep the matter under review through the instrumentality of informal consultation meetings. This was useful and was in fact first suggested by my delegation. This practice ought to continue. However, the informal meetings cannot be a permanent substitute for official meetings of the Council.

My delegation is deeply concerned that it has not been possible for the Council to meet formally even once on this matter since the expiry of the deadline, on 15 January, set by resolution 678 (1990). This has not reflected well on the prestige of the Council and the United Nations. The Secretary-General also referred to this in his statement to the Council members last week. The perception in which the Council is held by the international community ought to be of concern to the Council; at least, it is of concern to my delegation.

Many delegations - both those of members and those of non-members of the Council - have requested formal, open meetings of the Council to discuss the situation. The Council should welcome this interest on the part of Member States as evidence of the international community's confidence in the Council. In my delegation's view, it would be entirely proper and desirable that the meeting should be public, as is the Council's normal practice. A decision to go against this normal practice should be taken only in very special circumstances, since it

(Mr. Gharekhan, India)

could have the unintended effect of arousing avoidable doubts about the Council's functioning. My delegation is not convinced that circumstances today justify such an exception.

At the same time, my delegation is aware that there are some delegations - some of them not representing members of the Council - that would not like the Council to meet at all. On the other hand, there are several members of the Council that feel that, at least as an initial step, it might be useful for the Council to meet in a private session. My delegation is not unmindful of the preoccupation of those delegations. Should the Council decide, by majority, to convert this meeting into a private one, my delegation will of course respect that decision. The Council's provisional rules of procedure provide for it. But this would be the first time that the Council would have taken such an important decision through a vote. I wonder if such a division in the Council is wise or necessary at this stage.

It is my delegation's expectation that at some point in the near future the Council will revert to its traditional method of meeting in official public meetings.

The PRESIDENT: I thank the representative of India for his kind words addressed to me.

Mr. HOHENFELLNER (Austria): First of all, I should like to congratulate you, Sir, on your assumption of the presidency of the Security Council. Although this is the first time that you have presided over the Council, your leadership qualities are already known from our informal consultations. Let me assure you of our full cooperation. I should now like to thank your predecessor, Ambassador Bagbeni Adeito Nzengeya of Zaire, who exercised the function of President of the Council during the difficult month of January, for his work.

0269

(Mr. Hohenfellner, Austria)

When during our informal consultations, on 24 January, Austria put forward the idea of holding a private formal meeting of the Security Council, we were motivated by the following considerations: to make a compromise suggestion designed to break the deadlock between those who wanted no formal meeting of the Security Council at all as long as relevant Security Council resolutions had not been implemented and those who wanted an immediate public debate; to facilitate the difficult task of the President; to uphold rule 2 of the provisional rules of procedure, since we consider this rule to be of particular importance for the protection of the rights of members of the Security Council who find themselves in a minority; and to accommodate the concerns expressed by members as to the turn a public meeting might take and the wrong signals that it might be perceived to send. In order to give also other States which had already expressed an interest to participate in the debate an opportunity to do so, Austria favoured a liberal use of rule 37. Furthermore, we suggested to waive rule 51, thus allowing the verbatim records of the private meeting to be circulated in the usual fashion.

When we put forward these ideas almost three weeks ago, we were hoping for unanimous agreement by the members of the Council and the speedy convening of such a meeting. Alas, this was not to be. Although our original hopes were not realized, there is still a good case to be made for holding a private meeting. Austria will thus vote in favour. Our position on the substance of the matter will be stated later during the debate.

The PRESIDENT: I thank the representative of Austria for his kind words addressed to me.

Mr. BLANC (France) (interpretation from French): First of all, I should like to extend to you, Sir, my congratulations on the assumption of your country to the presidency. I should like to take this opportunity to thank our colleague His Excellency Ambassador Bagbeni Adeito Nzengeya, Permanent Representative of Zaire, who presided over our work during January.

I should like at the outset to thank you, Mr. President, on behalf of my Government, for your efforts to bring about the meeting our Council will hold. We wish also to thank your predecessor, the Permanent Representative of Zaire, who worked to the same end.

Some States Members of the United Nations, including two members of our Council, have asked for the Council to meet. A meeting must take place when at least one member of the Council has requested it. We also feel that this meeting is strictly in line with resolution 678 (1990), which stipulates that the Council decides to remain seized of the matter. Hence France was in favour of the convening of an official meeting so as to afford everyone an opportunity to state his position.

(Mr. Blanc, France)

From that point of view, the formula of a formal private meeting that has been proposed appears to us to be a good compromise between the views of those who would have preferred the Council not to meet and the views of others who would have preferred a public meeting. This formula is particularly welcome because participation in the debate will take place within the framework of accepted practices under our rules, and the verbatim records of the meetings will be published without recourse being made to the rules of the Council that would make it possible to limit the circulation of these records or to make them confidential.

For those reasons, we shall vote in favour of the proposal that has been made.

We feel, however, that at this stage the Security Council cannot take any concrete measure. Indeed, we must note, to our great regret, that Iraq's persistence in refusing to comply with the Security Council resolutions does not, for the time being, offer us any prospects.

The PRESIDENT: I thank the representative of France for his kind words addressed to me.

Mr. NOTERDAEME (Belgium) (interpretation from French): I should like first to tell you, Mr. President, that my delegation has every confidence about the way in which you will conduct the Council's proceedings this month. I take this opportunity also to express to your predecessor, Ambassador Bagbeni Adeito Nzengeya of Zaire, our sincere admiration for the way he led the Council's work in January.

I shall confine myself now to the procedural question before us. Later I shall have the opportunity to speak on the substance of the problems under discussion.

Belgium will vote in favour of holding a formal meeting of the Security Council on the situation between Iraq and Kuwait. We believe that, in accordance

0272

(Mr. Noterdaeme, Belgium)

with the Charter and the Council's provisional rules of procedure and practices, the Council should grant the request of those States that wish such a meeting.

My country, however, shares the concerns of those who, out of respect for the cohesiveness of the Council's work, would like this meeting to take place in private, but open to the participation of all delegations to the Organization that wish to participate in it.

My Government supports all the current diplomatic efforts designed to prevail upon Iraq to withdraw from Kuwait, in accordance with Security Council resolutions. We hope that the Council's meeting today will fall squarely within that context and will make it possible to give consideration to all useful proposals made to that end, particularly those emanating from the countries that have sought this meeting.

My delegation hopes that in that way the Council's meeting will contribute, responsibly and with restraint, to the achievement of a peaceful and rapid solution to a conflict that began on 2 August last year with the invasion and subsequent annexation of Kuwait.

The PRESIDENT: I thank the representative of Belgium for his kind words addressed to me.

Mr. AYALA LASSO (Ecuador) (interpretation from Spanish): I wish first to tell you, Sir, how pleased the delegation of Ecuador is that you will be presiding over the Security Council during the month of February. You have already demonstrated, during the meetings and talks we have had in the first days of this month, exceptional wisdom and even-handedness. This suggests that under your leadership we shall be able to follow the most appropriate path and attain the goal we all seek - the restoration of peace in the world.

0273

(Mr. Ayala Lasso, Ecuador)

I wish also to express my thanks and appreciation to our colleague the Permanent Representative of Zaire, who demonstrated great diplomatic skill and effectiveness in conducting the Security Council's proceedings last month.

I shall confine myself to expressing the position of the delegation of Ecuador on the procedural point that has been raised at this meeting of the Security Council. Like other representatives, I shall reserve my delegation's right to speak on substantive issues on a subsequent occasion.

As I stated this morning, in a way that I hoped was clear and unequivocal, my country is very pleased at the convening of this meeting of the Security Council. We have always believed that, in accordance with the applicable rules of procedure - in particular, rule 2 - the Security Council must meet whenever a request for a meeting is made by a Member State. In the present case, the request for a meeting of the Council was made by a considerable number of Arab Maghreb countries. Under resolution 674 (1990), the Council is obliged to

> "remain actively and permanently seized of the matter until Kuwait has regained its independence and peace has been restored in conformity with the relevant resolutions of the Security Council". (resolution 674 (1990), para. 11)

Under resolution 678 (1990), the Council must remain seized of the matter.

Consequently, it was obvious to the delegation of Ecuador that the Council had to meet, and to meet formally, to consider the item now before us. The Council has not met formally for a little more than two months now on the situation in the Gulf - a situation that has become more serious, indeed tragic, with every day that passes. Although the Council has dealt with the subject in many informal consultations that have taken place, Ecuador believes that the time has come for the Council to devote itself in a formal meeting to this complex subject, about which all the peoples of the world have expressed their concern and anxiety. It is

0274

(Mr. Ayala Lasso, Ecuador)

obvious that on so delicate and important an item not all the views will be the same. That is only natural because this situation is considered from differing political points of view. But we wish to state that the expression of differing views must not be taken as sending a mixed signal to anyone. On the contrary, it is an eloquent, positive demonstration that the United Nations, one of whose organs is the Security Council, was conceived as a forum for discussing and seeking ever-wider agreements in a democratic and constructive spirit.

(Mr. Ayala Lasso, Ecuador)

In proceeding in this way, our Organization is growing stronger, as is the common conviction that there are certain general principles we are all defending, on the basis of which we may well express different views to achieve a common objective: peace among all peoples and nations.

For these reasons, this morning I stated, and I state again now, that Ecuador would prefer a public meeting of the Council. We see no adequate reason for us to opt for a private meeting, which is also a possibility under the applicable rules. Nevertheless, if the majority in the Council should so decide, Ecuador would accept that democratic result and would not stand in the way of a private meeting of the Council.

The PRESIDENT: I thank the representative of Ecuador for his kind words addressed to me.

Mr. ALARCON de QUESADA (Cuba) (interpretation from Spanish): Clearly, Ambassador Pickering and I studied the same maths, and I know the conflict began 195 days ago. It would, however, be disingenuous indeed on Ambassador Pickering's part for him to assume he could convince anyone - with or without television - that what has been happening since 16 January is not something new and quite different from what was happening before.

From a certain point of view, I also agree with him that the war unleashed on 16 January truly did begin 195 days ago, when the United States began on the one hand to deploy its military forces and on the other to manipulate this organ of the United Nations.

With regard to the objective of those of us who asked for this meeting, let me, for my part, repeat what I said earlier. We have been very frank in our communications to the President of the Council. We requested a meeting of the Council some time ago to discuss, to exchange views and to hear differences of opinion - something that in our opinion is not wrong or condemnable, something

0276

(Mr. Alarcon de Quesada, Cuba)

that should not cause fear in those who claim they are speaking on behalf of the international community.

To sum up, we propose that this Council, so obedient in facilitating war, now give peace a chance.

Mr. BAGBENI ADEITO NZENGEYA (Zaire) (interpretation from French): Though I am speaking during a voting procedure, I could not fail to extend to you, Sir, the congratulations of my delegation on your accession to the presidency of the Security Council for the month of February. I would also take this opportunity to thank you sincerely for the kind words you addressed to me as your predecessor.

The background and circumstances of the Persian Gulf war are of course well known to everybody here. A member of our Organization, Kuwait, was on 2 August occupied and annexed by a militarily powerful neighbour having considerable human and material resources. Article 24 of the Charter states:

"In order to ensure prompt and effective action by the United Nations, its Members confer on the Security Council primary responsibility for the maintenance of international peace and security, and agree that in carrying out its duties under this responsibility the Security Council acts on their behalf."

Under that Article, the Council considered the situation that had arisen due to the occupation and annexation of a Member of the Organization. It adopted 12 resolutions calling on the occupier, another Member of the Organization, to comply with Article 25 of the Charter, which states:

"The Members of the United Nations agree to accept and carry out the decisions of the Security Council in accordance with the present Charter."

In so doing, the Council had the support of a very large number of Members of the Organization and of the Secretary-General in its démarches, actions and efforts

0277

(Mr. Bagbeni Adeito Nzengeya, Zaire)

aimed at persuading the occupying Power to order the withdrawal of its forces from Kuwait before 15 January 1991 in order to allow a peaceful and lasting settlement of the situation.

These initiatives and acts of good faith continue and are being stepped up through the good offices of the USSR, the 15 non-aligned countries and other Member States whose major concern remains the liberation of Kuwait, the restoration of the legitimate Government of that country and a lasting peace in the region.

My delegation continues to hope these diplomatic efforts will succeed so that an end can be put to the hostilities in the Persian Gulf.

Until these actions yield the hoped for and desired results, my delegation believes that the Security Council, which is still seized of the item "The situation between Iraq and Kuwait" under paragraph 5 of resolution 678 (1990), should actively follow the development and evolution of the situation in the Persian Gulf in connection with the implementation of the 12 resolutions it has adopted.

How can it discharge its mandate as a decision-making body? It must bear in mind its paramount responsibility to ensure that its resolutions are followed up and implemented.

The Council has several paths open to it. Unless it decides otherwise, it can meet in public under rule 48 of the provisional rules of procedure. But bearing in mind the diplomatic démarches of the Special Envoy of the USSR, Mr. Primakov and the 15 non-aligned countries, and the desire of the members of the Council to consider the situation in the Persian Gulf region in an atmosphere of serenity and resolve to explore and constructively seek new peaceful means of settling the conflict, my delegation feels a formal private meeting of the Council would enable

0278

(Mr. Bagbeni Adeito Nzengeya, Zaire)

its members to state their views and make their suggestions within the context of a fruitful exchange of views. The goal of course is a halt to the hostilities, to be immediately followed by the liberation of Kuwait and the restoration of peace to the Persian Gulf region.

As has so well been said by the representative of France, as President of the Council for January I worked along these lines with a view to such a compromise, which was almost achieved.

For all of these reasons, my delegation wholeheartedly supports a formal private meeting of the Council as proposed by the representative of the United Kingdom.

The PRESIDENT: I thank the representative of Zaire for his kind words addressed to me.

I shall now put to the vote the proposal made by the representative of the United Kingdom that this meeting of the Security Council be continued in private.

A vote was taken by show of hands:

In favour: Austria, Belgium, Côte d'Ivoire, France, Romania, Union of Soviet Socialist Republics, United Kingdom of Great Britain and Northern Ireland, United States of America, Zaire

Against: Cuba, Yemen

Abstaining: China, Ecuador, India, Zimbabwe

The PRESIDENT: The result of the voting is as follows: 9 in favour, 2 against and 4 abstentions. The proposal has therefore been adopted.

Keeping in mind the decision just taken, I propose to suspend the meeting now and resume it tomorrow morning at 11 o'clock. The agenda will be revised to reflect the private character of the meeting.

The meeting was suspended at 7.15 p.m.

0280

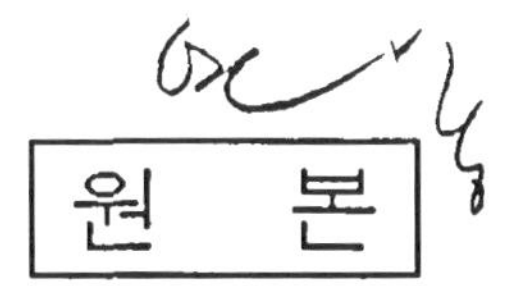

원 본

외 무 부

종 별 :

번 호 : UNW-0350 일 시 : 91 0214 2100

수 신 : 장 관(국연,중근동,기정)

발 신 : 주 유엔대사

제 목 : 안보리

1. 금 2.14. 표제 안보리 공식회의가 비공개리에 개최되었음.

쿠웨이트, 사우디, 카타르, 이락 및 영.중,루마니아등 13개 국가가 발언함.

2.쿠웨이트등 다국적군 소속 국가들 은 이락이 쿠웨이트로 부터의 철수등 걸프사태 관련 모든 안보리 결의를 조속히 이행 토록 모든 필요한 조치를 강구하여야 한다고 주장한 반면, 이락은 안보리 제반 결의는 불 법적인 조치이며, 이락에대한 공격은 이락을 파괴하고 중동지역내 미국 및 이스라엘의 패권을 강화 하기위한 음모의 결과라고 주장하고 이러한 국제적인 범죄행위를 조속히 종결 시키도록 필요한 조치를강구하여야 한다고 촉구함.

3.금일 주요국 발언요지는 아래와같음.

0.영국:다국적군의 군사행동은 안보리 결의의 테두리내에서 전개되고 있으며 이락의 군사력에 과도한 무력을 사용하는것이 아님.이락 대표는 이락이 무조건, 즉각 쿠웨이트에서 철수할것인지 분명한 태도를 밝히기 바람.

0.중국: 이락내 민간시설의 파괴, 민간인 사상에 대해 우려를 표명함.

모든 교전 당사국에게 전투행위가 확대되지 않도록 자제를촉구함.

평화적 해결을 위한 5개항 방안을 제시하고자함.즉 이락에의한 완전, 즉각 철수용의 표명, 관계 당사국들에 의한 평화적해 결의지 표명, 적대행위를 축소하기위한 7 모 교전 당사국의 자제, 중동 평화해결 방안일정작성,외군철수등임.

0.루마니아: 다국적군의 군사조치로 인하여 발생하고있는 이락내 비극적 사태에대한 궁극적 책임은 이락에있음. 이락에 대한 국제 법준수를 촉구함. 루마니아는 의료진및 화학전 오염 해소팀을사우디에 파견키로 결정하였음.

0.오지리: 안보리 결의는 이행되어야함.현사태하에서도 평화적 해결을위한 정치적 외교적 노력이 강화되어야함.

국기국 장관 차관 1차보 2차보 구주국 청와대 안기부 대책반

PAGE 1

91.02.15 11:39 CT

외신 1과 통제관

0281

4.표제건 토의를 위한 안보리는 추후 속개될예정임.끝

(대사 현홍주-국장)

PAGE 2

0282

원 본

외 무 부

종 별 : 지 급

번 호 : UNW-0354 일 시 : 91 0215 1900

수 신 : 장관(국연,중일,해기,기정)

발 신 : 주유엔대사

제 목 : 걸프사태(안보리)

연: UNW-0350 1. 금 2.15 오후 표제건 안보리(공식,비공개회의)가 속개되어 인도,프랑스,큐바일본 카나다 호주등 12개국의 발언을 청취함. 그일 회의에서 인도는 이락에 대한군사조치의 종결 또는 일시중지를 요청하였으며 큐바는 3개의 안보리 결의안 초안(상세하기참조)을 제시하였음.

2.금일 회의 종료후 안보리는 비공식협의회를 개최 금일 오전 주유엔 이락대표부 차석이 안보리 의장에게 전달한 2.15.자 이락혁명위 성명(조건부 철군 용의표명) 내용을 검토한것으로 알려짐.

3.금일 공식회의 에서의 주요국 발언요지

0.인도-금일 오전 이락측 성명에 비추어 사태의 평화적 해결을 촉진키 위해 대이락 군사조치의 종결또는 일시 중지를 제의함.아울러 유엔사무총장으로 하여금필요한 조치를 검토토록 안보리가 요청할것을 제의함.

0.프랑스-금일 이락측 성명은 안보리결의 660에 규정된 조건을 충족치 않음.현상황에서 안보리가 군사조치를 중지토록 하는것은 무의미함.

0.큐바-3개 안보리 결의안 초안을 제시함.

가.결의안(1) 요지

-이락에 대한 폭격의 즉각적인 중지

-사태의 평화적 해결을 위한 협상개시

나.결의안(2)요지

-유엔사무총장에 의한 자신의 1.15.자 대언론성명에 기초한 중재활동의 즉각적인재개

다.결의안(3)요지

-안보리내 모든 회원국으로 구성된 특별위원회 설치

국기국 장관 차관 1차보 중아국 정와대 안기부 공보처 대책반 정문국

PAGE 1 91.02.16 09:33 FA

외신 1과 통제관

0283

-동 위원회는 추가적인 파괴와 인명손실을 방지하기 위한 방안강구

-91.2.28까지 보고서를 안보리에 제출

0.일본-이락의 진정한 의도를 파악키 위해금일아침 이락제의를 신중히 연구하고있음.일본정부는 이락에 대해 철수를 계속 종용하고 있음.

0.카나다-이락사태이후 전후 처리문제는 해당지역 관련국들이 결정할 문제이나유엔이 국제적인 보장부여 가능

4.안보리 공식회의가 명 2.16(토) 11:00 속개될 예정임.

4.권참사관이 유엔사무국,타 대표부로 부터 입수한하기 자료를 별전 FAX 송부함.

1)큐바 결의안 초안

2)예멘 결의안 초안

3)91.1.15자 이락 혁명위 성명영문 요약문

4)상기 이락 성명에 대한 부시대통령의 코멘트.

첨부: UNW(F)-064

끝

(대사 현홍주-국장)

FEB 15 '91 18:41 KOREAN MISSION P.1

UNW-0664 10215 1900

(별첨1)

UNW-0354 첨부물

쿠바 결의안 초안

총5매

The Security Council,

Recalling its resolutions 660 (1990), 661 (1990), 662 (1990), 664 (1990), [6]65 (1990), 666 (1990), 667 (1990), 670 (1990), 674 (1990) and 678 (1990),

Guided by the Purposes and Principles of the United Nations, as embodied in [Ch]apter I of the Charter of the United Nations,

Mindful of the provisions of Article 29 of the Charter of the United [Na]tions, which states that "The Security Council may establish such subsidiary [or]gans as it deems necessary for the performance of its functions",

Acting on the basis of Rule 28 of the Provisional Rules of Procedure of the [Se]curity Council, which states that "The Security Council may appoint a [co]mmission or committee or rapporteur for a specified question",

Deeply concerned by the situation of war existing in the Gulf region, [en]dangering international peace and security, and determined to put a halt to [ho]stilities as soon as possible,

1. Decides to establish an ad hoc committee, composed of all members of the [Se]curity Council, to examine the present situation in the Gulf region and [po]ssible formulas for halting armed actions and for achieving a peaceful solution [o]f the conflict on the basis of the above mentioned resolutions of the Security [Co]uncil, thus avoiding further loss of life and destruction;

2. Decides also that the ad hoc committee mentioned in paragraph 1 above [wi]ll commence its work immediately after the adoption of the present resolution;

3. Decides further that the ad hoc committee will report back to the [Se]curity Council on its findings and concrete proposals not later than 20 [Fe]bruary 1991.

배부처	장관실	차관실	一차보	二차보	기획실	의전장	아주국	미주국	구주국	중아국	국기국	경제국	통상국	정문국	영교국	총무과	감사관	공보관	외연원	청와대	총리실	안기부	문공부	대책반
	/	/	/							/	/			/						/		/	/	/

5-1

0285

FEB 15 '91 18:42 KOREAN MISSION

(별첨2) Yemen

예멘작성 결의안 초안

The Security Council,

Deeply concerned about the state of war existing in the Gulf and, essentially about the loss of life and destruction of material property provoked by the massive bombings suffered by the Iraqi cities.

Commited to the restauration of the independance, sovereignty and territorial integrity of Kuwait,

Mindful of its primary responsibilities for the maintenance of international peace and security, as set out in Article 24 of the United Nations Charter,

Acting on the conviction that it is its duty to resort to all peaceful means for the resolution of international conflicts and differences in order to preserve international peace and security and "save succeeding generations from the scourge of war", as proclaimed in the Preamble to the United Nations Charter,

1. Demands that all bombings on Iraqi cities be immediately halted and requests that immediate negotiations geared at the peaceful resolution of the conflict without further resort to force be further intensified.

2. Requests further the ad hoc committee it has created by resolution ________ to immediately undertake the task of examining possible formulas for achieving a peaceful and just resolution to the conflict and inform the Council in the date foreseen;

3. Requests the Secretary General to renew his good offices and mediation efforts without delay, on the basis of his Press Statement of 15 January 1991 and report back to the Council as soon as possible;

4. Decides to remain seized with the matter.

☆☆☆☆☆

5-2

0286

(별첨3) '91.1.15자 "이라크 혁명위" 성명 요약

FBIS 064FEB15 (SEC 077FEB15)
UNCLAS 5K

Iraq: Government Announcement on 'Withdrawal' (Take 1 of 2)

NC1502124691 Baghdad Domestic Service in Arabic 1130 GMT 15 Feb 91

[Excerpt] [passage omitted] O dear Iraqis, O honest Arabs, O Muslims who truly believe in Islam, O honest and free men of the world: Proceeding from this firm and right feeling and this assessment of the nature of the showdown, and in order to rob the the evil U.S.-Zionist-Atlantic alliance of the opportunity to achieve their premeditated goals; and in appreciation of the Soviet initiative conveyed by the envoy of the Soviet leadership; and in compliance with the principles outlined in leader President Saddam Husayn's initiative on 12 August 1990, the Revolution Command Council has decided to declare the following:

First: Iraq's readiness to deal with Security Council resolution No. 660 of 1990 with the aim of reaching an honorable and acceptable political solution, including withdrawal. The first step that is required to be implemented as a pledge by Iraq regarding withdrawal will be linked to the following:

a. A total and comprehensive cease-fire on land, air, and sea.

b. For the Security Council to decide to abolish from the outset resolutions 661, 662, 664, 665, 666, 667, 669, 670, 674, 677, and 678 and all the effects resulting from all of them, and to abolish all resolutions and measures of boycott and embargo, as well as the other negative resolutions and measures that were adopted by certain countries against Iraq unilaterally or collectively before 2 August 1990, which were the real reasons for the Gulf crisis, so that things may return to normal as if nothing had happened. Iraq should not receive any negative effects for any reasons.

c. For the United States and the other countries participating in the aggression, and all the countries that sent their forces from the region to withdraw all the forces, weapons and equipment which they have brought to the Middle East region before and after 2 August 1990, whether in land, seas, oceans, or gulfs, including the weapons and equipment that certain countries provided to Israel under the pretext of the crisis in the Gulf, provided that these forces, weapons, and equipment are withdrawn during a period not exceeding one month from the date of the cease-fire.

(more)

15 FEB 1254z or

5-3

0287

NC1506125491

[Excerpt] D. Israel must withdraw from Palestine and the Arab territories it is occupying in the Golan and southern Lebanon in implementation of the UN Security Council [UNSC] and the UN General Assembly resolutions. In case Israel fails to do this, the UNSC should then enforce against Israel the same resolutions it passed against Iraq.

E. Iraq's historical rights on land and at sea should be guaranteed in full in any peaceful solution.

F. The political arrangement to be agreed upon should proceed from the people's will and in accordance with a genuine democratic practice and not on the basis of the rights acquired by the Al Sabah family. Accordingly, the nationalist and Islamic forces should primarily participate in the political arrangement to be agreed upon.

Second, the countries that have participated in the aggression and in financing the aggression undertake to reconstruct what the aggression has destroyed in Iraq in accordance with the best specifications regarding all the enterprises and installations that were targeted by the aggression and at their expense. Iraq should not incur any financial expenses in this regard.

Third, all the debts of Iraq and countries of the region--which were harmed by the aggression and which did not take part in the aggression, either directly or indirectly--to the Gulf countries and to the foreign countries that took part in the aggression should be written off. Besides, relations between the rich nations and poor nations in the region and the world should be based on justice and fairness in such a way that puts the rich nations before clear commitments regarding the realization of development in poor nations, and thus removes their economic sufferings. This should be based on the saying that the poor have a share to claim in the wealth of the rich. Moreover, the duplicitous approach pursued in handling the issues of peoples and nations should be halted, whether this approach is being pursued by the UNSC or by this or that country.

Fourth, the Gulf states, including Iran, should be given the task of freely drawing up security arrangements in the region and of organizing relations among them without any foreign interference.

Fifth, to declare the Arabian Gulf region a zone free of foreign military bases and from any form of foreign military presence. Everybody must undertake to observe this.

This is our argument, which we declare before the world, clear and shining against the traitors and their imperialist masters.

Our basic source of confidence, in addition to our reliance on the one and only God, will remain to be our great Iraqi people, our valiant and struggling Armed Forces, and those who believe in the path that we have chosen in fighting oppression and the oppressors. Victory will certainly be realized against the oppressors in the coming days, as it had been certain in past times. God is with us. May the despicable be damned.

[Signed] The Revolution Command Council

[Dated] 29 Rajab 1411 Hegira, corresponding to 15 February 1991.

(endall)
15 Feb 1313z mp

5-4

0288

열청취)

PRESIDENT BUSH

February 15, 1991

"When I first heard that statement, I must say I was happy that Saddam Hussein seemed to realize that he must now withdraw, unconditionally, from Kuwait in keeping with the relevant United Nations resolutions. Regrettably, the Iraq statement now appears to be a cruel hoax, dashing the hopes of the people in Iraq, and indeed around the world.

"It seems that there was an immediate celebratory atmosphere in Baghdad after this statement, and this reflects, I think, the Iraqi peoples' desire to see the war end -- a war the people of Iraq never sought.

"Not only was the Iraq statement full of unacceptable, old conditions, but Saddam Hussein has added several new conditions. We've been in touch with members of the coalition, and they recognize that there is nothing new here, with the possible exception of recognizing for the first time that Iraq must leave Kuwait.

"Let me state once again they must withdraw without condition; there must be full implementation of all the Security Council resolutions, and there will be no linkage to other problems in the area, and the legitimate rulers of Kuwait must be returned to Kuwait. Until a massive withdrawal begins with those Iraqi troops visibly leaving Kuwait, the Coalition forces, acting under United Nations resolution 678, will continue their efforts to force compliance with all the resolutions of the United Nations.

"But there's another way for the bloodshed to stop, and that is for the Iraqi military and the Iraqi people to take matters into their own hands, to force Saddam Hussein the dictator, to step aside and to comply with the United Nations resolutions and then rejoin the family of peace-loving nations.

"We have no argument with the people of Iraq. Our differences are with Iraq's brutal dictator. And the war, let me just assure you all, is going on schedule. Of course, all of us want to see the war ended, soon, and with a limited loss of life. And it can, if Saddam Hussein would comply unconditionally with these UN resolutions, and do now what he should have done long, long ago.

"So I'm sorry that, after analysis and reading the statements out of Baghdad in their entirety, there is nothing new here. It is a hoax. There are new demands added, and I feel very sorry for the people in Iraq, and I feel sorry for the families in this Country who probably felt as I did this morning when they heard the television that maybe we had a shot for peace today. But that's not the case, and we will continue. We will pursue our objectives with honor, decency, and we will not fail."

5-5

0289

관리번호	91-[illegible]

원 본

외 무 부

종 별 : 지 급

번 호 : UNW-0355 일 시 : 91 0215 1930

수 신 : 장관(중일,기정)

발 신 : 주 유엔 대사

제 목 : 이라크 쿠웨이트 철수

대:WUN-0309

1. 대호 이라크의 쿠웨이트 철수발표에 대해 미국을 비롯한 COALITION 측은이를 일축하면서 예정된 군사행동을 계속한다는 반응을 보이고 있는반면, 예멘,큐바등 친이락 입장국가들은 이라크가 안보리결의 660 호에 따라 쿠웨이트 철수를 천명하고 있다는점을 강조하면서 이는 걸프사태 해결을 위한 하나의 중요한진전인만큼 이를 계기로 걸프사태의 평화적 해결을 위한 진지한 노력이 있어야한다는 반응을 보임.

2. 한편 다수국가들은 이라크가 걸프전 발발이후 처음으로 쿠웨이트 철군의사를 밝힌점에 주목하면서도 서방측이 수락할수 있는 조건을 내세우고 있어 이라크의 진의를 좀더 확실히 파악해야 할 필요가 있으므로 앞으로 수일간 관련 진전상황을 지켜 보아야 할것이라는 견해를 표명하고있음.

3. 또다른 견해는 이라크의 금번 발표는 이라크가 그간의 MNF 의 대 쿠웨이트 및 이라크 공격으로 이제 더이상 이에 저항하기 어려운 상황에 처해 쿠웨이트로 부터 철수하지 않을수 없는 상황에 이르게 된 것으로 보면서 부대조건을 제시하고는 있으나 이는 대내외적인 철군 명분용에 불과함으로 결국은 적절한 방법으로 동 조건들을 완화해 나갈것이라고 함.

4. 한편, 금 2.15. 속개된 안보리 비공개회의에서 인도 대표는 이라크의 성명과관련, 걸프사태 해결을 위한 외교적 노력이 필요한 시점에 왔다고 말하면서 적대행위의 즉각중지와 유엔사무총장의 중재역할등을 제안하였으며 큐바대표는 상기 인도 입장을 지지하면서 적대행위 즉각중지, 사무총장의 중재역할및 걸프사태해결을 위한 AD HOC COMMITTEE 구성에 관한 3 개결의안을 안보리에 제출하였음.끝

(대사 현홍주-국장)

예고:91.6.30 일반

중아국	장관	차관	1차보	2차보	정문국	청와대	총리실	안기부
미주국								

PAGE 1

91.02.16 09:52

외신 2과 통제관 BW

0290

원 본

외 무 부

종 별 :

번 호 : UNW-0357 일 시 : 91 0216 2030

수 신 : 장관 (국연,중근동,해기,기정)

발 신 : 주 유엔대사

제 목 : 걸프사태 (안보리)

연: UNW-0350 (1), 0354(2)

1. 2.16.(토) 11:30-14:30간 안보리 (공식, 비공개회의)가 속개되어 아래 14개국의 발언을 청취하였음.

-파키스탄, 수단, 멕시코, 터키, 스웨덴, 사우디, 쿠웨이트, 이락, 영국, 미국,소련, 오지리, 예멘, 짐바브웨, 사이프러스 (답변권)

2.금일 발언국중 대부분이 2.15.자 이락혁명위 성명 (2.15.자 안보리문서 S/22229 로 금일 배포, 별첨 1)에 대한 입장을 표명한바, 영국, 미국, 사우디, 쿠웨이트, 터키 등 다국적군 소속 국가들은 금번 제안이 이락의 쿠웨이트로 부터의 무조건 즉각철수를 규정한 안보리 결의 660호에 반하여 여러가지 조건을 달고 있음을 지적하면서 평화적 해결방안 모색에 앞서 이락의 선철수를 강조한 반면, 이락, 수단, 파키스탄, 예멘, 짐바브웨 등은 동제안을 진지하게 검토할것을 요청하면서 외교적 해결을 모색할것을 역설함.

3.또한 다수국가들이 다국적군의 대 이락 공습으로 민간인 피해가 야기된것에 대하여 유감을 표명한바, 이락은 이와관련 다국적군의 제네바협약 위반 사실을 강조하였으며 반면 쿠웨이트 및 미국은 피점령 쿠웨이트내 민간인들의 피해 참상에 대하여 이락, 안보리 및 유엔회원국 들의 주의를 환기시켰음.

4.연호(2) 쿠바가 제출한 3개 결의안이 금일 안보리 문서로 배포된바 (첨부 2,3,4), 수단의 지지발언과 영국의 반대 발언이 있었음.

5.주요국 발언요지는 아래와 같음.

가.파키스탄

0파키스탄 수상의 6개항 제안설명

-안보리 결의 실행에 대한 이락의 분명한 언질이 있는대로 휴전실시, 모든

국기국 장관 차관 1차보 2차보 미주국 중아국 정문국 청와대
총리실 안기부 공보처 대책반

PAGE 1

91.02.18 06:13 DA
외신 1과 통제관

0291

외군철수, 이슬람 국가회의 개최, 범 아랍군 배치, 팔레스타인 문제등 안보리 기타 결의안 이행, 성지보호

나.수단

0즉각적이고 완전한 휴전실시

0이락 혁명위 성명에 제시된 평화적 해결방안 경청 요망

0안보리 결의안 범위를 초과한 무차별 공격 비난

다.스웨덴

0평화유지군 파견문제, 팔레스타인 문제, 군비통제 문제등 전후 중동지역 안보강화 대책강구 필요

라.사우디

0이락 혁명위 성명은 평화적 해결에 불길한 징조

-각종 조건 제시, 쿠웨이트 라는 용어조차 사용안함.

마.쿠웨이트

0 이락 성명은 기만책, 지연전술, 유엔 결의안 의무 회피 책략

0안보리결의 660호에 따라 이락군 철수후 모든 현안문제를 협상으로 해결 용의

바.이락

0이락은 전쟁포로에 관한 제네바 협약 준수, 반면 다국적군의 민간인에 대한 무차별 공격은 제네바협약 위반

0화학무기를 사용할 의도 없으나, 다국적군이 대량 파괴무기를 사용하거나 이에상응하는 대규모 공중포격 계속시 필요한 대응수단 강구할 권리를 유보함.

0비군사용 핵시설 공격 비난, 이로인한 방사능 오염 방지조치 강구 필요

0이락 외상 방쏘 회담 결과 기대

사.영국

0이락의 쿠웨이트 철수는 무조건적 이어야하며 NON- NEGOTIABLE ITEM 임

0이락의 제네바협약 준수여부 확인위해 ICRC 입국활동 허용 요망 (포로 처우현황 조사등)

0쿠바제출 결의안중 특별위원회 설치 및 사무총장 중재 재개 결의안은 불필요,이락공습중단 결의안은 수락 불가함.

아.미국

0이락의 각종 철수조건 제시는 실망스러움. (DISCOURAGING)

PAGE 2

0292

0 이락의 비타협적 태도에 비추어 군사적 및 외교적 수단등 모든 가용한 압력방안 사용 계속필요

0이락 민간인 희생 발생은 유감, 민간인 희생 극소화 노력 예정

0전후 안보장치 강구에 있어 중동국가들의 주도적 역할 지원

0전후 경제복구 노력에 적극 참여 용의

자.소련

0이락 외상의 방쏘 회담에 희망을 갖고있음.

0이락의 모든 안보리 결의안 준수 필요 입장 불변

6.상기 안보리 공식 비공개 회의 종료후 안보리는 비공식 협의를 개최 하였으며 2.19(화) 비공개 회의를 속개할 예정임.

7.금일 안보리 회의 개최 직전 VORONTSOV 소련대사는 이락 혁명위 성명에 대한소련 입장을 묻는 기자들의 질문에 대해 금번 제안중 일부는 흥미있으나 불필요한것도 있다고 하면서 소련으로서는 이를 신중히 검토할것 이라고 언급함.

끝

(대사 현홍주-국장)

FAX : UNW(F)-065

FEB 17 '91 08:20 KOREAN MISSION P.1

UNITED NATIONS UNW(F)-065 10216 2030 [첨부 1] S

Security Council 첨부물 UNW-0357 총 11매

Distr.
GENERAL

S/22229
15 February 1991
ENGLISH
ORIGINAL: ARABIC

NOTE VERBALE DATED 15 FEBRUARY 1991 FROM THE PERMANENT MISSION OF IRAQ TO THE UNITED NATIONS ADDRESSED TO THE PRESIDENT OF THE SECURITY COUNCIL

The Permanent Mission of the Republic of Iraq to the United Nations presents its compliments to the President of the Security Council and has the honour to transmit to him herewith the text of the decision announced by the Revolution Command Council of the Republic of Iraq on 15 February 1991. The Permanent Mission would be grateful if you would have this letter and its annex distributed as a document of the Security Council.

91-04935 2147g (E) /...

11-1

0294

In the name of God, the Merciful, the Compassionate,

Declaration issued by the Revolution Command Council

O, glorious Iraqi people,

Noble Arabs,

Muslims, true believers in Islam,

Free and noble people of the world,

Ever since the United States, the Zionists and America's Western colonialist allies have realized that a Power was coming into being in an Arab Muslim country, Iraq, a Power capable of counterbalancing the Zionist hegemony supported by imperialism in the region, a free and noble Power, determined with sincerity and self-denial to confront the aggression and the Zionist ambitions and to reject imperialist domination of the region, the United States, the Zionists and all the colonialist forces full of hatred for the Arabs and the Muslims have begun to take measures and decisions and to launch campaigns of intrigue and incitement against Iraq in order to prevent the formation and growth of this Power, to isolate, contain and punish Iraq because it had, with faith, determination and competence, overstepped the bounds drawn for it by the United States, the Zionists and the colonialist forces of the countries of the region.

In 1988 and 1989 there were constant attacks in the press and media, and on the part of officials in the United States and other colonialist countries, paving the way for the achievement of these wicked aims.

In 1990 these attacks escalated at a feverish and accelerating pace and on an ever-widening scale. The aim was patently obvious to us and to all conscious Arabs and true Muslims, to all free and noble people who believe in freedom and justice in the world. The aim was to prepare for the destruction of this rising Power and to restore predominance in the region to the United States, Zionists and the colonial Powers, this predominance which had for decades continued to prevent the Arabs from recovering their rights and their usurped and occupied territories in Palestine, the Golan and Lebanon, just as it had prevented the Arab nation from achieving its hopes of advancement, progress and justice in order that it might occupy the natural position it deserves in the world by reason of its glorious history and great contribution to human civilization.

During the first months of 1990 these attacks intensified and broadened and acquired a hysterical character. They began to urge daily that Iraq should be attacked and its leadership liquidated, and that it should be deprived of the means of advancement and progress. The United States, together with other colonialist countries, adopted a series of unfair decisions and measures prohibiting the export of everything which might contribute to the development of Iraq, and to its scientific and industrial advancement. These decisions comprised an effective economic boycott, one of the effects of which was the cancellation of foodstuff

/...

11 - 2

0295

contracts in March 1990. It was also clear that the United States was making preparations, in coordination with the Zionist entity, to strike at scientific and industrial facilities and sites and to liquidate the faithful national leadership of Iraq. When the United States discovered that this scheme, which depended to a large extent on the Zionist military capability, was insufficient to achieve its evil objectives, it recruited to the conspiracy its agents and protégés among the corrupt and imperious rulers in the region, the enemies of God.

The role of the latter was to weaken and exhaust the economy of Iraq, and bring it to the brink of economic collapse. At the same time the United States began to reinforce the network of the colonialist alliance in order to set up an American-NATO political and military coalition with the aim of attacking Iraq and gaining control of the region, since it had been afforded the opportunity to do so following the withdrawal of the Soviet Union from world affairs in order to pursue internal matters.

Iraqis,

Arabs,

Muslims,

Free and noble people of the world,

The essence and purpose of the events of 2 August 1990 were not as portrayed by American and colonialist propaganda nor as recounted by the treacherous rulers and followers of America. They constituted a patriotic, national, Islamic uprising against the conspiracy and against the imperious, an uprising against oppression and decadence, against corruption and the imperialist, Zionist and colonialist hegemony over the region, against the imperious rulers, whose role had been revealed in the American Zionist conspiracy. This is why the imperialist Zionist NATO alliance revealed its true aims and intentions from the very first hours of those events. It massed its armies and forces and organized the most evil campaign of delusion, lying and deception the world has witnessed in recent times. This evil, tyrannical imperialist, Zionist, NATO alliance coerced the United Nations into issuing against Iraq, with unparalleled rapidity, a series of iniquitous and unprecedented resolutions. At the same time, this Organization has for decades been incapable of satisfying the simplest claims of the Arab nation and of preserving the simplest rights of the Arabs in Palestine, despite the clarity of the Arab right and the violence of the tragedy endured by the heroic people of Palestine and from which other Arabs suffer, including the oppressed people of Lebanon.

This iniquitous alliance imposed its will on the world, pursued methods of intimidation, blackmail and bribery and employed all the means of viciousness, falsehood and deception in the arsenal of the imperialists, Zionists and forces of colonialism in order to prepare the way for aggression against Iraq.

/...

11-3

0296

O glorious Iraqis,

O noble Arabs,

O believing Muslims,

O those in the world who are noble and honourable,

The aggression that has befallen the courageous, proud, combatant, believing and steadfast country of Iraq, has no counterpart in history. In the entire history of mankind, there is no record of the likes of such a coalition, in which there participated the United States, two major Powers and many other States, som 30 in number, against combatant, courageous, steadfast Iraq, whose population doe not exceed 18 million. It is indeed an evil, iniquitous, malicious and disbelieving alliance against the stronghold of faith and principle, an alliance against the seat of freedom and the call for justice and fairness. For an entire month, the United States and its allies together with the Zionist entity, which h participated in the aggression from the outset, have been launching savage and devastating attacks against the people of Iraq, against its economic, scientific, cultural and services-related assets and its religious centres and against the country's sites of ancient civilization. History has not seen its like for intensity of fire nor means of slaughter and destruction, launched in the name of the United Nations, a fallacious international legitimacy and the new world order that they intend will be one of United States and NATO hegemony over the world.

The United States and the parties to the evil coalition have delivered, with aircraft that fire their missiles from afar and with long-range missiles, enormous quantities of bombs and explosives against women, children and elderly persons in all the towns and villages of Iraq and even the nomadic Bedouin of the desert. They have struck, in a premeditated manner, mosques, churches, schools, hospitals, civilian factories, bridges and major highways, telephone exchanges, electricity and water installations, irrigation dams, cultural centres and archaeological landmarks in the country. They have struck targets that have no connection of any kind whatever with the military effort or with the arena of the military clash of which they have spoken. The most recent such crime was that vile and heinous crim committed in the deliberate bombing of a civilian shelter, which killed and incinerated hundreds of women, children and elderly persons. The objective of thi brutal act of aggression was abundantly clear, and it was to advance the process o destruction that was their intention, and to punish the proud, noble and combatant people of Iraq because it had chosen the way of freedom, independence and honour and rejected humiliation, degradation and subjection to the will of colonialism an zionism.

The United States and its allies have launched a vile and cowardly war against a courageous and believing people. The history and destiny of peoples and nations are not determined by the material possessions of States and ruling regimes. Throughout history, many a strong and wealthy empire has fallen because it adopted the way of shame, cowardice, oppression and dissoluteness. This is the destiny of iniquitous America and its vile regimes, and it is the destiny of zionism and all the forces of colonialism, God willing. Iraq has triumphed in this confrontation. It has triumphed because it has remained steadfast, courageous, believing, noble,

/...

11-4

0297

and strong-willed. It has triumphed because it has maintained principles and spiritual values derived from its true religion and its centuries-old heritage. Its losses in terms of material assets in this battle, despite their enormity, are of slight importance when set against its preservation of its resolute spirit, its faith deeply rooted in principle and its strong determination to pursue the road of resurgence and progress.

O noble Iraqis,

O honourable Arabs,

O Muslims ... who truly believe in Islam,

O those in the world who are noble and perceptive,

On the basis of this strongly entrenched feeling and of this assessment of the character of the conflict, in order to deprive the vicious United States, Zionist and NATO alliance of the opportunity to achieve its planned destructive goals, in appreciation of the initiative of the Soviet Union conveyed by the envoy of the Soviet leadership, and in keeping with the principles set forth in the initiative of President Saddam Hussein, announced on 12 August 1990, the Revolution Command Council has decided to announce the following:

I. Iraq's readiness to deal on the basis of Security Council resolution 660 (1990) with a view to reaching an honourable and acceptable political solution, including withdrawal. The first step that must be taken, as an undertaking on Iraq's part with regard to the matter of withdrawal, is linked with the following:

(a) A complete and comprehensive cease-fire on land, at sea and in the air;

(b) That the Security Council should, from the outset, decide to annul its resolutions 661, 662, 664, 665, 666, 667, 669, 670, 674, 677 and 678 and all the consequences to which they give rise. Similarly, the annulment of all decisions and measures of boycott and embargo and the other adverse decisions and measures adopted by certain States against Iraq, jointly and severally, prior to 2 August 1990, and which were the true cause of the Gulf crisis, so that matters may be restored to their normal status as if nothing had happened and without any adverse consequences for Iraq for any reason whatever;

(c) The United States, the other States participating in the aggression and all States that have dispatched forces to the region shall withdraw from the Middle East region and the Arabian Gulf region all the forces, armaments and matériel that they introduced before and after 2 August 1990, whether they are on land, at sea, in the oceans or in the gulfs, including the weapons and matériel provided by certain States to Israel on the pretext of the crisis in the Gulf, it being understood that the withdrawal of such forces, armaments and matériel shall take place within a period not to exceed one month from the date of the cease-fire;

(d) That Israel should withdraw from Palestine and from the Arab territories it is occupying in the Golan and in Lebanon, in implementation of the resolutions of the Security Council and the General Assembly of the United Nations. In the

/...

11-5

0298

event that it should refuse to do so, the Security Council shall apply against Israel the same resolutions that it adopted against Iraq;

(e) The guarantee of Iraq's full and undiminished historical rights on land and at sea in any political solution;

(f) The political arrangement to be agreed upon shall be based on the will of the people in accordance with genuine democratic practice and not on the acquired privileges of the House of Al Sabah. On this basis, national and Islamic forces must participate in a fundamental manner in the political arrangement to be agreed upon.

II. Those States that have participated in the aggression and in financing it shall undertake to rebuild that which the aggression has destroyed in Iraq, in accordance with the highest specifications for each of the activities, projects and installations targeted by the aggression, at their own expense and without Iraq's incurring any financial outlays.

III. Cancellation of all the debts incurred by Iraq, as well as by the States of the region damaged by the aggression which have not participated in it either directly or indirectly, to the Gulf States and those foreign States which participated in the aggression; the establishment of relations between the poor and wealthy States of the region and of the world based on justice and fairness so as to confront the wealthy countries with unequivocal obligations for the achievement of development in the poor countries and for the elimination of their economic sufferings, on the basis of the principle that the poor have a right to the resources of the wealthy; and a halt to the use of double standards in dealing with issues affecting peoples and nations, whether on the part of the Security Council or on the part of one State or another.

IV. To the States of the Gulf, including Iran, shall be left the freedom and the duty to establish security arrangements in the region and to organize relations among themselves without any external interference.

V. The declaration of the Arabian Gulf region as a zone free of foreign military bases and of any form of foreign military presence; and universal commitment to that effect. This is our case, and we have announced it to the world. We have set it forth clearly and plainly to the treacherous and perfidious and their imperialist masters. Our fundamental assurance, having placed our trust in the One and Only God, is in our mighty Iraqi people, in its combatant and valiant armed forces, and in those who have believed in the road that we are taking in resisting oppression and the oppressors. In the coming days, victory over the oppressors shall be assured, just as it was assured in former days. God is most great. May the infamous be driven out.

Revolution Command Council

29 Rajab A.H. 1411
15 February 1991

11-6

0299

(첨부 2)

UNITED
NATIONS

Security Council

Distr.
GENERAL

S/22231
15 February 1991
ENGLISH
ORIGINAL: SPANISH

Cuba: draft resolution

The Security Council,

Recalling its resolutions 660 (1990), 661 (1990), 662 (1990), 664 (1990), 665 (1990), 666 (1990), 667 (1990), 669 (1990), 670 (1990), 674 (1990), 677 (1990) and 678 (1990),

Guided by the purposes and principles of the United Nations, as set out in Chapter I of the Charter of the United Nations,

Mindful of the provisions of Article 29 of the Charter of the United Nations, which provides that "the Security Council may establish such subsidiary organs as it deems necessary for the performance of its functions",

Acting in accordance with Rule 28 of the Provisional Rules of Procedure of the Security Council, which states that "the Security Council may appoint a commission or committee or a rapporteur for a specified question",

Deeply concerned by the war situation existing in the Gulf region, which endangers international peace and security, and determined to put an end to the hostilities as soon as possible,

1. Decides to establish an Ad Hoc Committee, composed of all members of the Security Council, to examine the situation currently prevailing in the Gulf region and consider possible formulas for halting armed actions and achieving a peaceful settlement of the conflict on the basis of the above-mentioned resolutions of the Security Council, thus avoiding further loss of life and destruction;

2. Decides also that the Ad Hoc Committee referred to in paragraph 1 shall begin its work immediately after the adoption of the present resolution;

3. Decides further that the Ad Hoc Committee shall report back to the Security Council on its findings and on any specific proposals which may have been made not later than 28 February 1991.

91-05025 3133Z (E)

11-7

0300

(첨부 3)

UNITED NATIONS

Security Council

Distr.
GENERAL

S/22232
15 February 1991
ENGLISH
ORIGINAL: SPANISH

Cuba: draft resolution

The Security Council,

Deeply concerned by the state of war existing in the Gulf and, above all, by the losses of human life and the destruction of material property caused by the mass bombings suffered by the cities of Iraq,

Committed to restoring the independence, sovereignty and territorial integrity of Kuwait,

Considering its primary responsibility for the maintenance of international peace and security, as established in Article 24 of the Charter of the United Nations,

Convinced that it is its duty to use all peaceful means for the settlement of international conflicts and differences in order to maintain international peace and security and "save succeeding generations from the scourge of war", as proclaimed in the Preamble to the Charter of the United Nations,

1. Demands that the bombings of the cities of Iraq be immediately halted and requests that the negotiations for seeking a peaceful resolution of the conflict be immediately intensified without further resort to force;

2. Decides to remain seized of the matter.

91-05031 3132Z (E)

11-8

0301

(청부 4)

UNITED NATIONS

Security Council

Distr.
GENERAL

S/22233
15 February 1991
ENGLISH
ORIGINAL: SPANISH

Cuba: draft resolution

The Security Council,

Reaffirming the need to take steps with a view to reaching a peaceful solution to the present situation in the Gulf,

Committed to restoring the independence, sovereignty and territorial integrity of Kuwait and to avoiding further losses of life and material property,

Considering the role which the Secretary-General has played in the elimination and avoidance of situations of conflict and the role he has to play in achieving a peaceful solution to the situation of war prevailing in the Gulf,

Considering also the efforts which the Secretary-General made to that end before hostilities erupted on 16 January 1991,

1. *Requests* the Secretary-General to renew his good offices and mediation efforts without delay, on the basis of his statement to the press of 15 January 1991, and to report back to the Council as soon as possible;

2. *Decides* to remain seized of the matter.

91-05037 3131Z (E)

11-9

0302

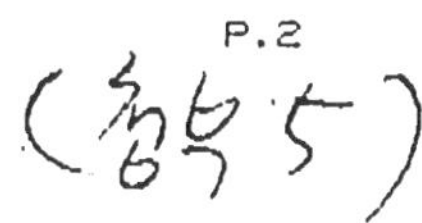

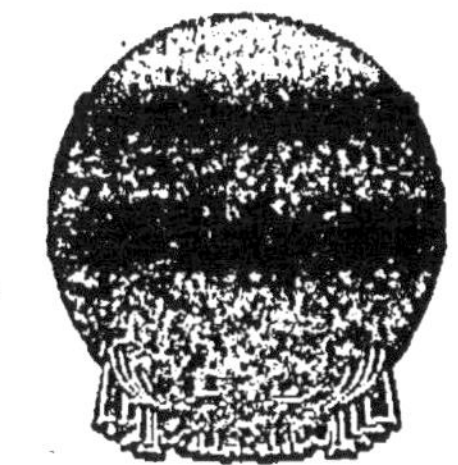

PEOPLE'S REPUBLIC OF CHINA

MISSION TO THE UNITED NATIONS

155 WEST 66th STREET, NEW YORK, N.Y. 10023

PRESS RELEASE

No.15
16 Feb. 1991

ANSWER BY SPOKESMAN OF CHINESE FOREIGN MINISTRY

February 16, 1991

Question: What is your comment on the conditional withdrawal of troops from Kuwait as announced by Iraq?

Answer: On February 15, Iraq announced that it would accept, with certain conditions, Security Council resolution 660 calling for withdrawal of Iraqi troops from Kuwait. This is the first time that Iraq has indicated a willingness to withdraw its troops from Kuwait which represents a positive step towards a political settlement of the Gulf conflict. It is our hope that Iraq's indication of troop withdrawal will be accompanied by specific measures and will be translated into action.

The Chinese government has always advocated that the Gulf crisis be resolved through political and diplomatic channels within the framework of the relevant U.N. Security Council resolutions. Right now, the Gulf war is at a critical moment, with its escalation and extension imminent. We strongly call on all the parties concerned to exercise maximum restraint, take steps to lower the intensity of hostilities and demonstrate a willingness for a peaceful settlement so as to help create conditions for the efforts of the international community to seek a peaceful settlement.

****

11-10

0303

(참부 6)

PEOPLE'S REPUBLIC OF CHINA

MISSION TO THE UNITED NATIONS

155 WEST 66th STREET, NEW YORK, N.Y. 10023

PRESS RELEASE

No. 14
15 Feb. 1991

ANSWERS BY SPOKESMAN OF CHINESE FOREIGN MINISTRY

1. Question: What is your comment on the death of 400 and more civilians in a air raid shelter in Baghdad as a result of bombing on 13 February?

Answer: The Gulf war is going on for nearly a month, causing heavy losses of life and property of many civilians. One of air raid shelters in Baghdad was bombed on 13 February, causing death of more than 400 innocent civilians, including many women and children. We hereby express our deep regret and anxiety. This incident further proves the urgency of a political solution to the Gulf conflict. If the war continues and extends, it will surely cause even more tragedies of great casualties. We once again call on all the warring parties to exercise maximum restraint to prevent the war from extending and escalating, and take steps to lower the intensity of hostilities so as to help create conditions for the efforts of the international community to seek a peaceful solution to the Gulf conflict.

2. Question: What is your comment on the failure to reach agreement on the Gulf crisis by the foreign minister meeting of the Non-Aligned countries held in Belgrade?

Answer: The foreign minister consultation of the Non-Aligned countries held in Belgrade decided to send missions to Baghdad, Washington and other places in a continued search for ways to resolve the Gulf conflict peacefully. The Chinese government welcomes this decision and holds that the peace efforts made by the Non-Aligned Movement are an important part of the peace efforts by the international community. We sincerely hope that these efforts will be successful.

****

11-11

0304

외 무 부

종 별 :

번 호 : UNW-0388 일 시 : 91 0220 2230

수 신 : 장 관(중일,국연,기정)

발 신 : 주 유엔 대사

제 목 : 걸프사태

1.소련의 최근 중재노력과 관련하여 주유엔 소련대사가 유엔 사무총장에게 송부한 2.19자 서한이 동일자 안보리 문서로 (S/22241) 금 2.20배포되었음.

2.상기 서한은 소련의 중재안이 안보리관련 결의안 준수를 기초로하고 있으며, 핵심요소가 이락군의 신속한 철수개시를 확보하는 것이라고 설명하고있음.동 텍스트는 별전 FAX송부함.끝

첨부:상기 FAX:UNW(F)-069

끝

(대사 현홍주-국장)

중아국 1차보 국기국 정문국 안기부

PAGE 1

91.02.21 13:18 WG

외신 1과 통제관

0305

-UNW_FEB 20 '91 22:00 KOREAN MISSION P.1

UNW(F)-069 10220 2730 (중일. 국연. 기정) 총104

UNITED NATIONS

S

Security Council

Distr.
GENERAL

S/22241
19 February 1991
ENGLISH
ORIGINAL: RUSSIAN

LETTER DATED 19 FEBRUARY 1991 FROM THE PERMANENT REPRESENTATIVE OF THE UNION OF SOVIET SOCIALIST REPUBLICS TO THE UNITED NATIONS ADDRESSED TO THE SECRETARY-GENERAL

I have the honour to request you to have circulated as a document of the Security Council of the United Nations the following information about the Soviet-Iraqi talks held in Moscow on 18 February 1991.

"During the talks with the personal representative of the President of Iraq, the Soviet side proceeded from the assumption that the current spiralling crisis in the Persian Gulf called for immediate and resolute measures to avoid further escalation of the conflict, to save thousands of lives, and to prevent the threat of disruption of the ecological balance of the whole region.

In the course of a prolonged and substantive exchange of views on the situation in the military-operations theatre and on the whole range of issues that brought about those operations, President Gorbachev proposed a plan of specific measures.

This plan is predicated on the necessity of strictly abiding by the mandate set forth in the resolutions of the Security Council regarding the Gulf crisis. The key element of the plan consists in securing a rapid start of a withdrawal of the Iraqi forces from Kuwait, which would make it possible to put an immediate end to the bloodshed.

We hope that our proposals will be considered in a most serious manner. We are now awaiting a reaction from Baghdad, which we expect very soon. On the basis of that reaction, a substantive discussion of practical measures would be possible.

The current situation calls for a cautious, responsible approach. This is no time for loud and spectacular initiatives, but for a serious diplomatic process. The effectiveness of such a process will determine the prospects for a rapid movement towards political settlement on the basis of the decisions of the Security Council, with due regard for the important role of that body in maintaining international peace and security."

(*Signed*) Y. VORONTSOV

91-05331 2309b (E)

1-1

0306

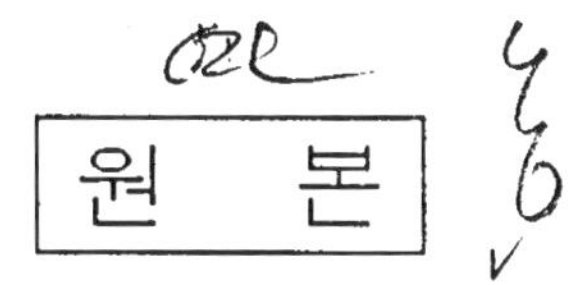

외 무 부

종 별 :

번 호 : UNW-0422 일 시 : 91 0222 1630

수 신 : 장 관 (국연,중동,기정)

발 신 : 주 유엔 대사

제 목 : 걸프사태

2.21. 오전 유엔사무총장이 소련의 종전 제안관련 기자질문에 대해 답변한 내용을 별첨송부함. 끝

(대사 현홍주-국장)

첨부: FAX (UNW(F)-074)

국기국	장관	차관	1차보	2차보	중아국	정문국	청와대	종리실
안기부								

PAGE 1

91.02.23 09:23 WG

외신 1과 통제관

0307

UNW(F)-074 10222 1630 첨부 UNW-0422 총2매 (국연, 중동 기자)

Remarks of the Secretary-General upon entering the Secretariat building at approximately 9:45 a.m. on Friday 22 February 1991.

Q. Now that the Soviet plan is public, could you tell us what you think of it?

S-G First of all, I think we have to express gratitude to the Soviet Union for having made such an important effort. It is a plan which deserves very serious consideration. There are some points which are extremely encouraging. The fact that Iraq has confirmed its determination to withdraw from Kuwaiti territory is something which I consider very important, as well as some other points in the eight-point peace plan I consider positive, for instance the reference to prisoners of war is something which I very much appreciate. Of course, it is now up to the Security Council to consider the whole proposal in the light of the information which the Soviet Ambassador will provide to the Council, I think today.

Q. Any time?

S-G What I gather is that the Foreign Ministers of Iraq and the Soviet Union are still working on the details. Once it is completed certainly the Soviet Ambassador will come to the Security Council.

Q. Are you discouraged that the United States has already said, in effect, that it does not find it acceptable?

S-G All countries have the right to express some reservation. What is important is that so far nobody has said "no", nobody has rejected it, that is important. It proves the seriousness with which all countries are considering these proposals.

Q. Do you think that the coalition forces would be acting in haste if they were to go ahead at this point with a ground defensive?

S-G For me, as Secretary-General of the United Nations, which is theoretically a peaceful organisation, I think that everything which can be done in order to save human lives is really very important.

2-1

0308

Q. Now that there is a peace proposal, and an Iraqi acceptance of unconditional withdrawal from Kuwait, why do you find it difficult to say that a ground war should not begin and give peace a chance?

S-G I have no difficulty, I just expressed my real concern about the losses of human lifes. It is very clear, from the very beginning, that the fact that there are hostilities concerns and saddens me.

* * *

2-2

0309

외 무 부

종 별 :

번 호 : UNW-0433　　　　　　일 시 : 91 0223 2230

수 신 : 장관 (중근동,국연,해기,기정)

발 신 : 주유엔대사

제 목 : 걸프사태 (안보리)

1.표제 관련 안보리 비공개 회의가 지난 2.16.에 이어 2.23.11:30-13:30 열린바, 주요 경과를 아래보고함.

가. Y.VORONSTOV 소련대사와 T.PICKERING 미국대사가 각각 자국안에 대해 설명하였으며(소 6개항 평화안, 미 최후통첩안), 이어 여타 이사국중 중,인도, 영, 오스트리아, 쿠바, 불, 벨기에,에쿠아돌, 예맨, 루마니아, 자이르가 발언하였으며 사태 관련국으로서 쿠웨이트, 이집트, 이락이 발언함.

나.중, 인도, 오스트리아, 쿠바, 에쿠아돌, 예멘,자이르는 조속한 사태해결을 위한 안보리의 책임과 대책마련의 필요성을 제기하였으며, 이와 관련 특히 인도는 비상임이사국 들의 역할을 강조함.

다.영, 불, 특히 쿠웨이트, 이집트는 사태해결을 위해서는 이락이 안보리 제반 관련 결의안들의 즉각적인 전면 이행을 수락해야 함을 지적하였으며, 영, 벨기에, 루마니아는 소련안의 제4항 (이락군 철수후 안보리 결의안 자동 해제)과 관련 결의안해제여 부는 안보리가 결정할 문제라고 언급함.

라.소련은 통합적인 해결방안에 관심을 표명하면서 자국안과 미국안의 절충 가능성을 시사하였음. 반면 미국은 자국안에 관해 단호한 견지입장을 확인함.

마.이락은 자국의 소련안 수락 입장만을 간단히 언급함.

바.한편 동회의에 참석한 PEREZ DE CUELLAR사무총장은 안보리 결의안 이행과 전쟁종결이라는 두가지 요건을 충족시켜야 한다고 짧게 언급함.

2.상기 회의시 VORONSTOV 대사는 T.AZIZ 이락외상이 미국안에 대해 적극적 검토입장을 소측에 밝혔다고 언급하였으나 더이상의 부연설명은 없었음.

3.안보리는 상기 비공개 회의에 이어 2.23. 오후 양자및 다자간 비공식 협의를 진행중임. 끝

(대사 현홍주 - 국장)

중아국 장관 차관 1차보 2차보 국기국 정문국 청와대 총리실
안기부 공보처

PAGE 1　　　　　　91.02.24 15:07 DN

외신 1과 통제관

0310

원 본

외 무 부

종 별 : 지 급

번 호 : UNW-0449 일 시 : 91 0225 2230

수 신 : 장 관(국연,중근동,기정)(사본:노창희대사)

발 신 : 주 유엔 대사

제 목 : 걸프사태(안보리)

1.표제관련 안보리 비공식협의가 소련측 요청으로 금 2.25(월) 16:30-17:30 간 개최된바, 우방국관계관들로부터 파악한 협의요지는 아래와같음.

2.협의요지

가. VORONTSOV 소련대사 발언요지

0.안보리 제반결의안의 목적이 충족될수 있다고 믿을만한 근거가있음.(REASON TO BELIEVE)

0. 이락측으로 부터 아래와같은 걸프사태해결 방식에 대하여 건설적인 반응 (CONSTRUCTIVERESPONSE) 을 접수하였음.

- 유엔이 이락철군개시 일자를 확정하는대로 이락은 먼저 제시된 철군기간 (3주) 보다 훨씬짧은 기간에 철수함.

- 상기철군 조건이 수락되면 안보리는 철군방식 (MODALITY) 및 확인장치 (VERIFICATION)를 검토함.

나.안보리의장

0.금 2.25.중 2회 이락대사와 접촉, 상기제안과 관련한 이락정부의 공식수락 여부를 확인한바, 이락대사는 본국정부로 부터 아무런 훈령을 받은바없다고 언급한바 있음.

다.미,영국대사

0.현재로서는 소련측 설명내용의 사실 여부를 확인할 근거가 없는바, 이것이 사실이라면 우선 이락 정부가 안보리앞 공식문서를 통해 이를 확인하는것이 선행되어야할것임.

3.상기협의 종료후 HANNAH 영국대사는 기자들의 질문에 대해 소련측 설명내용을 알려주면서 현재로서는 안보리에서 어떠한 MAGIC SOLUTION 을 취할수가 없을 것으로

국기국	장관	차관	1차보	2차보	중아국	국기국	정문국	청와대
총리실	안기부							

PAGE 1

91.02.26 13:14

외신 1과 통제관

0311

본다고 언급함.

4.한편 17:40 당지 CNN 방송은 후세인 대통령이 소련측 제안에 따라 이락군의 쿠웨이트 철수를 지시하였다는 바그다드방송의 보도가 있었음을 보도함.끝

(대사 현홍주-국장)

안보리 비공식 협의결과 (속)

이락 철군 통보관련 안보리 비공식 협의는 현지시각 2.26(화) 03:30분경 종료

지금까지 밝혀진 각국입장

o 인도/쿠바/예멘

- 이락이 660호를 수락한 이상 안보리로서는 결의안을 채택하고, 철군을 이행하는 조치를 취해야 함.

o 미, 영 대부분

- 아직도 공식적으로 철군을 수락한 것이 확실치 않음. (서면 제시아님)
- 소련을 통해 재시된 것도 660호만으로 여타 결의안 언급없음.
- 이 문제에 대하여는 본국정부와의 상의 필요

o 소 련

- 중간입장으로 중재자 역할

한가지 특징

o 철군기간에 관하여 1주일보다는 길어야 한다는 일반적 인식

결 론 (의장 언급사항)

o 금 오전 11:00시에 비공식 협의 재개

o 그간 각국대표와 접촉하여 결의안 Text 준비문제를 협의하겠음.

전 망

o 안보리 재개되더라도 쉽게 결의안 채택될것 같지는 않음.

(주유엔대표부 17:45분 전화 보고)

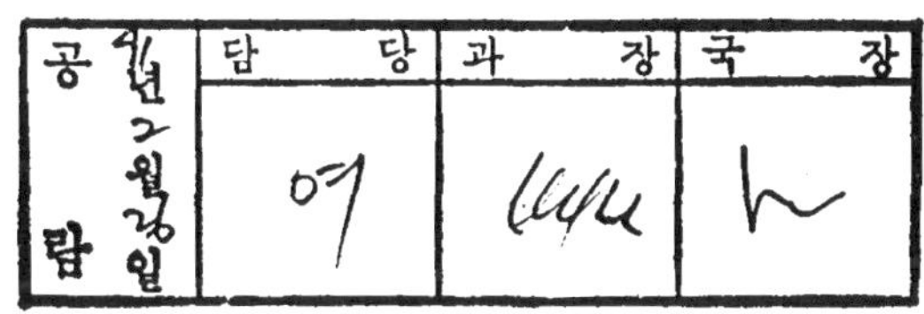

0313

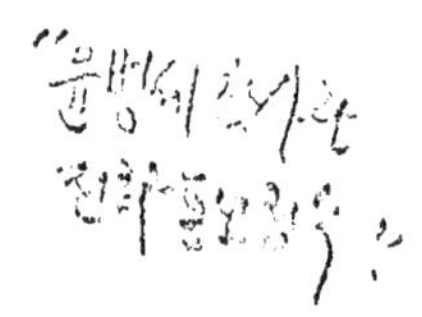

걸프전 관련 안보리 Private Meeting 결과

91.2.26. 15:00
주유엔대표부 보고

1. 개 요

   ㅇ 일시 : 91.2.25(월) 11:15 PM-12:40 AM

2. 회의진행

   ㅇ 소련의 제안설명

   - 수시간전 「후세인」이 고르바쵸프에게 메시지 전달 "660호 결의에 따라 쿠웨이트로부터 무조건 철수 공식 결정. 최단기간내 철수 예정인 바, 안보리가 휴전에 필요한 조정 역할하여 줄 것을 요청"
   - 안보리의 적절한 심의, 결정 기대

   ㅇ 각국 발언내용 및 반응

   - 예 멘
     · 이락의 철수 및 유엔주도하 철수감시를 위한 결의안 채택 필요성 강조
   - 인 도
     · 메시지의 중요성에 비추어 진지한 검토 필요
   - 쿠웨이트
     · 660호만 언급, 여타 결의안에 대한 언급없음.
     · 이락의 선택적 수용자세 받아들일 수 없음.
     · 이락의 의사가 서면으로 제출되어야 함.
   - 이 락
     · 소련 언급내용 확인
     · 안전하고, 질서있는 철군이 되도록 안보리 협조 요구

앙 고 재	국제연합과	91년 2월 26일	담 당	과 장	국 장	차관보	차 관	장 관
			[signature]	[signature]	[signature]			

0314

- 영 국

  · 660호 결의와 기타관련 결의는 불가분의 관계

  · 본국정부와 상의, 의견 밝힐 예정

- 중 국

  · 긍정적 사태 진전으로 평가

  · 진지한 검토와 사태의 평화적 해결 강조

- 쿠 바

  · 예멘 제의와 같이 결의안 채택 요구

0315

원 본

외 무 부

종 별 :

번 호 : UNW-0451 일 시 : 91 0226 0700

수 신 : 장관 (국연,중근동,해기,기정)사본:노창희 대사

발 신 : 주유엔대사

제 목 : 걸프 사태 (안보리)

1. 이락측 철군 용의 표명과 관련, 안보리 공식 비공개 회의가 소련의 요청에 따라 2.25.23:15-2.26.00:40 간 개최되었으며 이어 비공식협의가 03:30 까지 약 3시간동안 개최된바 요지 아래 보고함.

2.공식 비공개 회의

가.소련대사의 모두 발언에 이어 예멘, 미국, 인도,쿠웨이트, 이락, 영국, 중국, 자이르, 쿠바, 벨지움이 발언함.

나. VORONTSOV 소련대사는 고르바쵸프 대통령이 수시간전 후세인 이락대통령으로부터

1) 이락정부는 안보리 결의 660호에 따라 쿠웨이트로 부터 이락군을 철수할것을결정하였음.

2) 이에따라 이락군이 90.8.2. 이전의 위치로 철수하도록 명령을 시달하였음.

3) 안보리로 하여금 조속히 휴전 (CEASEFIRE) 조치를 취해주도록 요청함.

4) 휴전과함께 이락군은 가능한 최단 기간내에 철군을 완료함 등을 요지로 하는메세지를 접수하였으며 소련은 이락이 이미 철군을 개시하였다고 발표한점에 유의한다고 하면서 안보리가 적절한 결정을 채택할것을 요망함.

다.이어 이락대사 (약 30분 늦게 참석)는 소련대사 설명 내용을 재확인 하면서 아지즈 외상이 소련외상에게 동 메세지를 전달하였음을 밝히고 휴전에 필요한 조치와이락군의 안전한 철군 보장조치를 안보리가 조속히 강구해 줄것을 요망함.

라.예멘, 쿠바, 인도는 이락의 철수 결정을 환영하면서 이에따른 안보리 결의 채택 지지입장을 표명한 반면, 미국, 영국, 쿠웨이트등 다국적군 측은

1) 철군의사 통보가 이락 정부에 의해 공식적으로 통보되지 않았다는점

2) 철군의사와 반대되는 적대행위가 강화되고 있다는점

국기국 장관 차관 1차보 2차보 미주국 중아국 정문국 대사실
청와대 총리실 안기부 공보처

PAGE 1 91.02.27 02:33 DQ

외신 1과 통제관

0316

3) 이락측이 안보리 결의 660호 준수만을 언급하고 있는바 여타 결의안을 모두 준수해야 한다는점

4) 본국정부의 훈령이 필요하다는점등을 들어 안보리의 결의 채택에 반대함.

마. 주요 발언 요지

0 예멘

-휴전, 이락군의 최단시일내 철수, 유엔에 의한 철군감시 등을 골자로 하는 안보리 결의안을 조속 채택할것을 제의

0 미국

-현재로서는 군사작전 계속 수행, 이를 변경시킬 이유 없음.

-소련측이 설명한 이락의 철수 결정의 진위를 가릴 방법이 없음.

-이락이 철군 용의와는 반대로 SCUD 미사일 공격 강행함

-과거 이락의 DUPLICITY STATEMENT 사례에 비추어 후세인 대통령이 직접 (PERSONALLY) 그리고 공개적으로 (PUBLICLY) 이를 밝혀야 될것임.

0 인도

-소련측이 전달한 이락측 메세지는 의심의 여지없이 분명함.

-금번 제안은 다국적군 측 제안에 매우 근접해있으므로 이를 지지

0 쿠웨이트

-이락이 12개 안보리 결의 모두를 수락한다는 입장을 서면으로 안보리 의장 또는 사무총장에게 공식 통보 필요

- 이락의 수많은 기만 사례 지적

- 안보리 결의 660호 만 선별적으로 수락하는것은 용납 불가 (예컨데 쿠웨이트 병합 철수에 관한 662호등 불언급)

0 이락

-이락정부는 안보리 결의 660호를 충실히 이행하기로 결정하였음. (소련대사 설명 재확인)

-쿠웨이트의 존재를 GEOGRAPHICAL FACT 로서 인정함.

-안보리 결의 660호가 모든 결의의 모체가 되는것이므로 이의 이행을 보장코자 하는것임.

-여타 결의안은 상당수가 이미 시행되고 있다고 봄.

0 영국

-안보리 결의 660호와 여타 결의안은 불가분의 관계이며, 부분적으로 수락하는것은 용납 불가

-소련측을 통한 메세지를 경시코자 하는것은 아니나, 갑작스러운 사태발전임에비추어 어떠한 조치를 취하기 앞서 본국 정부의 공식 훈령을 받아야함.

0 중국

-이락의 철군 결정을 POSITIVE 한것으로 평가,환영함.

-걸프사태의 조기 평화적 해결을 지지하는바,안보리가 이락의 결정에 진지한 고려를 하기 희망함.

0 쿠바

-예멘이 제시한 요지의 안보리 결의안 채택 지지

-660호 수락 결정이 여타 결의안 불수락을 의미하는것도 아님.

-안보리의 조치 없을경우 이는 SCANDALOUS한것임.

0 벨지움

-만약 안보리 결의안 채택시 (서문 또는 본문)660호 및 여타 결의안을 이락이 모두 수락하기로했다는 식으로 규정할 경우 이락의 수락 여부 문의

3.비공식 협의

가.상기 공식 비공개 회의시 각국 입장이 되풀이된바, 미,영,벨지움, 프랑스는 분명하고도 공식적이고 확인가능한 철군의사 표명과 모든 안보리 결의안의 준수를 재촉구한 반면, 인도,쿠바, 예멘은 660호 이행문제를 여타 결의안 이행과 반드시 결부시킴이 없이 먼저 안보리가 검토할것을 주장함.

나.소련은 이락이 660호를 수락하겠다고 한 이상,여타 결의안 문제로 인해 철군하지 말라고 할수도 없지 않은가 라고 말하고, 철군일정은 최단기간이어야겠으나 다국적군 측이 제시한 1주일 보다는 좀더 걸리지 않겠는가 하는 입장을 표명함.

다.안보리 의장은 각 이사국에게 조속히 본국정부와 상의토록 요망하면서 결의안 제출문제에 관하여는 관계국 (예멘, 인도등이 문안제시 의사 표명) 들과 상의한것이라고 언급함.

4.안보리는 2.26.(화) 11:00 비공식 협의를 재개 예정임. 끝

(대사 현홍주-국장)

첨부: FAX (UNW(F)-079)

1. 소련정부의 지상전 개시관련 성명 (2.25)

2. 이락의 소련제안 수락 서한(2.24)

PAGE 4

0319

UNITED NATIONS

⇒779 UNW(Fi)-~~0461~~ 10226 0700 총 3매

S

첨부 UNW-0451

Security Council

Distr.
GENERAL

S/22262
24 February 1991
ENGLISH
ORIGINAL: ARABIC

LETTER DATED 24 FEBRUARY 1991 FROM THE PERMANENT REPRESENTATIVE OF IRAQ TO THE UNITED NATIONS ADDRESSED TO THE PRESIDENT OF THE SECURITY COUNCIL

On instructions from my Government, I have the honour to inform you that the Government of the Republic of Iraq endorses the Soviet peace initiative.

I should be grateful if you would have this letter circulated as a document of the Security Council.

(Signed) Abdul Amir A. AL-ANBARI
Ambassador
Permanent Representative

3-1

91-06126 2165g (E)

배부처	장관실	차관실	一차보	二차보	기획실	의전장	아주국	미주국	구주국	중아국	국기국	경제국	통상국	정문국	영교국	총무과	감사관	공보관	외연원	청와대	총리실	안기부	문공부
										/													

0320

UNITED
NATIONS

Security Council

PROVISIONAL

S/22265
25 February 1991
ENGLISH
ORIGINAL: RUSSIAN

LETTER DATED 25 FEBRUARY 1991 FROM THE PERMANENT REPRESENTATIVE OF THE UNION OF SOVIET SOCIALIST REPUBLICS TO THE UNITED NATIONS ADDRESSED TO THE SECRETARY-GENERAL

I have the honour to transmit to you the text of the statement by the Soviet Government concerning the start of ground operations in the Persian Gulf region.

I should be grateful if you would have the text of the statement circulated as a document of the Security Council.

(Signed) Y. Vorontsov

2831E

3-2

/...

0321

Annex

STATEMENT BY THE SOVIET GOVERNMENT

United States President George Bush announced at dawn on 24 February that he had ordered the start of ground operations against Iraq.

The instinct to rely on a military solution prevailed, despite the fact that Iraq's agreement to withdraw its forces from Kuwait in keeping with United Nations Security Council resolution 660 (1990) had created a basically new situation, clearing the way to channelling the Gulf conflict towards a political settlement. As is known, Iraqi Foreign Minister Tariq Aziz told a news conference in Moscow on 23 February that the Iraqi leadership was prepared to withdraw all its forces immediately and unconditionally from Kuwait to the positions in which they were located on 1 August 1990.

The Soviet Union, which had done much to impel Iraq to take that step, urged the international community to take advantage of the opportunity to prevent the conflict from escalating into a still more acute and bloodier phase. In the course of 23 February, the Soviet President had telephone conversations with the leaders of the United States of America, the United Kingdom of Great Britain and Northern Ireland, France, Italy, Germany, Japan, Syria, Egypt and the Islamic Republic of Iran. Before that, the Soviet President had sent personal messages to the Heads of State and Government of all countries members of the Security Council, as well as to the Secretary-General of the United Nations, briefing them on the results of the latest round of talks with Tariq Aziz in Moscow, which produced qualitative shifts in Iraq's position. The Governments of Arab States were informed of the steps we were taking. The Soviet representative to the United Nations took steps aimed at convening an emergency meeting of the Security Council to examine on an urgent basis the situation that had arisen, set the date for the start of the withdrawal of Iraqi troops from Kuwait, and resolve the issue of confirming, verifying and monitoring the cease-fire and the troop withdrawal.

The Soviet Union expresses regret that a very real chance of securing a peaceful outcome to the conflict and achieving the objectives set by the Security Council resolutions without further casualties and destruction has been missed.

The differences between the formulas accepted by Iraq and the proposals by a number of other countries were slight, and lent themselves to resolution in the Security Council framework within a day or two. It is still not too late to do this. The Security Council, which is now meeting, should get down to examining without delay the new situation that has taken shape.

-----

3 - 3

0322

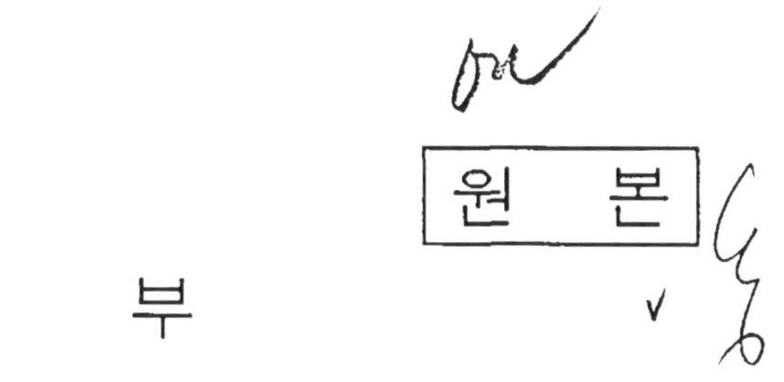

외 무 부

종 별 :

번 호 : UNW-0455 일 시 : 91 0226 1730

수 신 : 장 관(국연,중근동,해기,기정) (사본:노창희 대사)

발 신 : 주 유엔 대사

제 목 : 걸프사태(안보리)

연: UNW-0451

1. 안보리는 연호에 이어 2.26 12:00 경 부터 약 2시간 비공식 협의를 가진바, 당관에서 탐문한 동협의 결과를 아래보고함.

가. 미, 영은 이락이 모든 안보리 관련 결의안 수락의사를 표명하지 않고있는 상황에서 여하한 휴전논의도 불가하다는 입장을 밝혔으며, 불란서도 이에 동조함.

나. 쿠바는 이락이 제660 호 결의안을 수락하였으므로 여타 결의안 수락문제와 별도로 안보리가 우선 휴전조치를 취하여야 한다고 주장하였음.

다. 소련은 이락의 제660 호 결의안 수락 및 휴전의사를 재확인하면서, 안보리의 휴전조치를 촉구함.

라. 인도는 휴전조치도 중요하나 이락의 여타 결의안 수락의사 여부도 확인할 필요가 있음을 제기하면서 안보리 의장과 소련이 이문제를 이락측에 확인토록 요청함.

마. 쿠바, 예멘은 이락의 여타 결의안 수락이 휴전의선결조건이 되어서는 안되며 안보리가 즉각 휴전조치를 취해야함을 재주장함.

바. 안보리 의장은 관련국과 개별회의를 계속 진행해 나가겠으며 필요시 비공식 협의를 속개하겠다고 밝힘.

2. 상기관련 쿠바측은 별첨 안보리 결의안 초안을 2.26 비공식으로 배포한바, 참고 바람.

첨부: UNW(F)-082

끝

(대사 현홍주-국장)

국기국	장관	차관	1차보	2차보	중아국	국기국(대사)	정문국	청와대
종리실	안기부	공보처						

PAGE 1

91.02.27 10:26 WG

외신 1과 통제관

0323

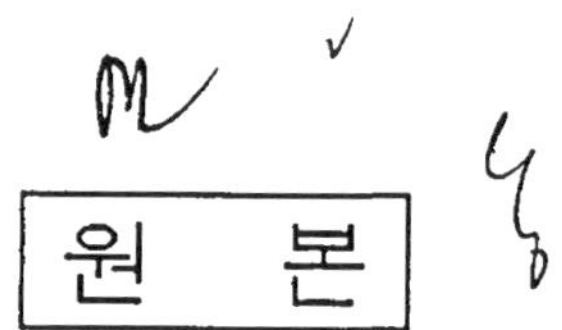

외 무 부

종 별 :

번 호 : UNW-0463 일 시 : 91 0227 1530

수 신 : 장 관 (국연,중근동,해기,기정)사본:노창희대사

발 신 : 주 유엔 대사

제 목 : 걸프사태 (안보리)

1.금 2.27.오전 11:00 경 L.AL-ANBARI 이락대사는 안보리 S.MUMBENGEGWI 의장(짐바베) 에게 다음요지의 이락 제의를 전달한 것으로 알려졌음.(상세 별첨 참조)

가.이락의 안보리 제 660호 결의안 수락 및 이행재확인

나.안보리의 즉각적인 휴전결의안 채택시 제662, 674호 결의안 이행 동의

다.제 661, 665, 670 호 결의안은 이미 실효한 것으로 간주

라.휴전 즉시 포로석방 및 귀환조치 용의

2.동 이락제의에 따라 안보리 비공식 협의가 금일 12:30 긴급 소집 되었다가 15:00로 개최가 연기된바 동 결과는 추보 위계임.

3.상기에 앞서 금일자 NYT 지는 2.26. 유엔본부발로 소련이 이락의 모든 유엔 관련 결의안 수락의 중요성을 인정함으로써 당초의 휴전조치우선 입장에서 변화를 보이고 있다고 보도한바있음. 끝

(대사 현홍주-국장)

첨부: FAX (UNW(F)-085)

국기국	장관	차관	1차보	2차보	중아국	국기국	청와대	총리실
안기부	공보처							

PAGE 1 91.02.28 08:51 WG

외신 1과 통제관

0324

UNW(FI)-085 1+0227 1530 첨부물 =UNW-0463 총1매

Your Excellencies,

I have the honor to inform you that the Iraqi government again confirms its full acceptance of resolution 660 (1990). The Iraqi armed forces have begun withdrawal to the positions which they held on 1 August 1990. We hope that full withdrawal will be completed in the next few hours, despite the fact that the American and other forces are continuing to attack the Iraqi armed forces while they are withdrawing.

I also wish to inform you that the Iraq government agrees to fulfil resolutions 662(1990) and 674(1990) on condition that the Security Council adopts a resolution for an immediate cease-fire and cessation of military operations on land, sea and in the air. It also agrees to consider the basis for adoption of resolutions 661(1990), 665(1990) and 670(1990) as out of force and, therefore, these resolutions are no longer in effect.

The Iraq government also confirms its full preparedness immediately after the cease-fire to release prisoners of war and return them to the countries in the course of a very short time, in accordance with the Third Geneva Convention of 1949, with the assistance of the International Red Cross.

I request you to communicate this message immediately to the Security Council and to have it issued as a document of the SC.

[complimentory closing]

Tarik Aziz

[TITLE]

0325

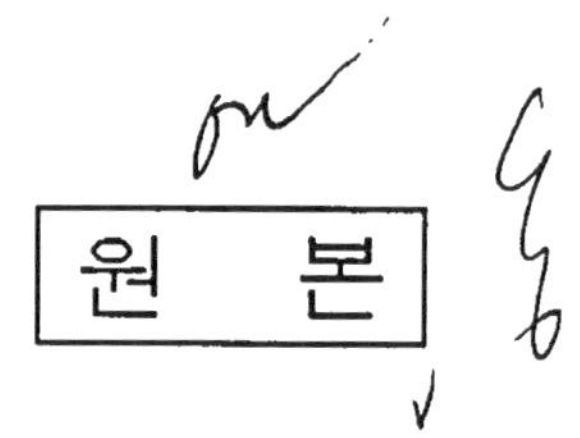

원 본

외 무 부

종 별 :

번 호 : UNW-0470 일 시 : 91 0227 2030

수 신 : 장 관(국연,중근동,해기,기정)(사본:노창희대사)

발 신 : 주 유엔 대사

제 목 : 걸프사태(안보리)

연: UNW-0463

1. 연호 이락제의 관련 안보리 비공식협의가 2.27 16:00 부터 약1시간반 동안 진행된바, 동협의결과 다수 이사국의 의견에 따라 안보리 S.MUMBENGEGWI 의장이 L.AL-ANBARI 이락대사와 접촉, 모든 안보리 관련 결의안의 수락, 포로 및 억류민간인의 즉각 (48시간이내) 석방을 촉구하기로함.

2.상기 비공식협의중 방침에 미, 영, 인도, 중, 에쿠아돌, 오스트리아, 불, 자이르, 루마니아, 벨기에, 소련이 지지의 뜻을 나타낸 것으로 알려졌음.

3.한편 이락은 연호 제의서한 (S/22273) 에 이어 이락군의 쿠웨이트 철군완료를 통보하는 별첨서한 (S/22274) 를 안보리에 제출해온바 미측은 상기 비공식협의중 이락군의 철군완료 사실을 부인하였다고함.

첨부:상기 이락측서한: UNW(F)-089

끝

(대사 현홍주-국장)

국기국 장관 차관 1차보 2차보 중아국 국기국 정문국 청와대
총리실 안기부 공보처 대책반

PAGE 1 91.02.28 11:08 WG

외신 1과 통제관

0326

#UNW-0470 의
첨부물

UNW(F)-089 10227 - 30
(국연 종료등. 해기. 기재) 사본: 노창희 대사

총 104

THE PERMANENT MISSION OF IRAQ
TO THE UNITED NATIONS
New York N.Y. 10021

المثلية العراقية الدائمة لدى الأمم المتحدة
نيويورك

S/22274

Excellency, 27 February 1991

Upon instruction from my Government I have the honour to inform you that all Iraqi forces have withdrawn from Kuwait, the last unit of which left Kuwait at down today February 27, 1991 local time. The American and other pro-aggressor forces continued to attack our forces during their withdrawal.

I will appreciat it if Your Excellency have this letter circulated as an offical document of the Security Council.

Please accept, Your Excellency, my highest consideration.

Abdul Amir Al-Anbari
Ambassador
Permanent Representative

H.E. President of the Security Council

1 - 1

0327

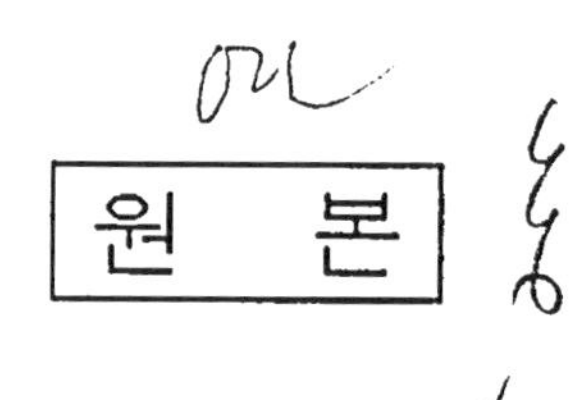

외 무 부

종 별 :

번 호 : UNW-0473 일 시 : 91 0228 0700

수 신 : 장관 (국연,중근동,기정,해기)

발 신 : 주유엔대사

제 목 : 걸프 사태 (안보리)

연: UNW-0470

2.27.21:00 부쉬 미대통령의 다국적군 공격 작전 중지 조치 발표에 이어 이락 유엔대사가 안보리 의장에게 모든 안보리 관련 결의안 수락을 통보하였다는 미확인 보도가 나도는 가운데 2.28.01:00 까지 긴급 안보리 회의 소집 움직임이있었으나 안보리 의장의 관련국들과의 개별 협의 결과 2.28. 10:30 비공식 협의를 열기로 된바,동비공식 협의 동향은 추보 위계임. 끝

(대사-국장)

국기국 장관 차관 1차보 2차보 미주국 중아국 정문국 청와대
총리실 안기부 공보처

PAGE 1

91.02.28 23:54 DQ

외신 1과 통제관

0328

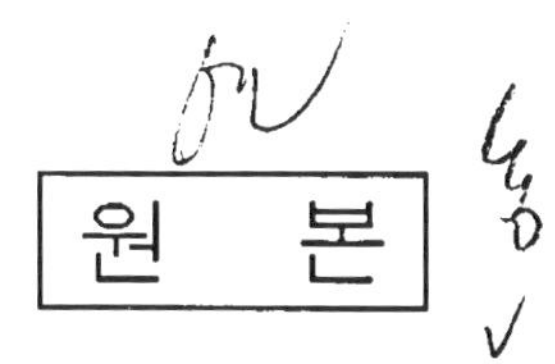

외 무 부

종 별 :

번 호 : UNW-0479　　　　　　　　일 시 : 91 0228 1800

수 신 : 장 관 (국연,중근동,해기,기정)(사본:노창희대사)

발 신 : 주 유엔 대사

제 목 : 걸프사태(안보리)

연: UNW-0470

1. 연호 안보리 비공식협의가 2.28 11:30-13:00 간 열린바, 정식휴전 (FORMAL CEASE-FIRE) 조치를 포함한 제반현안에 관하여 안보리 의장이 이사국, 이락, 쿠웨이트와 개별협의를 더진행키로함.

2.상기 협의중 인도, 쿠바등이 U.N.OBSERVER MISSION파견 검토문제를 제기한 것으로 알려진바, 동문제도 개별협의시 논의가 있을것으로 보임.

3.이락대사는 미국대사와 어제밤 및 금일 오전 2회에 걸쳐 양자간 협의를갖고 , 전쟁포로 및 이락억류 쿠웨이트 민간인 (쿠웨이트 대사는 약 22,000 명으로 추산)석방문제를 중점논의한 것으로 보도됨.

4.한편 UNIIMOG (U.N.IRAN-IRAQ MILITARY OBSERVER GROUP)임기는 안보리의 다른 조치가 없는한 유엔사무총장의 권고에 의거 금 2.28 종료예정이며, 대신 소규모 민간사무소 (SMALL CIVILIAN OFFICES)설치가 추진될 것으로 관측됨.

첨부: UNW(F)-091:1.안보리의장앞 이락 안보리제반관련 결의안 수락통보문 (S/22275)

2.사무총장 기자문답(2.28),3.쏘 외상기자회견내용(2.28)끝

(대사대리 신기복-국장)

국기국　장관　차관　1차보　2차보　중아국　국기국　정문국　청와대
종리실　안기부　공보처

PAGE 1

91.03.01　10:28 WG
외신 1과 통제관

0329

FEB 28 '91 17:36 KOR MISSION P.1

UNW-0479 첨부물 UNW(F)-091 10228 1800 총4매

(국연.중근동.해기.기정) 사본: 노창희 대사

UNITED NATIONS S

Security Council

Distr.
GENERAL

S/22275
27 February 1991
ENGLISH
ORIGINAL: ARABIC

LETTER DATED 27 FEBRUARY 1991 FROM THE PERMANENT REPRESENTATIVE OF IRAQ TO THE UNITED NATIONS ADDRESSED TO THE PRESIDENT OF THE SECURITY COUNCIL

On instructions from my Government I have the honour to transmit herewith a letter addressed to you from Mr. Tariq Aziz, Deputy Prime Minister, Minister for Foreign Affairs of the Republic of Iraq.

I should be grateful if you would have this letter and its annex circulated as a document of the Security Council.

(Signed) Abdul-Amir AL-ANBARI
Ambassador
Permanent Representative

91-06533 2321d (E) /...

4-1 0330

177 P01 LENINPROTOCOL '91-03-01 07:47

Remarks made by the Secretary-General upon entering the Secretariat building at approximately 9:40 a.m. on Thursday 28 February 1991.

Q. Can we have your reaction to President's Bush call for a ceasefire?

S-G Of course it is a reaction of great satisfaction because we hope it is the beginning of the end of this terrible tragedy. And now it is for the Security Council to take the necessary conclusions and we hope very much that the Security Council meeting will take place this morning.

Q. What about the conditions that Mr. Bush has imposed on Iraqis?

S-G Let us see what the reaction of the Iraqis is. As you know, I received yesterday a letter from the Iraqi Foreign Minister accepting all United Nations Security Council resolutions. And I think that all in all, what you call conditions put by Mr. Bush are in some ways in accordance with the United Nations Security Council resolutions. If Iraq accepts all UN Security Council resolutions, it wouldn't be too difficult for them to comply with what you call conditions.

Q. Can the allied forces impose additional conditions without the United Nations?

S-G It is conditions for a pause and not conditions for the end of the war. It is just a pause.

Q. What about peace-keeping forces?

S-G We are prepared to send out, as soon as possible, some observers or whatever we are asked for by the Security Council.

Q. Will they be UN or coalition forces?

S-G I hope UN forces.

* * *

4-2

0331

.BESSMERTNYKH'S STATEMENT ON THE ENDING OF GULF HOSTILITIES.
28/2 TASS 39

MOSCOW FEBRUARY 28 TASS - BY TASS CORRESPONDENTS IGOR PESKOV AND LEONID TIMOFEYEV:

SOVIET FOREIGN MINISTER ALEXANDER BESSMERTNYKH ARRANGED A PRESS CONFERENCE HERE TODAY IN CONNECTION WITH THE ENDING OF THE GULF HOSTILITIES. HE MADE THE FOLLOWING INTRODUCTORY STATEMENT:

+TODAY NIGHT, A FEW HOURS BEFORE THE U.S. PRESIDENT ANNOUNCED THE DECISION TO SUSPEND THE GULF HOSTILITIES, I HAD

URGENT CONSULTATIONS WITH U.S. SECRETARY OF STATE JAMES BAKER ON FURTHER STEPS TO BE TAKEN BY THE USSR, THE UNITED STATES AND OTHER MEMBERS OF THE COALITION IN CONNECTION WITH THIS NEW IMPORTANT TURN OF EVENTS.

IMMEDIATELY AFTER THAT, I REPORTED ON THE EMERGING SITUATION PERSONALLY TO PRESIDENT GORBACHEV AND RECEIVED CONCRETE INSTRUCTIONS ABOUT OUR CURRENT ACTIONS VIS-A-VIS BAGHDAD, THE U.N. SECURITY COUNCIL AND WASHINGTON, AS WELL AS ABOUT OUR FURTHER POLICY IN RESPECT TO THE PERSIAN GULF AND THE MIDDLE

EAST. SEVERAL PRIORITY TASKS HAVE NOW EMERGED. FIRSTLY, IT IS NECESSARY TO RULE OUT COMPLETELY ANY RESUMPTION OF HOSTILITIES IN THE CONFLICT AREA. CONTACTS ARE NOW BEING ESTABLISHED FOR THIS PURPOSE BETWEEN MILITARY REPRESENTATIVES OF THE SIDES INVOLVED AND WE ARE DOING OUR BEST TO PROMOTE THEM.

SECONDLY, IT IS VERY IMPORTANT TO HOLD A MEETING OF THE U.N. SECURITY COUNCIL, WHICH MUST GET DOWN TO THE PROMPT AND THOROUGH DISCUSSIONS OF PROBLEMS LINKED WITH THE OVERALL POLITICAL

SETTLEMENT OF THE IRAQI-KUWAIT CONFLICT. WE AGREE, AND WE HAVE DISCUSSED THIS MATTER WITH SECRETARY OF STATE BAKER, TO HOLD A MEETING OF THE FIVE PERMANENT SECURITY COUNCIL MEMBERS BEFORE THE COUNCIL'S OFFICIAL MEETING. WE PROCEED FROM THE PREMISE THAT THE TASK OF THIS MOST IMPORTANT INTERNATIONAL BODY IS TO CREATE RELIABLE POLITICAL AND LEGAL PREREQUISITES FOR THE FORMAL AND COMPLETE ENDING OF THE WAR. AS BEFORE, THE SOVIET UNION WILL CONTINUE ITS ACTIVE EFFORTS TO FIND JUST SOLUTIONS, WHICH WILL BE

ACCEPTABLE TO ALL THE SIDES CONCERNED.

THIRDLY, THE INTERNATIONAL COMMUNITY IS CONFRONTED WITH THE TASK OF GETTING DOWN WITHOUT FURTHER DELAY TO THE ELABORATION AND HARMONIZATION OF POST-CRISIS ARRANGEMENTS IN THE REGION. THE MOST IMPORTANT POINT IS TO ESTABLISH A SECURITY SYSTEM, WHICH WOULD NOT ONLY DRAW A LINE UNDER THE RECENT EVENTS, BUT GUARANTEE AGAINST FUTURE ARMED CLASHES IN THE REGION. THE SOVIET UNION HAS MAINTAINED AND CONTINUES TO MAINTAIN ACTIVE CONTACTS WITH THE

4-3 0332

PRINCIPAL STATES OF THE REGION, AS WELL AS WITH THE MAIN EUROPEAN AND ASIAN STATES IN ORDER TO FIND COMMON APPROACHES TO THE SOLUTION OF THIS FUNDAMENTAL TASK.

OF COURSE, WE ARE CONTINUING OUR CONTACTS WITH THE AMERICAN SIDE. FOR INSTANCE, WE HAVE AGREED WITH THE U.S. SECRETARY OF STATE TO CONTINUE OUR EXCHANGES OF VIEWS ON THIS MATTER, INCLUDING ON HIS FORTHCOMING TRIP TO THE REGION. WE HOPE TO FIND MANY COMMON POINTS IN THE POSITIONS OF THE USSR, THE UNITED STATES AND OTHER NATIONS. WE REALIZE THAT THE FUTURE LARGELY

DEPENDS ON HOW WE WILL ABLE TO CREATE, THROUGH INTERNATIONAL EFFORTS, A STRUCTURE FOR ENSURING SECURITY IN THE REGION AND GUARANTEE ITS RECONSTRUCTION.

AT THE SAME TIME, I WISH TO STRESS PRECISELY, THAT THE FUTURE OF THE REGION BELONGS AND MUST BE DETERMINED PRIMARILY BY THE PEOPLES INHABITING IT. FOR OUR PART, WE MUST ONLY HELP THEM ENSURE AND GUARANTEE THE EFFECTIVENESS OF THE SITUATION'S FUTURE DEVELOPMENT, AFFECTING THESE COUNTRIES. WE ARE RESOLVED TO GET

DOWN URGENTLY, TOGETHER WITH THE ARAB STATES, ISRAEL, AND ALL OTHER SIDES INVOLVED IN THE CONFLICT, TO THE SETTLEMENT OF THE MIDDLE EAST PROBLEM, WHICH IS THE MAIN SOURCE OF INSTABILITY, LACK OF TRUST AND CONTINUING ARMS RACE IN THE REGION.

TO SUM UP, I WISH TO SAY THAT THE ENDING OF THE GULF HOSTILITIES IS A MAJOR AND VERY IMPORTANT INTERNATIONAL EVENT. WE WELCOME THE LIBERATION OF KUWAIT AND THE RESTORATION OF ITS INDEPENDENCE, SOVEREIGNTY AND TERRITORIAL INTEGRITY, THE RETURN OF ITS LAWFUL GOVERNMENT TO THE COUNTRY. WE BELIEVE THIS IS THE

FIRST TIME THE INTERNATIONAL COMMUNITY HAS DISPLAYED ITS COMMON WILL TO OPPOSE THE ANNEXION OF ONE STATE BY ANOTHER.

FROM THE VERY OUTSET OF THE CRISIS THE SOVIET UNION, AS YOU KNOW, HAS SOUGHT AN OPTIMAL SOLUTION OF THE SITUATION PRIMARILY BY PEACEFUL MEANS. THIS POLICY OF OURS COULD BE TRACED THROUGHOUT THE PERIOD FOLLOWING AUGUST 2. PRESIDENT GORBACHEV HAS CONSISTENTLY SHAPED OUR POLITICAL AND DIPLOMATIC POLICY IN THIS ISSUE, INCLUDING THROUGH ACTIVE CONTACTS WITH LEADERS OF ALL THE

PRINCIPAL STATES INVOLVED IN THE CRISIS. AND EVEN AT THE LAST DRAMATIC STAGE MIKHAIL GORBACHEV HAD AN ACTIVE DIALOGUE WITH LEADERS OF SEVERAL MAJOR POWERS FOR THE PURPOSE OF FINDING A PEACEFUL SOLUTION.

PERHAPS, THIS PRECEDENT IS NOT ENTIRELY PERFECT, BUT IT MAY, AND WE WISH TO BELIEVE IT WILL PREVENT SIMILAR SITUATIONS IN THE FUTURE, SITUATIONS THAT DO NOT CORRESPOND TO THE NEW EPOCH OF PEACEFUL POLICY THAT IS NOW MAKING HEADWAY, THOUGH NOT WITHOUT DIFFICULTY. IF THESE NEW TENDENCIES ARE ALLOWED TO STRIKE ROOT, MANKIND WILL BE ABLE TO LIVE IN CONDITIONS OF GENUINE SECURITY.+

ITEM ENDS +++

4-4

0333

177 P04 LENINPROTOCOL '91-03-01 07:49

외교문서 비밀해제: 걸프 사태 19

걸프 사태 유엔안전보장이사회 동향 2

초판인쇄 2024년 03월 15일
초판발행 2024년 03월 15일

지은이 한국학술정보(주)
펴낸이 채종준
펴낸곳 한국학술정보(주)
주 소 경기도 파주시 회동길 230(문발동)
전 화 031-908-3181(대표)
팩 스 031-908-3189
홈페이지 http://ebook.kstudy.com
E-mail 출판사업부 publish@kstudy.com
등 록 제일산-115호(2000. 6. 19)

ISBN 979-11-6983-979-2 94340
979-11-6983-960-0 94340 (set)